THE TRUE HISTORY OF MERLIN THE MAGICIAN

THE TRUE HISTORY OF
MERLIN
THE MAGICIAN

ℰꙅꙅℛ

ANNE LAWRENCE-MATHERS

YALE UNIVERSITY PRESS
NEW HAVEN AND LONDON

For information about this and other Yale University Press publications, please contact:
U.S. Office: sales.press@yale.edu   www.yalebooks.com
Europe Office: sales@yaleup.co.uk   www.yalebooks.co.uk

Set in Adobe Caslon Pro by IDSUK (DataConnection) Ltd
Printed in Great Britain by TJ International Ltd, Padstow, Cornwall

Library of Congress Cataloging-in-Publication Data

Lawrence-Mathers, Anne, 1953–
  The true history of Merlin the Magician/Anne Lawrence-Mathers.
    p. cm.
  ISBN 978-0-300-14489-5 (cl : alk. paper)
1. Merlin (Legendary character)   2. Arthurian romances—History and criticism.   3. Geoffrey, of Monmouth, Bishop of St. Asaph, 1100?–1154—Characters—Merlin.   I. Title.
  PN686.M4L39 2012
  809'.93351—dc23

                                                              2012017297

A catalogue record for this book is available from the British Library

10 9 8 7 6 5 4 3 2 1

CONTENTS

ഌരു

Illustrations

ℰↃCℛ

1. Merlin prophesying for Vortigern. © The British Library Board. All Rights Reserved (Ms Cotton Claudius B vii, fol. 224r).

2. J.M.W. Turner, *Snowdon and Dinas Emrys from above Beddgelert*, 1799. © Tate, London, 2012.

3. Stonehenge, 2008.

4. William Lilly, engraved by Thomas Cross, title page of *Merlini Anglici Ephemeris*, 1680. © National Portrait Gallery, London.

5. The 'Chaucer Astrolabe', 1326. © The Trustees of the British Museum.

6. Sketch and translation of a horoscope datable to August 1151. © The British Library Board. All Rights Reserved (Ms Royal App. 85, fol. 2r). Martin Brown.

7. Merlin's begetting, from *L'Histoire de Merlin*, c.1280-90. Bibliothèque Nationale, Paris, France/The Bridgeman Art Library (Ms Fr. 95 fol. 113v).

8. Merlin as prophet, from the *Prophecies de Merlin*, c.1320. Fondation Martin Bodmer, Cologny, Genève (Cod. Bodmer 116, p. 13r).

INTRODUCTION

෨ᗡᏟᏒ

M ERLIN THE PROPHET-MAGICIAN is a figure in whom super-human power and tragic loss are always in tension. His powers have fascinated audiences from the Middle Ages to the present day, and have emphasized his difference from ordinary humans, yet the tragedy which always hangs over him means that he evokes as much sympathy as fear. His most familiar incarnation is that of a 'mage' of great power, who can appear and disappear at will, read minds and change physical appearances. These powers, together with apparently unlimited knowledge of past, present and future, enable him to guide the destinies of kings, to provide magical weapons and to prophesy the future of kingdoms. With his powers he ensures the birth of King Arthur, and then shapes him into an ideal, if tragically fated, ruler. Yet Merlin is human enough to be fallible, and to feel love and desire – and it is this capacity which makes him vulnerable to the seductions of the 'damsel of the lake', even though he knows that she will destroy him once she has learnt all his secrets. This Merlin first appeared in the twelfth century, and was put into his 'classic' form by Sir Thomas Malory in the fifteenth century. This is the direct ancestor of the Merlin who reappeared, for instance, in the television series 'Camelot', shown in the UK in the summer of 2011, where once again he led King Arthur into his fated future.

In the nineteenth century, Merlin's powers and his tragic fate were described in very similar terms. The most famous version is Tennyson's 'Merlin and Vivien' (published in 1859). Here the great magician is

> the most famous man of all those times,
> Merlin, who knew the range of all their arts,
> Had built the King his havens, ships, and halls,
> Was also Bard, and knew the starry heavens.

Merlin's nemesis as described by Tennyson is a temptress and serpent all in one, who pursues Merlin to Brittany and into the enchanted forest of Brocéliande in order to seduce him. He yields, gives her the knowledge she seeks – that of how to destroy him – and succumbs to the living death which he has foreseen:

> Then, in one moment, she put forth the charm
> Of woven paces and of waving hands,
> And in the hollow oak he lay as dead,
> And lost to life and use and name and fame.[1]

A less eroticized version of this same great magician, again the more than human creator and guide of King Arthur, was given highly influential shape in the twentieth century by T. H. White. This 'twinkly tutor' appeared in *The Sword in the Stone* in 1939 and in *The Book of Merlyn* (which was written in 1941, though not published until after White's death). White's Merlyn takes the form of a 'very old gentleman', dressed in an astrological gown and a pointed hat, and possessing not only a 'wand of lignum vitae' but also a magical corkin-drill, a phoenix and a talking owl, as well as too much antiquarian and alchemical apparatus to list.[2] Once again he uses his powers of magic and prophecy to guide King Arthur; and this time he reappears even after Arthur's final defeat, making one last, tragic effort to teach both king and reader, before recognizing that his role has come to its end, and simply disappearing.

This is the familiar and apparently timeless Merlin, versions of whom have appeared in both histories and fictions for nearly six hundred years. But Merlin was not only and always an aged figure, nor was he the creation of Sir Thomas Malory. Under the name of Merlin he appeared first in the twelfth century as a child wizard, the son of a demon and a Welsh Christian princess.[3] This heritage enabled him to see all the secrets of the earth and to prophesy not only the death of kings but the whole destiny of Britain. Still more surprisingly, this Merlin brought about the conception of King Arthur, but disappeared from human society before Arthur's birth and was certainly not a member of Arthur's court. This Merlin has been less frequently evoked, but a version has recently reappeared in the twenty-first century as the boy-magician hero of the BBC series 'Merlin'. Here he was shown learning to handle his own powers whilst also preserving both Arthur and Camelot for future greatness.

However, these creative reworkings across many centuries conceal an essential divergence. For from the twelfth to the sixteenth century, Merlin was believed to be a real historical personage, whilst by the seventeenth he had come to be a figure of legend. From the perspective of the twenty-first century it is hard to believe that Merlin was ever accepted as real, but the evidence is incontrovert-ible. In this book, I take seriously the importance of Merlin's mediaeval existence as a historical figure, separate from his fictional representations. This challenges the established tradition of treating Merlin as an archetypal figure, based on legends which grew over many centuries and which retained their symbolic power throughout all the changes of shape imposed upon the magician himself. But this new approach is vital for understanding the impact and significance of Merlin's own shift from historical personage to legendary archetype.

The BBC's Merlin, like those of White, Tennyson and even Malory, is openly a fictional figure, the product of a creative engagement between new authors and old themes. For writers in this tradition, the adding of adventures, love affairs and magical combats is both an important part of the creative process and entirely acceptable – such alterations and additions are central to the creation of historical fictions. But historical fictions should be considered separately from histories, and that is what I set out to do in this book. Of course, it is perfectly possible for a well-known figure to be presented in both historical and fictional forms. If reworking in fictional form were proof of non-existence, then Alexander, Charlemagne and Queen Victoria, to name only a few, would need to be taken out of history. But modern readers would be startled by any suggestion that they might struggle to tell the difference between a history book and a historical novel. And is it not condescending to the past to suggest that mediaeval and early modern readers and authors were not equally sensitive to varying genres, even if their categories differed from modern ones?

What makes Merlin a particularly exciting subject for this approach is that the relationship between history and fiction is especially complex and revealing in his case. For Merlin the Magician, creator of King Arthur, was himself created by a twelfth-century churchman known as Geoffrey of Monmouth, in his apparently serious Latin work, *Historia regum Britanniae* (*History of the Kings of Britain*). The word 'created' is fitting here since, although he clearly used old sources, Geoffrey's book was certainly not the simple translation of a long-lost chronicle that it purported to be. It was largely an outrageous fraud, far outstripping the *Hitler Diaries* in this respect and infinitely more successful. It wove reputable chronicles together with outright fabrications and transmuted Celtic sources into a deeply attractive, invented tradition, for twelfth-century England in particular and mediaeval Europe in general. Its success was such that before the end of the century it had not only been placed amongst the ranks of key historical texts, but had also inspired further research by writers who proceeded to publish their own findings in the archives of numerous Welsh churches, as well as Winchester and Glastonbury cathedrals.[4]

Geoffrey of Monmouth's Merlin was both boy wizard and the magus of the twelfth-century renaissance. He was an astrologer, prophet and natural philosopher, and he provided almost all the basic material for the later versions. What is more, this Merlin was given not only a new name (easier to pronounce and less likely to make French speakers giggle than the Celtic Myrddin) but also a new habitation and a new identity. The Merlin of the *History of the Kings of Britain* was a learned magician and a prophet equal to those in the Bible, who helped British kings at the time of the Anglo-Saxon invasion of post-Roman Britain. He used his powers to shape the politics of this formative period (with the magical creation of Arthur central to this), and he prophesied the whole destiny of Britain and its rulers, up to the end of the world itself. He quite literally left his mark on the landscape, by creating the great monument later known as Stonehenge, magically transporting the stones from Ireland to Salisbury Plain. And then he suddenly disappeared, without indulging in love affairs or taking any place at Arthur's court.

5

The texts used in creating this twelfth-century Merlin, the supposedly historical Dark-Age magician based upon early Welsh sources, have inevitably been much discussed by historians. They have established, as far as this can be done, the pre-history of Merlin the Magician in the shape of the princely Celtic poet and prophet, Myrddin.[5] But Merlin is not only significant for his early origins; he is arguably even more fascinating and more important precisely because he was accepted for so long as a real historical figure. For nearly five hundred years he provided not just proof of the reality of magic (this was never really in doubt until the eighteenth century) but detailed and factual examples of just what magic could achieve. This historical Merlin was an embodiment of all the major types of magician: a seer, an inspired prophet, an astrologer, a proto-alchemist, an expert in natural magic, and an adept in cosmology. He also had the unique advantage of having no need to summon demons to work his magic, since he was himself the son of a demon (whilst also being a Christian). He was no figure from folklore or the creation of popular tradition: he embodied the cutting edge of mediaeval science, and his powers were convincingly real. This needs to be understood: Merlin's powers and prophecies, which appear so obviously fantastical – if not nonsensical – to a modern audience, were taken wholly seriously. They even helped to add credibility to the 'long-lost' history which first revealed them to a wide European public. Merlin, therefore, quite literally helped to change history, and in particular he helped to put British history into world history, from which it had largely been excluded.

The twelfth and thirteenth centuries produced a great outburst of scholarly and literary activity, with the writing of history playing a key role in expressing a new understanding of the world. This was the context that made the *History of the Kings of Britain* so welcome for the highly satisfactory way in which it filled in gaps in people's knowledge of the past. It first provided an origin story for the inhabitants of Britain, tracing them back to the survivors of fallen Troy, and putting them on a par with the Romans (who claimed descent from Aeneas) as well as all the new, post-Roman nations who were claiming similar Trojan ancestry. In the process, the history of Britain was explicitly correlated with biblical and classical history, to take its place on a world stage. The conclusion to Book One of the *History* tells us that Brutus, the founder of the British nation, gave his code of laws to his people at the same time that Eli the high priest ruled in Judea and Aeneas Silvius reigned in Italy. Book Two, chapter 6, tells of Brutus' grandson, Maddan, who was a contemporary of the prophet Samuel and the poet Homer. Chapter 11 tells the much more exciting story of Bladud, necromancer-king and creator of the city and hot baths of Bath. His time was that of the prophet Elijah, and his son was King Leir (Shakespeare's Lear), father of Goneril, Regan and Cordelia. Leir's story leads on to that of his grandson, Cunedagius, whose reign coincided with the prophecies of Isaiah and the foundation of Rome by Romulus and Remus. The history of Britain thus rivals, in both length and significance, the history of any other nation – and it began long before the arrival of Julius Caesar and his conquering legions.

To see the grandeur of this history, it is only necessary to contrast it with the sparse fragments on pre-Roman Britain which were all that the Venerable Bede could assemble. Bede's *Ecclesiastical History of the English People* valiantly began with an account of Britain and its earliest inhabitants.[6] This follows classical precedent in giving a description of the country's size, location and natural resources, but of its early history all Bede can say is: it was first called Albion; its earliest inhabitants were the Britons, who came from Brittany; they were followed by the Picts from Scythia, and then the Scots from Ireland. Book One, chapter 2 then moves immediately to the arrival of Julius Caesar, 'the first Roman to reach Britain', and chapter 3 moves on to 'Claudius, the second Roman to reach Britain'. Bede's main story is, of course, that of the Anglo-Saxons and their conversion to Christianity, but the absence of any detailed information on the Britons, the Picts and the Scots has an inevitable effect. Whether or not Bede intended it, the impression given is that Britain was brought into world history only by its conquest by the Romans. Bede's work remained the main source for the early history of the English (as it is still), but by the twelfth century the English had been conquered by the Normans, and had declined in historical significance.

The impact of the *History of the Kings of Britain* on the development of world histories is demonstrated by the *Speculum Historiale* (*Mirror of History*). This made up one-third of the encyclopaedic *Speculum Maius* (*The Great Mirror*) assembled by Vincent of Beauvais in the thirteenth century, under the patronage of the Capetian royal house. The *Mirror of History* tells the history of the world (up to the middle of the thirteenth century) in thirty-one books, subdivided into 3,793 chapters.[7] Book Twenty-One covers (so the list of contents says) the reigns of five emperors, from Theodosius the Younger to Zeno, in 111 chapters. The material summarized here includes the death of St Augustine of Hippo, the ravages of the Huns and the career of St Patrick in Ireland. Bede's account of the incursions of the Angles in Britain would fall within the scope of this Book – but only the visits of St Germanus to the Pelagian heretics in Britain are deemed worthy of notice by Vincent of Beauvais. The *Mirror of History* is not very much interested in the Angles. Instead, Britain reappears in chapter 30 of Book Twenty-One, under the heading 'Concerning certain incidents of that time, and about Merlin and his prophecies'. The 'incidents' occupy roughly the first third of the chapter, and take place in Rome, Constantinople and branches of the Christian Church. With a brief 'In the following year', the chapter then moves abruptly to Britain, and to Merlin's appearance as a youthful prophet in the reign of King Vortigern. The rest of the chapter is taken up with an account of Merlin, his 'spirit' father, and his ability to reveal things hidden and prophesy things to come. Selected prophecies are even summarized, with special attention given to the reign of Arthur, but including the Norman Conquest. After that comes the cautious comment that many other things that Merlin prophesied cannot be clearly understood until the events actually take place, but the chapter ends by linking Merlin's prophecies to the inspiration of the Holy Spirit, even whilst placing him in the rather ambiguous company of Balaam and the Sibyl.

There is no sense here that the *History of the Kings of Britain* should be taken with a pinch of salt. Geoffrey's narrative has been incorporated into the mainstream of history – and Merlin is a world figure. The *Mirror of History* is just as fascinated by his supernatural parentage and his superhuman powers as were other readers for many centuries. It is only fair to mention here, in the role of honourable exception (or perhaps troublesome maverick), the Yorkshire chronicler William of Newburgh. In the dying years of the twelfth century, and at the very end of his life, William took the trouble to compose a Prologue to his own chronicle, dedicated to a special attack on the 'writer' (William would not dignify Geoffrey with the title of historian) who had filled his work with the 'ridiculous lies' concocted by the Britons about Arthur, and with the 'false divinations of some Merlin'.[8] However, William's dying effort attracted scarcely any attention, except amongst the Cistercians of Northern England. Virtually no copies of his work were made, whilst the *History of the Kings of Britain* became and remained not only a bestseller in its own right but also the source of a great and steady stream of further best-sellers. And the significance of Merlin in this success is inescapable.

To return briefly to the *Mirror of History*, chapter 49 of Book Twenty-One covers 'Various Deeds', once again placing events in Rome and in the Christian Church first and second in order. This section ends with a note of the discovery of the head of John the Baptist by two monks, and then the chapter moves to the sudden appearance of 'a star of wonderful magnitude above the island of Britain'. The star is described in great detail, following Geoffrey closely, and its interpretation by 'Merlin the prophet' is included. Chapter 49 then comes to what is, for such a dry history, a resounding conclusion, with the conception of 'that most famous Arthur'. The conclusions are clear: Merlin is the only British figure who occupies the world stage until the birth of Arthur, and it is Merlin's super-natural heritage and prophetic powers which give him this stature.

The relationship between Merlin and the book that launched him into the European scholarly world was clearly one of complex mutual dependence. Geoffrey of Monmouth had the skill and the scholarship to cast his fraudulent history in the style which was to be adopted for the comprehensive histories of the thirteenth century, and this, together with the sheer attraction of his content, helped to make Merlin the magician/prophet convincing as a historical figure. It was equally the case that Merlin's powers as a reader of the stars, and as a prophet who stood comparison both with biblical figures and with the classical sibyl, acted as guarantors of the truth of the *History*. But – and it is a very important but – Merlin's powers also made him a dangerous subject for mediaeval and early modern writers of history. Geoffrey of Monmouth himself was safe, since he made it very clear that he did no more than to translate a long-lost and very ancient book. Moreover, he sheltered behind his friend and patron Archdeacon Walter of Oxford, the person (according to Geoffrey) who had actually discovered the momentous manuscript and decided that its contents should be brought to the attention of the world. Thus Walter and Geoffrey both took care to share and to dissipate responsibility for the *History of the Kings of Britain*, and neither took personal responsibility for what it said.

But no later writer about Merlin could be so protected. Each would be responsible for what he (or very occasionally she) said about the greatest magician/prophet of 'modern times'. Poets and writers of historical romances could safely handle him with freedom, since everybody knew that they sought mainly to entertain (if in an improving fashion). Those who attempted serious comment, however, on the real, historical Merlin, on his demonic father and supernatural powers, needed skill in theology and natural philosophy if they were not to fall into serious error and to suffer unwelcome consequences. One of the most striking things about Merlin is that his glamour and fame were strong enough to make him almost instantaneously the subject of a great demand for information, despite the dangers for those who sought to supply it. This attraction, potentially fatal though it might be, drew numerous historians, natural philosophers and even theologians to write about Merlin. He was far too important to be left only to poets.

Study of Merlin, therefore, needs to take account of this powerful combination of reality and danger, which for more than four hundred years made him a major, but perilous, subject for serious analysis. The historical facts about Merlin were recorded in the *History of the Kings of Britain* – could any historian go beyond them? The potential rewards were great, so it is hardly surprising that many ambitious scholars tried – even though, as it turned out, there was little for them to find. Of course, the fact that no tomb or skeleton was found for Merlin (unlike Arthur, Guinevere or

Gawain) was not necessarily surprising. Was a half-demon actually mortal? Given that Merlin was real, his total disappearance could act as further proof of his magical powers (which had always included the power to appear at will, wherever he chose). That it had this effect is shown by the romances, and by their creation of the story retold by Tennyson and depicted by numerous Victorian painters. This tragic story of doomed love and female wiles accounted for Merlin's disappearance, and consigned him to a form of death even whilst stressing the immortality of his suffering. But it could form no part of historical accounts of Merlin, which had to stay within the limits imposed by the factual record on the one hand and philosophical acceptability on the other. Or at least they did until the late sixteenth century, when Merlin finally ceased to have a historical record, and was consigned wholly to the realms of fiction and legend.

The title of this book reflects the challenging fact that, from the appearance of the *History of the Kings of Britain* down to the critical comments of the Italian historian Polydore Vergil in his *Historia Anglica* (published under royal patronage in 1534), Merlin was accepted as a real historical magician and prophet. Indeed, Polydore Vergil's rejection of the great heroes of the *History of the Kings of Britain* made him very unpopular in England despite his royal protection, and the antiquary John Leland rapidly composed a *Defence of Geoffrey* (of Monmouth) in 1536 and a *Proof of Arthur* in 1544. Moreover, Merlin's removal from the historical record did nothing to lessen his appeal as a theme for fiction. His popularity with the Tudors is demonstrated by his important role in Spenser's *Faerie Queene* of 1590, where once more he uses his unique knowledge to guide Prince Arthur and the Redcrosse Knight to their fated future. Indeed, since the historical account of Merlin was now available to be used as fiction, Spenser could give details of the prophet-magician's hidden dwelling in the western forests, locating it in a cave beside the River Barry at 'Dynevowre' (Carmarthenshire).[9] A century later, in 1691, Purcell and Dryden staged their semi-opera *King Arthur*, which plays even more freely with the 'historical' Merlin whilst still envisaging him as magical protector of the Island of Britain.[10] In this version, Arthur is already king, but his realm is menaced both militarily and supernaturally by the wicked Saxons and their evil magic. It is Merlin who leads the supernatural combat on the side of good, and who ensures not only that the Saxons are defeated and all their magics dispelled, but also that the beautiful Emmeline of Cornwall is cured of her blindness in time to marry Arthur. Merlin's dominance over the story is emphasized at the end, when he conjures a magical masque to celebrate Britain's protection by the ocean.

This seventeenth-century emphasis on Merlin as magical protector of Britain, and particularly of England, was exploited in great numbers of pamphlets and almanacs that popularized new prophecies and attributed them to the Great Wizard. The connection between political crisis in England and widespread interest in Merlin's prophecies leapt effortlessly over Merlin's debunking, and continued from the twelfth century into at least the seventeenth. Through the period of the Civil War and Cromwell's Protectorate, William Lilly achieved enormous fame as an astrologer, and made impressive amounts of money by publishing almanacs and predictions under the name of 'Merlinus Anglicus'. It was only in the eighteenth century that Merlin's prophecies, whether old or new, became a subject for fashionable mockery. Until that time, it could be argued, Merlin had survived the unmasking of Geoffrey of Monmouth's fraud rather better than Arthur. This was because the separation of Geoffrey's creations from history left most of them, Arthur included, simply as subjects for romance. When mediaeval romances fell catastrophically from fashion, their subject matter was also in danger of falling. But Merlin's prophetic freedom from being bound to any one time period, and the existence of an established tradition of composing/'finding' new political prophecies by him, enabled him to surpass such trifling problems. Hence the issuing of new prophecies attributed to Merlin not only continued but even grew from the twelfth century to the seventeenth – it kept Merlin alive as a contemporary figure, with important things to say about modern events.

There were, I argue, no fewer than three streams of writing about Merlin: the historical, the prophetical and the fictional. As is always the case, these streams could influence and draw upon one another, and authors could play with the conventions of their chosen genres. But it is crucial for the distinctions to be acknowledged. And it is even more crucial for acknowledgement to be given to the fact that, for at least four centuries, Merlin the early mediaeval magician-prophet was a real historical figure. Without this reality, he could not have achieved the near universal fame which made him a world figure. And without that international reputation as the most famous magician of all time he could not have survived the destruction of his historical role as the creator and prophet of King Arthur. But in fact his reputation as prophet and astrologer was deliberately (if ironically) maintained into the eighteenth century, even whilst antiquarians began to delve into Dark-Age remains for any surviving traces of the Celtic Myrddin whom Geoffrey of Monmouth had so fatefully transformed. From that time on, the tension between history and fiction has tended to be resolved through the growth of a legendary Merlin, whose Celtic origins have been emphasized. The construction of that Merlin is a fascinating story in itself, but it is not the subject of this book. This *True History* is about the time when Merlin was real.

CHAPTER 1

ഇരു

THE DISCOVERY OF MERLIN

ERLIN THE MAGICIAN, like his name, was a creation of the twelfth century. This is no attempt to deny the existence of earlier Welsh sources, but Myrddin the princely bard of the Cymry, driven mad by a disastrous battle and expressing himself in cryptic poetry, needs to be separated from the twelfth-century Merlin. The latter is the shape changer, star reader, prophet and creator of King Arthur who is still familiar to modern audiences. The story of the search for the 'original' Myrddin has been told in other books. Merlin, the magus of the high Middle Ages, deserves one of his own. This mediaeval Merlin was not a figure of legend but an apparently documented, long-lost maker of British history. This Merlin's impact has been such that, despite his gradual move from the pages of history to those of literature, the key elements of his magical powers have not changed significantly. The name of Merlin is still instantly recognizable, and is still associated with that of the great and tragic King Arthur. The events of this Merlin's life, as first told by a cleric who called himself Geoffrey of Monmouth, are both familiar and fascinating.[1]

Geoffrey's Merlin was the semi-human child of a Welsh Christian princess and a demon. He could see into the depths of the earth, and could interpret the motions of the stars; he could also, if he chose, reveal his knowledge to powerful kings, although he was never under their control. Merlin was the great, magical engineer who brought Stonehenge from Ireland to England, and his skill with potions was so great that he could transform his protégés from one shape to another. He could communicate with animals and birds, and could make them do his will. Like a biblical prophet he was also an infallible interpreter of dreams. In other words, he was master of all the forces, and of all the languages and meanings, of the earth and of the stars above it. But his powers went even beyond this, for as a prophet he had knowledge of the distant past and of the whole of the future, at least for Britain. His prophecies were an instant sensation: copies were in high demand, and commentaries and interpretations multiplied rapidly.[2]

This is the Merlin who became the archetype of the great magician, in control of superhuman knowledge as well as power. Unlike shaman figures, he does not merge into the natural world – instead he interprets and dominates it. His enormous appeal derives from bringing together the magical traditions of the ancient world, the Christian Church, and the Celtic past as re-imagined in the mediaeval court. Even in the nineteenth century, this Merlin remained a potent and remarkably unchanging figure, although he had moved from history to the realm he still occupies: that of literature.

This power as a symbolic figure is inseparable from his historical complexity – from the fact that he was discovered, during the twelfth-century renaissance, as a real person who had lived just as classical civilization was dying. Merlin was not an alien figure from a wild, Dark-Age past. Rather, he was a prophet-magician who had helped to shape a world of great empires, and was master of both natural forces and advanced technology. Merlin had an immediate impact in mediaeval Europe. He was accepted as a genuine historical figure, and he brought together key themes in both magic and politics. His powers of prophecy were perhaps of greatest importance in the Middle Ages. But he was also an embodiment of forms of magic that remained serious and real throughout the renaissance as well as the mediaeval period. This enduring power could not have been achieved without two necessary conditions. The first was the fact that he was accepted as real for over four hundred years. The second was his capacity to offer examples of all the major forms of magic practised down to the seventeenth century. His impact is demonstrated by his extraordinary longevity as an archetype of a great magician. It is this unique status which makes Merlin so important as a subject for historical study.

The first puzzle is what made this mediaeval Merlin so completely convincing when he was first revealed to scholars and political leaders in England, Normandy and France in the 1130s. What was it that made him both so compelling and so apparently factual? Geoffrey of Monmouth's account of Merlin needs to be given particular attention, since this launched Merlin into his career that still continues to the present day, and that makes it something very special. Geoffrey was clever enough to start from an older Welsh historical work, the *History of the Britons* attributed to Nennius, and to make sure that his additions had classical and biblical parallels.[3] Moreover, he claimed that his work was simply a translation of a long-lost 'ancient book in the British tongue' discovered by his patron, Walter the Archdeacon of Oxford.[4] He also kept his information on Merlin tantalizingly brief, whilst making it deeply sensational in content. It is placed towards the middle of Geoffrey's long, historical account of the

Britons, so that the reader has to work through many centuries' worth of material, all carefully cross-referenced with biblical and classical events, before coming to Merlin.

Book Six, chapter 16 of the *History of the Kings of Britain* tells how the tyrant-king, Vortigern, traitor to his own British people, was himself betrayed and defeated by the Saxons. Forced to hide in the mountains of Wales, he ordered his subjects, under the instruction of his *magi*, to build him a fortress. But they laboured in vain, since every night the solid stone walls were swallowed up by the earth. Confronted with this, Vortigern's magicians showed their true wickedness, by advising the king to find a boy who had never had a father, to sacrifice him and to use his blood to hold the fortress together. The tyrant saw nothing amiss with this plan, and sent his soldiers out to scour the country for such a boy. At 'Kaermerdin' they found Merlin, and took the boy and his mother to Vortigern. Merlin's mother was of high birth, being the daughter of the king of Demetia, and of impeccable piety, being a nun. Her account of Merlin's birth was troubling, since she swore on her immortal soul that she had never slept with a man. She had become pregnant inside the nunnery itself, in its most private apartments, and without the other nuns perceiving anything. A mysterious being, in the form of 'a very handsome young man', had materialized beside her at will, had engaged her in conversation, and had made love to her. More shockingly still, this had happened not just once but 'often'. And this being, clearly no human, had made the royal nun pregnant.[5]

The boy Merlin then showed his own power by questioning the king, and by challenging his court magicians to a sort of magical trial. Vortigern was so impressed that he summoned his *magi* and allowed Merlin to shame them. Merlin's first question to these murderous magicians was: What is it that is hidden under the foundations of the tower and prevents it from standing? Merlin's own answer to this problem was that a subterranean pool would be found under the foundations, and when the king ordered his workmen to dig, the hidden pool was duly found. However, the revelations did not end there. Merlin next challenged the magicians to say what lay under the pool – and once again they did not know. Sensationally, what Merlin could see was that at the bottom of the pool there were two stones; and inside the stones there were two dragons. This also was proved there and then to be true, and it is hardly surprising that Vortigern's courtiers 'realized that there was something supernatural about Merlin'. This forms the conclusion to Book Six. Still more impressively, the next whole section of the *History*, Book Seven, tells of how Merlin, having had the hidden dragons released to fight one another in the pit excavated in front of the king, went into a prophetic trance and recounted the whole future of Britain from the fifth century down to the end of time.

It was the success of the great series of prophecies that established Merlin immediately as a trustworthy figure for almost all patrons and scholars. The importance of prophecy as a direct revelation from God was enormous (and continued to be so at least into the sixteenth century). The Book of Genesis provides a visionary, prophetic account of how God brought the universe, the world and humanity into being. The Book of Revelation gives an equally visionary description of the wars, sufferings and supernatural events that will precede the Second Coming of Christ. Merlin's prophecies, as presented by Geoffrey of Monmouth, rival these great prophetic accounts and are expressed in language nearly as rich and strange. For readers in the twelfth century the sudden availability of Merlin's prophecies was a sensation. Copies of the prophecies themselves, accompanied by commentaries and interpretations, began to spread very fast.[6] Merlin offered knowledge of the future, and his revelations, like Geoffrey's *History*, gave the people of Britain a central position in world affairs.

Merlin's prophecies are now regarded as an obvious deception, written in deliberately obscure language of a particularly otiose sort, and providing proof of nothing but Geoffrey of Monmouth's impudence. But they achieved immediate fame, and were crucial in establishing Merlin's reputation as a great historical figure. Geoffrey himself interrupted his historical narrative to boast: 'I had not yet completed work on my narrative when Merlin began to be talked about very much, and from many different places people urged me strongly to publish his prophecies.'[7] Chief amongst them, it seems, was Alexander, bishop of Lincoln, and Geoffrey inserts his letter to that powerful churchman at the same point. This begins: 'Alexander, Bishop of Lincoln, my admiration for your nobility compels me to translate the *Prophecies of Merlin* from the British language into Latin for you, before finishing the history of the deeds of the kings of the Britons.' What could be more effective? Geoffrey seems at the time to have been living in Alexander's diocese, and working for one of Alexander's archdeacons, whose name he also brought into the *History*. The power and reputation of the diocese of Lincoln is thus brought to bear in supporting Merlin, his history and his prophecies.

After this triumphant demonstration of Merlin's credentials as a prophet, Geoffrey then recounted how Merlin fearlessly foretold Vortigern's downfall and death, and outlined the reigns of the next kings of Britain. Book Eight proceeds to bear out Merlin's words. Merlin reappears in person only after long years of war, when Aurelius Ambrosius has become king and has embarked on the post-war reconstruction of his kingdom. Aurelius's desire to build a fitting memorial to the British war dead was the occasion for this return to the public gaze. His courtiers advised him that only

Merlin, 'the prophet of Vortigern' had sufficient knowledge and sufficient skill with 'inventive mechanisms' to create something both unprecedented and everlasting. Merlin, by this time adult, did consent to come to court but refused Aurelius's requests for prophecies on demand, and made it clear that he had no desire to become a royal adviser or entertainer. His own suggestion that Aurelius have the great stones of the 'Giants' Ring' brought all the way from Ireland and re-erected on Salisbury Plain was in turn treated with sarcasm, but was accepted when Merlin revealed that the stones had been brought from Africa long ago by giants, and retained magical healing properties. The result was that Merlin himself travelled to Ireland with Aurelius's brother, Uther Pendragon, and used his skill in magic and technology to move the stones and to construct the memorial (which commentators have unhesitatingly identified as Stonehenge).

After this triumph, Merlin once again withdrew from court, but consented to advise Uther Pendragon at the next time of great British need. The occasion was the treacherous poisoning of Aurelius at Winchester, whilst Uther was on campaign. A terrifying portent in the form of a dragon-spewing star appeared in the sky one night, and led Uther to summon all his wise men, Merlin included. Merlin was once again possessed by his prophetic spirit, and revealed that Aurelius had been assassinated, and that Uther must become king as well as beget a son who would be one of the greatest kings of all. Once again Merlin then vanished, and his prophecies were borne out by events, until the next crucial and fated moment arrived, the story of which also appears in Book Eight.

This moment was when Uther fell in love with Ygerna, wife of the Duke of Cornwall. Uther's desire was so fierce, and the duke's sense of honour so strong, that the result was civil war. Even this did nothing to lessen Uther's passion, and he confided to his advisers that he feared he would suffer a physical breakdown, or even die, if he could not possess her. Once again at such a point of crisis the king was advised that only Merlin could offer a solution, and once again Merlin summoned spectacular powers to bring about the necessary conclusion. This time Merlin used 'potions' to transform Uther into the likeness of the Duke of Cornwall and himself into the appearance of the duke's faithful companion. The magic succeeded so well that the faithful Ygerna had no suspicion that she had spent the night with Uther rather than with her husband – and the result was the conception of Arthur. During the night the duke was killed in battle, and Uther was thus able to marry the widowed duchess and to ensure the legitimacy of his son, Arthur. And this is Merlin's last actual appearance in the *History*. The great prophet-magician is referred to later, but bringing about the conception of Arthur is his last recorded act in Geoffrey's narrative, and by the time of Uther's death at the end of Book Eight he has effectively disappeared.

Merlin was thus revealed as a long-lost historical figure from the fifth century, who had moulded the British past and predicted the Anglo-Norman future. And what is perhaps most striking in all of this is that the astonished early readers of Merlin's story and of his prophecies were so eager to accept both as genuine. Geoffrey of Monmouth showed consummate skill not just as a writer of persuasive history and stunning prophecy, but also as a creator of convincing provenance for both. Moreover, Geoffrey chose his moment with equivalent skill, for he revealed both the *History* and Merlin to the world in the 1130s. This was a time when churchmen across Europe were writing up histories in a new, scholarly style, and the Anglo-Norman realm was in need of a new narrative to replace Bede's account of the Anglo-Saxons. Even so, it is surprising that Merlin managed to be accepted almost without discussion. His integration was so fast that it almost appeared as if he had always been there – but this still requires an explanation.

It must have helped that the 1130s, when this transformation of British and European history took place, also saw a period of high political tension in both England and the northern and western parts of France. The writing of history always has a political dimension, but this was especially true when the conquering Norman dynasty was in danger of disintegrating. The 1130s were a time of the potential fall (and rise) of dynasties, when any insight into the future would be welcome – especially in England. Henry I had been king of England since 1100, when his brother, William Rufus, was mysteriously shot by an arrow. From 1106 Henry had also maintained a contested rule over Normandy, whilst holding his other brother, Robert, prisoner. In England itself, Henry's status as youngest son of a foreign invader was doubly insecure. He took steps to make himself more acceptable to the Anglo-Saxons by marrying Edith-Matilda, a nun and princess, and one of the last to claim membership of the Anglo-Saxon royal dynasty. Their marriage took place on 11 November 1100, at the very start of Henry's reign, and succeeded, within three years, in producing a legitimate son and daughter. The daughter, Matilda, was married to the Emperor Henry V, whilst the son, William, was educated as his father's heir.

However, this dynastic security was suddenly destroyed in 1120 when William was drowned. Edith-Matilda had died in 1118 but Henry, the acknowledged father of more than twenty illegitimate children, had not remarried. After the loss of his heir, he married Adeliza of Louvain within a matter of weeks. This marriage, unfortunately, remained notably childless, something which must have placed the young queen under enormous pressure, given Henry's large number of illegitimate children. Unlike the kings of France when facing similar problems, Henry did not repudiate his queen.

But neither could he legitimate one of his bastards. He schemed in other ways to secure a safe succession and to ensure that Robert of Normandy's son could not become heir to Normandy and England. These schemes created political factions both at court and across Henry's realm as potential successors built rival groups of supporters, and as the king grew older the tensions rose ever higher.[8]

A leading figure at the court of the ageing king during this troubled time was his nephew, Stephen of Blois, son of Henry and Robert's sister Adela. Stephen had been brought up at Henry's court, was allowed to marry a niece of Henry's first wife and was poised to be Henry's heir. However, in 1125 Henry's daughter Matilda was left a childless widow. Henry summoned her back to England and required his supporters to take oaths that they would accept Matilda as his successor. In 1128 came a further shock, when Henry married Matilda to Geoffrey, the fifteen-year-old heir of the Count of Anjou. Henry brought Matilda back to England in 1131, for renewed oaths of acceptance as her father's successor. Matilda proceeded to give birth to three sons in three successive years. However, they were all small children when Henry I died in 1135. These, then, were the very dangerous times which led up to the revelation of Merlin and his prophecies.

When Stephen of Blois broke his oath to accept Matilda as queen, and had himself crowned king of England in 1135, the search for both an acceptable explanation of the present and some insight into the future became even more pressing. Moreover, any such analysis had to be addressed to a political class which had changed radically since 1066. The Anglo-Norman aristocracy in no way identified with the Anglo-Saxon past. There was also a new interest in the writing of dynastic and national histories. Both political and intellectual developments therefore led to a pressing need for new accounts of 'British' history and new ways of understanding the current situation. Bede's account of the early Anglo-Saxon kingdoms could never be challenged. It was in need of updating, however, and, even more seriously, it dealt with a people, the English, whose history had fallen from the world stage. Moreover, it contained little information about the British inhabitants of the island. Geoffrey's *History* thus filled an urgent gap, whilst Merlin's prophecies offered information (however hard to interpret) on the future of Britain.

In order to show how badly Geoffrey's work was needed, it is necessary only to see how little Bede offered on the early history of Britain. Britain, he said, was formerly known as Albion, and its first inhabitants, the British, had migrated from Brittany, changing Albion into Britain as they did so. The Picts arrived later, and were themselves followed by the Scots, who migrated from Ireland into northern Britain. Early Britain therefore had three population groups: the British, the Picts and the Scots.[9] This is essentially all the information Bede had, until he reached the conquest by Julius Caesar, and the incorporation of Britain into the well-recorded Roman Empire. Moreover, an almost equally great obscurity descends on Bede's account when, in the fifth century, the Romans abandon the British to their fate at the hands of the Picts and the Scots.

Bede managed to put together an account of events roughly down to the mid-fifth century and the reign of the Emperor Valentinian III, to which he dated the fall of the empire in the west (*c*.444). Thereafter, he had only the sixth-century monk Gildas's description of the degeneracy of the Romano-British, with one brief mention of how the 'tyrant' Vortigern invited the Angles and Saxons into Britain in the mid-fifth century. He then had to leap directly to the time of Pope Gregory I and the mission of Augustine to the Anglo-Saxons at the end of the sixth century.[10] It is clear that for historians seeking to bring the Anglo-Norman realm into world history, this left an enormous gap. Still more unsatisfactory for their purpose was the compound work now known as the *Anglo-Saxon Chronicle*.[11] This was almost certainly begun as a political initiative by King Alfred, and gave a year-by-year set of entries for the histories of the Anglo-Saxon kingdoms. It was written in Old English and was concerned almost entirely with local events. It had little to add to Bede's account of the early period except Anglo-Saxon king lists and some doubtful name derivations. This history was clearly unsatisfactory for the new kings of England, who needed something much more cosmopolitan.

Bede's account of the migration of the British into the empty island of Albion did fit well into established world history in one way. The Bible made it clear that all known peoples had to be descended from Noah and his sons, so that the post-Flood emptiness of Britain, and the arrival of migrants, made sense. However, as historical writing took a new turn in the early decades of the twelfth century, there was a growing requirement for histories of individual peoples both to be updated and to be placed within the great structures of unfolding world history, based on the Bible. These had first been worked out in the fifth century by the Fathers of the Church, who had established that history, like time itself, was a matter for the Church and not just for secular rulers. For all these reasons, a great wave of historical research and writing was under way in England during the reign of Henry I. The dynastic insecurity of the 1130s made history a matter of still more urgent concern, and made prophecy, quite literally, a godsend.

However, early twelfth-century researchers looking for a complete history of Britain met only with frustration. This generation of scholars, trained in the post-Conquest monasteries with their enlarged libraries, searched hard – to little avail. This was the crucial first audience for Geoffrey's great discovery, and its response would decide the fate of Merlin. Perhaps the most influential Anglo-Norman historian of all was William of Malmesbury (c.1090–c.1143).[12] He was of mixed Norman and English parentage and, after a youth dedicated, as he himself says, to historical research, he became determined to track down 'anything concerning our country'. He found the results disappointing in comparison with the 'historians of foreign nations' whose works he obtained, and therefore began to 'bring to light events lying concealed in the confused mass of antiquity'. His two great contributions to English history were his *History of the English Kings* and *Acts of the Bishops*, and he seems to have been allowed to search the ancient records of Glastonbury and Worcester, as well as those of his own monastery of Malmesbury. William's fame was such that none other than Henry of Blois, brother of King Stephen, commissioned from him a book *On the Antiquity of Glastonbury*. This was written after 1126, when Henry became abbot of Glastonbury and needed an up-to-date account of the historic claims of his abbey.[13]

William was also called upon to write an authoritative version of unfolding events in the reign of Henry I. He called this his *Modern History* (*Historia Novella*), and he wrote it for Robert of Gloucester, the powerful but illegitimate son of Henry I.[14] In this work, one of William's central issues is the legitimacy of the claim of Henry I's daughter, Matilda. Her unbroken descent, on her mother's side, from Egbert, king of the West Saxons and over-king of 'the Island', is stressed. The fourteen generations of these kings, from Egbert to Edward the Confessor, are carefully enumerated, thus establishing both her claim and her exact place in history. In William's account, the seriousness of recent political events is emphasized by linking them to natural disasters and wonders. For instance, the death of Henry I was accompanied by an eclipse and an earthquake and Stephen's arrival, forsworn, to claim England was marked by an unseasonal thunderstorm. By contrast, Matilda is described as a heroine, and arrives in England 'to assert her right'.[15] William of Malmesbury was not only an acknowledged expert on the history of England but also a sort of court adviser on history. His expertise and his knowledge of the ancient historical and religious centres of England made him someone useful to contemporary politicians, and their commissions showed that they were well aware of the importance of getting the 'right' history.

At a rather more utilitarian level, twelfth-century England also had new generations of school students requiring authoritative historical textbooks. The cathedrals, including those newly founded by the conquerors, were now providing education for future clerics and for the sons of their own clergy by establishing new schools. The role of history was important in shaping such pupils' sense of identity. This milieu produced the second of the leading 'English' chroniclers of the period – Henry, later archdeacon of Huntingdon.[16] He seems to have been the son of a canon of Lincoln cathedral, and was educated in the cathedral school. His cleverness brought him to the attention of Bishop Alexander of Lincoln, who appointed him an archdeacon and also chose him to write a *History of the English*. This historical work was explicitly intended to explain 'the origins of our people', and Henry executed his commission so well that he provided the basic shape of English history for centuries to come.[17] Henry structured his history of Britain around the successive invasions of the Romans, the Picts and Scots, the English, the Danes and the Normans. He also greatly clarified Anglo-Saxon history by inventing the idea that there had been seven main kingdoms in Anglo-Saxon England and outlining the history of each. This work seems already to have made him well known by the late 1130s, and to have positioned him as potential successor to William of

Malmesbury (who died *c*.1143). It was this status as an up-and-coming writer of history which made his decision to support Geoffrey of Monmouth's *History of the Kings of Britain* so crucial. Geoffrey might have timed his new history perfectly, so that it appeared at a time when insight into the currents of events in Britain was sorely needed, but it also had to survive scholarly scrutiny. Henry both publicized the *History of the Kings of Britain* and gave it his support. It will probably never be known whether Henry was aware that he was taking part in a fraud.

The first steps in revealing to the world the 'newly discovered' British magician and prophet, Merlin, were taken whilst Henry I was still alive. Geoffrey produced a pamphlet of the *Prophecies of Merlin*, with his letter to Bishop Alexander of Lincoln as an introduction, and claimed that he was responding to existing public demand for information about Merlin and his prophecies. Given that Geoffrey is a wholly untrustworthy witness, it is impossible to know whether there is any truth in this claim. But the fact that the *Prophecies* were issued before the *History* is supported by evidence. This comes from the work of Orderic Vitalis, monk and chronicler of the Norman abbey of St Evroult, who was working on his own *Ecclesiastical History* in the 1130s.[18] As part of this he had constructed an impressive chronology of world history, bringing together a great range of historical and theological sources. He also revealed that he had read the *Prophecies of Merlin* before Henry I's death in 1135, and that he accepted them as genuine, inspired insights into past, present and future.

Orderic's testimony is important for several reasons. First, it proves that the *Prophecies of Merlin* did indeed spread rapidly, at least within the Anglo-Norman realm. Second, it shows that highly educated historians such as Orderic enthusiastically accepted Merlin as a genuine magician and prophet of the fifth century. Orderic was no amateur when it came to British and English history; he records that he knew and used 'the books of Gildas the British historian and Bede the English writer'. His expertise was proved when he identified Merlin with the child-prophet Ambrosius, who appears in the *Historia Brittonum*, believed in the twelfth century to be the work of Gildas. It was this expertise which led Orderic to state that he would make available selections from the prophecies in order to help scholars who did not have their own copy. He even went on to make his own interpretations of selected prophecies, which was a bold thing to do in a period when prophecy was as much a theological as a political and historical issue. Orderic is regarded as an entirely honest witness, and his evidence does more than just provide a date for the first revelation of Merlin. It shows that Merlin and his prophecies were so attractive to their audience that they spread both rapidly and without needing support from the *History of the Kings of Britain*. If anything, it seems to have been the other way around: the acceptance of Merlin helped to establish the credentials of the *History*.

The next stage of the great revelation began in 1139, when Henry of Huntingdon, already established as both cleric and historian, was chosen to travel to the papal court in Rome, in the retinue of Archbishop Theobald of Canterbury. The party stopped en route at the Norman abbey of Bec, the home of Robert of Torigny, author of a history of the Norman dukes. Robert, welcoming Henry as a fellow historian, showed him a book he described as 'a whole history of the Britons'. It is clear that this was the *History of the Kings of Britain*. Robert was cautious, noting that this 'history of the Britons' was clearly unknown to the great Christian historians, Eusebius and Jerome. This was a problem, since they had lived in the late years of the Roman Empire, and should have known of a history that begins soon after the Fall of Troy and continues through the early Christian period, which they had covered. The fact that they knew nothing even of Arthur, who had conquered most of Europe, including Rome itself and its allies, was therefore worrying.[19]

Henry of Huntingdon, however, had no such reservations. He not only read this exciting, and even stunning, work straight through, but also composed a letter announcing the great discovery. In the letter is a list of all the newly discovered kings of the Britons, Arthur included. The letter was addressed to Henry's otherwise unknown friend 'Warin the Briton', who appears to have been an expert on British history. Warin, according to the letter, had read Henry's own historical work and asked him why he had omitted the great British kings 'between Brutus and Julius Caesar'. Henry recorded that he had searched, but had been unable to find any information on these figures – but now 'the great book of Geoffrey Arthur, which I found at the Abbey of Bec' had provided a complete list. Both the list of kings in Henry's letter and the mention of 'Geoffrey Arthur' as author of the book in which their stories were told make it clear that the work in question was Geoffrey of Monmouth's *History of the Kings of Britain*. Was Henry a co-conspirator with Geoffrey of Monmouth, or was he taken in by Geoffrey's fraud? The answer will never be known, but it is certain that Henry, an accredited historian, gave enthusiastic endorsement to a book that appears to have worried Robert of Torigny. Moreover, he strongly suggested that he had heard some of the story from another British historian.[20]

Several aspects of Henry's letter are very odd. First, Henry seems to imply that he himself has been searching for sources on British history, even though his great work was on the history of the English. Much more odd is the fact that Henry had to travel all the way to Bec to find Geoffrey's work. After all, Geoffrey was another scholar seeking the patronage of the bishop of Lincoln, and was also a friend and associate of another Lincoln archdeacon. Indeed, Geoffrey claimed in the *History of the Kings of Britain* itself that he also had Bishop Alexander as a patron for his writing. Could Henry really have known nothing of Walter and Geoffrey's great discovery? The name by which Henry refers to Geoffrey actually suggests otherwise. In most copies of the *History of the Kings of Britain* Geoffrey's name is given as 'Geoffrey of Monmouth', perhaps in order to explain how he was able to read the 'very ancient book in the British tongue' that he claimed to be translating. 'Geoffrey Arthur' was the name he used when witnessing a series of documents, as associate of Archdeacon Walter of Oxford, from 1129. That Henry of Huntingdon should know that a translator-historian called Geoffrey of Monmouth was also 'Geoffrey Arthur' and yet know nothing of his historical work is very strange.

However, if Henry's motives remain mysterious, the outcome of his support is very clear. It was when Henry placed his reputation behind the *History of the Kings of Britain* that Robert of Torigny was convinced. Thus the story of Merlin and his 'creation' of Arthur was launched by Geoffrey, Walter and Henry, all educated churchmen linked to the bishop of Lincoln, and henceforth the history was as eagerly received as the prophecies. Geoffrey showed awareness of the political significance of both when he wrote to Robert of Gloucester, son of Henry I and patron of William of Malmesbury. According to Geoffrey, Robert was a great figure for all who belonged to 'our island of Britain' and thus a natural patron for British history. Geoffrey's view was that he was offering something that neither William of Malmesbury nor Henry of Huntingdon could, since their territory was 'the kings of the Saxons'. Similarly, the Welsh kings were separate again, and their historian was (according to Geoffrey) to be Caradoc of Llancarfan. Geoffrey's proof that he had unique knowledge to offer was that only he had access to the mysterious and ancient book in the British tongue discovered by Walter, Archdeacon of Oxford.[21]

Merlin and his prophecies were therefore already a sensation before the *History* gained wide acceptance. He, and the knowledge of the future that he offered, were perhaps all the more attractive at a time of great and growing political uncertainty. What is certain is that, as news of the great discoveries spread from the royal and ecclesiastical courts, followers of fashion wanted copies. Representative of the lesser aristocrats who wanted to know about Merlin, Arthur and their times were Lord Ralf fitzGilbert and his wife, Lady Constance, who commissioned the first popular version of the new history. Little is known about Lord Ralf, but it seems that his wife had connections to the court of Queen Adeliza, the widow of Henry I. Lady Constance seems to have been something of a collector of up-to-date histories, since she paid a mark of 'refined silver' for a copy of a verse 'Life of Henry I' that had been written for Adeliza by a poet called David. We are told that Constance often read this work 'in her chamber'. Constance also had sufficient connections to hire a professional writer who had worked at the court of Henry I. This is Master Geoffrey Gaimar, who could read Latin, French and English, as was necessary for writers at the time.[22]

For his ambitious patrons, Gaimar produced translations, in fashionable French verse, of both Geoffrey's version of British history and an account of Anglo-Saxon history. These were the *Estoire des Bretuns*, now lost, and an *Estoire des Engleis*, which survives. Gaimar followed the convention of immortalizing his patrons by writing an epilogue which named them. He also said that it was Lady Constance who helped him acquire the sources for his version of 'British' history, from Troy to William Rufus. Gaimar was apparently working in around 1135–40, and his description of the books he used leaves no doubt that they included the work of Geoffrey of Monmouth. Moreover, he acquired multiple versions of Geoffrey's work from different contacts, and talks of these as separate sources. It seems clear that the news of Merlin was spreading as rapidly as Geoffrey claimed.

One version of the story came from Walter Espec, a powerful baron of the north of England and one-time ally of Robert of Gloucester. According to Gaimar, Robert had a *History of the Kings of Britain* that had been translated for him from Welsh books. Walter Espec had acquired this history from Robert of Gloucester. And it was from Walter Espec that Lord Ralf, at the request of Lady Constance, had borrowed it for Gaimar to translate into French. Gaimar also used contacts of his own to obtain a text which he calls the 'good book of Oxford which belonged to Archdeacon Walter'. Like Walter Espec's book, this too can have been none other than a copy of the new/long-lost history of Britain. Both had been brought to the fitzGilberts' castle in the Midlands for Gaimar's use before 1139. It thus seems that the prophecies of Merlin and the new version of British history were spreading in fashionable circles at least as fast as Latin versions of the work were spreading amongst scholars.

Before starting on his own work Gaimar had made a copy of the Espec/Gloucester book, and had compared it with Archdeacon Walter's book. He had found, he said, that the 'Oxford' book had material not found in the Espec/Gloucester volume. Word of the new historical discoveries was clearly widespread in the late 1130s, in both fashionable and scholarly circles. By the 1140s, the 'new' history was so well known that the saintly Cistercian abbot Ailred of Rievaulx could incorporate a brief reference to stories about Arthur into one of his own works, clearly confident that his audience would know what he meant.[23] Alfred, the treasurer of Beverley Minster, also in Yorkshire, was so enthusiastic that he undertook to produce a version for the less learned. According to Alfred, to lack knowledge of ancient Britain and its prophet was to be guilty of *rusticitas* (that is, being out of touch and old-fashioned). Alfred also makes it clear that there was much discussion of the great discovery amongst the 'chattering classes'; and that it was important to stress that one did not believe all of it.[24] As for Gaimar's handling of Merlin, sadly it was lost along with his *Estoire des Bretuns*.

It is clear that news of Merlin and of the long-lost British history spread wide and fast. What also emerges is that demand for the *Prophecies* seems rapidly to have outstripped even that for the *History*. This is especially remarkable since no fewer than 220 mediaeval manuscript copies of the *History* survive (in versions containing both the main history and the prophecies), and this is an enormous number given the rate of loss of mediaeval manuscripts. The *History* can thus be claimed to be one of the most popular and most long-lasting works of the mediaeval period. Yet over and above the enormous distribution of this text, there are a further eighty-five separate copies of the *Prophecies*. The seriousness with which the latter in particular were taken is shown by the speed with which detailed commentaries on them began to circulate. Their longevity is shown by the fact that new commentaries were produced for at least a century. Moreover, if imitation is the sincerest form of flattery, then Geoffrey and Merlin were much complimented – and continued to be so until at least the seventeenth century.

Still more striking, whilst Geoffrey and his account of Arthur were accused outright of invention by a few historians (though amazingly few, given the scope of Geoffrey's claims), Merlin the Magician and his prophecies were accepted. Two factors played important roles in this acceptance. The first was the high status given to prophecy in twelfth-century culture. The second was that

Orderic Vitalis was not the only learned writer who identified Merlin with the boy-prophet Ambrosius, who had appeared in the *Historia Brittonum*. This was believed by most mediaeval scholars to be the work of the sixth-century monk and historian Gildas, and to have been used by Bede. Gildas's actual text had in fact virtually disappeared by the eleventh century. However, a ninth-century Welsh historian, later known as Nennius, had put together a collection of the historical records he could find, including Gildas. This collection, the *Historia Brittonum*, became increasingly known to historians in the twelfth century. The fact that it circulated under Gildas's name added greatly to its prestige. Thus the saintly Gildas, whose relics were claimed by Glastonbury Abbey, was believed to be the source of a story about a boy-magician who was clearly identifiable as Merlin.

The account in the *Historia Brittonum* that did so much to verify Merlin went as follows.[25] The rule of the Romans in Britain came to a slow end after the reign of Magnus Maximus, the last Roman-British emperor. In the time of the tyrant Vortigern, the Saxons were invited into Britain under the command of their warlike leaders Hengist and Horsa. Vortigern attempted to maintain power but was ultimately forced to flee into the mountains of Wales. Here he attempted to make himself safe by having a fortified tower constructed in an impregnable position, but the tower kept collapsing as soon as it was built. Vortigern consulted his 'court magicians', who told him that the blood of a boy who had no father must be poured on to the foundations of the tower. Vortigern accordingly sent out his soldiers, who discovered a boy 'in the district of Glevesing' whose mother testified that he had no human father. Brought to Vortigern, the mysterious boy could see into the bowels of the earth underneath the tower, where he divined two dragon-serpents below a subterranean lake, whose presence kept causing the tower to fall. In addition, he foretold the wars between the Britons and the Saxons, which were represented by the fights between the two dragons. The parallels with the *History of the Kings of Britain* are clear.

This Gildas/Nennius account concluded with a rather confused statement that the boy, who called himself simply Ambrosius, then claimed the mountain fortress as his own. Vortigern departed to found a new city, named after himself. Equally confusing royal genealogies are given, as well as outlines of Vortigern's misrule and conflicting statements as to how he died. In the course of these, the 'great king Ambrosius' is mentioned, before a time of battles between the Saxons under Hengist's son, Octha, and the Britons under their war leader, Arthur. Finally, the list of Arthur's victories concludes with the twelfth, and greatest, at Mount Badon. The location of Mount Badon is not specified, but Arthur alone is said to have killed 960 men. After this Arthur is mentioned no further, and there is no account of his death.[26]

For twelfth-century readers there was little problem in identifying the Ambrosius of Gildas/Nennius with the Merlin of Geoffrey of Monmouth's *History of the Kings of Britain*. The 'long-lost' work 'translated' by Geoffrey gives an almost identical account of Merlin's first appearance, though with more detail on the sensational story of Merlin's mother's seduction by a demon. And Merlin's prophecies are located by Geoffrey in this same encounter between the boy-magician and Vortigern. Merlin the Magician, then, came to twelfth-century readers with the authority of Gildas/Nennius behind him. By contrast, Arthur is not called a king in this history, and although he is described as a great war-leader his adventures are apparently confined to Britain. There is no mention of his successful reign in Britain, let alone his conquest of Rome before his betrayal by his wife and nephew. It is hardly surprising that

Merlin was more immediately convincing than King Arthur. Moral reservations were expressed about Merlin's unmarried mother and demonic father, and learned theologians debated the question of just how much foreknowledge a demon could have, but Merlin and his powers had immediate and lasting success.

Even William, the late twelfth-century theologian and historian of the Augustinian priory of Newburgh in Yorkshire, who accused Geoffrey of Monmouth outright of lying about British history and King Arthur, accepted Merlin.[27] William went out of his way to incorporate into his own version of post-Conquest English history a furious attack on Geoffrey's *History*, but his comments on Merlin were relatively restrained. William pointed out that demons cannot share divine knowledge, although they have knowledge which goes well beyond that of humans. Thus, Merlin could not derive his prophetic powers simply from his demonic father. He also referred to Merlin, scornfully, as a mere source of 'lying divinations'. But the very fact that he pointed out that some of the prophecies had turned out to be false suggests that he had taken the trouble to interpret them. Beyond that, he simply argued that Geoffrey had concocted prophecies of his own, and had passed them on together with the 'traditional' ones.[28] William wrote at the end of the twelfth century, by which time it might be expected that the craze for Arthur and Merlin would have passed its peak, but that was not so. Moreover, very few people wanted to hear what William had to say. Only two mediaeval copies of William's work survive, and one of those is the manuscript that William seems to have left to his priory of Newburgh at his death.[29]

Merlin had therefore made his appearance by the end of 1135, and was instantly accepted as a genuine historical figure. Indeed, his appeal was greater the more the reader knew of obscure historical works. For the most historically learned, Merlin was the most acceptable figure of the 'new history'. For everybody he was a truly great prophet and magician. News of Merlin spread rapidly, not only amongst churchmen and scholars but also in court circles and then amongst ambitious members of the minor aristocracy. For everybody, it seems, Merlin was crucial in establishing the authenticity of the *History of the Kings of Britain*. This was both because he could be identified as a fuller version of a figure in a long-accepted British history, the *Historia Brittonum*, and because the apparent truth of his prophecies proved the reality of his powers. Figures in the prophecies themselves could be identified (by experts) with rulers named in other historical sources, and these identifications could themselves be circulated.

By 1150 at the latest, Merlin had been proved to be a real historical being, and this had the inevitable effect of making his magical powers, as well as his prophecies, part of the historical record. This is what makes Merlin so very important. His feats of magic were, at least potentially, real historical events in themselves, and thus they provided evidence of what magical power could do. Were they challenged as impossible? Were they criticized as demonic and unsuitable for sober historical works? Did they provide material for theological discussion? What else was discovered about Merlin? These are questions which the rest of this book will address.

CHAPTER 2

WRITING THE HISTORY OF MERLIN

MERLIN, THE GREAT magician and 'prophet of Vortigern', was established as real in the 1130s and remained so until the 1530s. Moreover, excited discussion of the magician and his prophecies spread rapidly, both amongst the political class and in the Church. It was never likely that such a major discovery would be ignored by commentators, and another chapter will look at the interpretations of Merlin's prophecies which were produced by numerous writers. But first, the extent of further work on Merlin himself needs to be established. Did other historians and chroniclers find more on Merlin – and if so, what was it? Did news of Merlin reach those who could not read Latin chronicles, or commission French translations? Was the new version of British history, in which Merlin played such a central part, accepted? If it was, how much did British history change?

The last two of these questions are the easiest to answer, since the new British history was almost universally accepted, copied and shelved in libraries along with other serious histories. The *History of the Kings of Britain* was one of the great bestsellers of the Middle Ages, and copies survive from most European countries in very large numbers. The impact on British history was radical. For centuries the dominant story of Britain in the post-Roman period had been a brief and inglorious account of how the sinful British people, misled by rulers both wicked and foolish, were punished by plagues and foreign invaders. Still more depressingly, the Britons were shown not only as sinful but also as very poor fighters, which was a far greater ignominy. The main authorities for this history were the Venerable Bede and his source, Gildas 'the Wise'. Gildas, a sixth-century monk, missionary and biblical scholar, had named and shamed the worst of the British rulers and church leaders of the late fifth and early sixth centuries. He compiled an impressive list of prophecies and denunciations, drawn from the Bible, and applied them all to the leaders of the British.[1] This denunciation established Gildas's own reputation for scholarship and wisdom, whilst giving the British rulers of his own time a lasting character as villains and fools. According to Gildas, the Romanized British, stripped of soldiers as the Roman Empire collapsed, could not fight off the Picts and the Scots, even though the Romans had left a wall to defend their northern frontier and a string of forts to defend their coasts. Their leaders, headed by the tyrant Vortigern, added folly to this failure by inviting in the pagan Saxons to do their fighting. Thus the decline of the British was a story of wickedness and stupidity receiving predictable punishment. The 'new history', however, turned the Britons back into the heroes of their own story, and it also went far to replace Gildas the Wise with Merlin the Prophet as a figure of authority for British history.

Careful correlation of the *History of the Kings of Britain* with the works of Gildas, Nennius and Bede could produce dates for the period of Merlin's activity, for those who wished for such things. It also showed up just how vague existing accounts of the British were. Gildas had given no actual dates, but his account made it possible for Bede to link Vortigern's career to the joint reign of Martianus and Valentinian in Rome, and to suggest a date of around 449. Bede also followed Gildas's version of the disastrous collapse of Roman Britain, but clarified the sequence of events and added new information from continental Saxon sources. This produced the well-known outline of how the Saxon mercenaries rebelled against their British employers and allied themselves with the Picts. The British were overwhelmingly defeated, but recovered under Ambrosius Aurelianus, the last leader of 'the Roman race'. This culminated in the great triumph of the British at the Battle of Badon Hill, around 495, and a brief time of peace for the British before their final decline into wickedness. Thereafter, Bede could find nothing until 596, when, 'about one hundred and fifty years after the coming of the Angles to Britain', Pope Gregory I sent Augustine to convert the English to Christianity.[2]

To this skeletal account the *History of the Kings of Britain* added a series of kings, culminating in Arthur. Ambrosius Aurelianus's victory over the tyrant Vortigern was recounted in detail, as was the reign of his brother, Uther Pendragon, who does not appear in Bede or Gildas at all. Tantalizingly, no dates are given for these kings, or for the coronation of Arthur, but we are told that Arthur was fifteen when he became king after the treacherous assassination of his father, Uther. By this time Merlin has already disappeared from the account, but a date is given for the fateful battle which ends Arthur's reign. This is the tragic battle at the River Camblan, fought after Arthur has been betrayed by his queen, Guinevere, and his nephew, Mordred. The date of this battle is given as 542, and at the end of it Arthur, fatally wounded, is taken to the Isle of Avalon and, like Merlin before him, vanishes from the story.[3]

Nevertheless, Merlin's name and prophecies appear again at the end of the *History of the Kings of Britain*. Following Arthur's death the inexorable decline of the British had resumed, although with more heroic resistance on their part, and with plague and famine completing what the Saxons could not. Eventually King Cadwallader, the last great king, is ordered by an angelic voice to depart from Britain. The voice gives Cadwallader a message directly from God, instructing him to go to Rome, where he will die. The voice also gives divine approval to Merlin's prophecy. Cadwallader is told that God does not intend the Britons to rule Britain again 'until the time prophesied by Merlin to King Arthur'.[4] No such prophecy has been narrated in the *History*, and yet the power of Merlin's prophecies effectively concludes the work. Merlin was thus introduced to fascinated readers in the 1130s and 1140s as a great prophet, an artificer to rival Daedalus and Wayland the Smith, and a half-demon who transcended human time and space. The *History of the Kings of Britain* ends by demonstrating the accuracy of Merlin's prophecies, whilst also emphasizing that they were in accordance with the will of God.

It is hardly surprising that word of Merlin and his powers spread quickly from the circles of monastic historians and their powerful patrons to those of courtiers and ambitious aristocrats. By the 1140s Alfred, the treasurer at Beverley Minster, wrote that not to have read the *History* was to be rustic and backward. He could not have been clearer, and it is likely that the fashionable would pay well for copies of this essential reading. It is therefore unsurprising that other researchers went looking for further information on Merlin and his times. The *History of the Kings of Britain* itself makes repeated mention of two authors, Gildas and Bede, in order to establish its credentials. Copies of Bede's historical work were widespread in Anglo-Saxon and Anglo-Norman England, but

Gildas was a more difficult issue. Bede's use of him as a source had created the impression that Gildas had written an actual history of Britain, although in fact his attacks on Vortigern and other kings were part of a 'prophetic' warning to the British to change their behaviour before it was too late. This in turn contributed to the mistaken belief that the collection of historical records compiled by the Welsh monk Nennius incorporated Gildas's work. Gildas's actual sermon or treatise, the *De Excidio et Conquestu Britanniae* (*On the Fall and Conquest of Britain*), had become extremely rare by the twelfth century, and the *Historia Brittonum* of Nennius was often shelved under the name of Gildas.[5] This work thus experienced a surge in demand from the 1140s on – but what did it add to the story of Merlin?

First, it confirms the existence and prophetic powers of a mysterious boy who prophesied for Vortigern. This boy, although named Ambrosius, is easy to identify as the Merlin Ambrosius of the *History*. Moreover, in this version he states that his father was a Roman consul (even though his mother has, as in the *History*, declared that she knows nothing of his father). This helps to explain his Roman name, and is perhaps why he goes on to make a successful claim for power in his own right:

'Do you [Vortigern] depart from this place, where you are not permitted to erect a citadel; I, to whom fate has allotted this mansion, shall remain here; whilst to you it is incumbent to seek other provinces, where you may build a fortress.' 'What is your name?' asked the king; 'I am called Ambrose [in British Embresguletic],' returned the boy; and in answer to the king's question, 'What is your origin?' he replied, 'A Roman consul was my father.' Then the king assigned him that city, with all the western Provinces of Britain; and departing with his wise men to the sinistral district, he arrived in the region named Gueneri, where he built a city which, according to his name, was called Cair Guorthegirn.[6]

Gildas/Nennius gives no more information than that, and says nothing about the prophecies of Merlin 'translated' by Geoffrey of Monmouth. But this did not mean that there were no other long-lost British books to be found. The era offered special hopes of new discoveries, as French-speaking bishops and abbots employed researchers to study the archives of their abbeys and cathedrals in the expectation of finding records from the British past that Anglo-Saxon dignitaries had ignored or rejected. This was both in order to establish the credentials of their own institutions and to link them to the new history. Antiquity was such an important source of authority and power that the abbey of Glastonbury, under the leadership of Henry of Blois (brother of King Stephen and also a papal legate), had set out to establish its own claims even before Geoffrey of Monmouth, Walter of Oxford and Henry of Huntingdon had unveiled their great discovery.

The claims of Glastonbury were on a very large scale, and included the assertion that it had the relics, and at least some of the books, of Gildas himself. If this were not enough to establish its leading position in the race to establish pre-Saxon credentials, there was also its claim to have the relics of both St Patrick and St David. For these to be made believable, especially in the face of apparently stronger claims by churches in Ireland and Wales, an acceptable and authoritative history was required. William of Malmesbury, no less, was the historian invited to Glastonbury at the end of the 1120s, and he made an astonishing stream of discoveries about British history and Glastonbury's place in it.[7] These did not include anything relating to Merlin, but they are still important for our story.

When he was commissioned to prepare a history of Glastonbury, William was already working on his *Deeds of the Kings of the English*. As he lamented, no one had attempted a serious Latin history of 'this people' since the death of Bede. He drew upon his enormous knowledge of 'chronicles from far and wide' in writing this, and his work makes clear that his researches were impressive.[8] He included an account of the reign of Vortigern, and the first arrival of the 'English', for which he names the Gildas/Nennius *History of the Britons* as his source. However, William says nothing about the dramatic incident of the boy-prophet Ambrosius. Instead, breaking off his narrative, he gives a learned disquisition on the northern peoples who took over various parts of the Roman Empire, amongst whom were the Angles, Saxons and Jutes. He also explains how these pagans, believing the ancestors of their kings to have been deities, named Wednesday and Friday after them.[9] This displayed his antiquarian research on the 'English', and was much repeated by English chroniclers. Not even the *magi* of Vortigern's court mentioned by Gildas/Nennius are included by William – which is odd, since elsewhere he shows his enthusiasm for such supernatural tales as that of the 'witch of Berkeley'.[10] It is possible that William's copy of the *History of the Britons* was abbreviated, since he follows the Old English annals known as the *Anglo-Saxon Chronicle* for most of his account of the foundation of the Anglo-Saxon kingdoms. He does, however, suddenly insert Gildas/Nennius's heroic war leader Arthur into his story and comments: 'It is of this Arthur that the Britons tell many fables, even up to the present day.'[11] This has the effect of leaving William's own stance nicely ambiguous, since he rejects the 'fables' whilst accepting the actual existence of Arthur.

At Glastonbury, William found a 'mass of sources' and of annals, documents and carved stones. Glastonbury, he confirmed, dated back to the time of Pope Eleutherius and the British king Lucius.

Bede had dated these men to around 167 AD, which made Glastonbury nearly three centuries old in the reign of Vortigern (and approaching its first millennium in William's time). William was more dubious about the Glastonbury documents' claim that Glastonbury's church of St Mary was founded by the actual disciples of Christ, but he did accept that not only St Patrick but also Gildas 'the Historian' had spent time there.[12] He collected oral testimony on the wonders of the place and its relics. He also carefully recorded the inscriptions on the ancient stones in the churchyard and collated them with records of abbots and with local place-names.[13] In analysing Glastonbury's claim to the relics of St David (which he accepted) he also examined the history of the British church in the fifth century. St David is stated to be King Arthur's uncle in the *History of the Kings of Britain*, but William shows no knowledge of this. William did accept that St David was an archbishop, and that he came to Glastonbury with his seven bishops (the same number as in Geoffrey's work). Finally, in his *Deeds of the Kings of England*, William records another discovery. He describes a mysterious tomb on the coast of Wales, in the district of Ros. This was found in the late eleventh century and was no less than fourteen feet long. It was identified as the tomb of Walwin (Gawain), whom William calls 'the noble nephew of Arthur'.[14] None of this provided further information on Merlin, but it certainly made the *History of the Kings of Britain* and its account of the sixth century more acceptable.

William's work at Glastonbury is datable to around 1129–39, overlapping the period in which Geoffrey of Monmouth was making known his discoveries on British history and the prophecies of Merlin. Once those great discoveries spread, William's work was no longer enough for the monks of Glastonbury. The belief that their 'old church' of St Mary had been founded by the disciples of

Christ is clearly linked to the claims that none other than Joseph of Arimathea had come to Glastonbury, with relics of the Crucifixion. William of Malmesbury had been characteristically careful when discussing this church, but he himself helped to support another legend when he found in the Glastonbury archive a document dated 601, which named Glastonbury as 'the land called Ineswitrin'. He commented that this was the British name for the region, and that Glastonbury had once been an island. The monks subsequently built on this idea to claim that Ineswitrin was none other than the Isle of Avalon, to which the wounded Arthur had been taken.[15]

Another researcher into the British past was the Welsh historian and hagiographer, Caradoc of Llancarfan, whom Geoffrey of Monmouth called the historian of the kings of the Welsh. In fact Caradoc seems to have been something of a specialist in writing the Lives of British saints.[16] For Glastonbury he wrote a Life of St Gildas (that is, Gildas the Wise). In this he depicted Gildas as one of the twenty-four sons of Nan, king of Scotia, and a faithful subject of King Arthur, even after Arthur has killed one of his brothers. Caradoc also wrote that Gildas spent a year teaching in the schools at Glastonbury, and left at least one book in his own handwriting to the church.[17] Gildas is also said to have died at Glastonbury, after living there for some time as a hermit. Like William, Caradoc discussed the British name for Glastonbury:

Glastonia was of old called Ynisgutrin, and is still called so by the British inhabitants. Ynis in the British language is *insula* in Latin, and *gutrin* (made of glass). But after the coming of the English and the expulsion of the Britons, that is, the Welsh, it received a fresh name, Glastigberi, according to the formation of the first name, that is English *glass*, Latin *vitrum*, and *beria* a city; then Glastinberia, that is, the City of Glass.

Caradoc also said that Somerset was once the 'summer country' and that its king in the time of Gildas and Arthur was Melvas, a wicked king who kidnapped Arthur's queen, Gwenhwyfar. Only the intervention of Gildas and the abbot of 'Glastonia' persuaded Melvas to return the queen to Arthur and prevented war between the two kings.[18]

Caradoc's work for the bishop of Llandaf, believed by some historians to be his brother, added still further to this growing history of the 'world' of Merlin. The *Book of Llandaf*, also largely produced in the 1130s and also now notorious as a forgery, set out a history of the bishopric of Llandaf going back to the fifth century.[19] Unsurprisingly, this work confirms parts of the new history found also in the prophecies of Merlin and the work of William of Malmesbury. As the history of a bishopric and cathedral, the *Book of Llandaf* deals mostly with records relating to gifts, estates and properties. Merlin was not a patron of the church of Llandaf and thus does not appear directly in Caradoc's text. Nevertheless, William and Caradoc between them added considerably to the official record on the British Church, its saintly scholars and hermits, and its prestigious connections to early Christianity. William's researches at Glastonbury lay behind his Lives of the local saints, Patrick, Indract and Benignus, whilst Caradoc's Life of Gildas has already been discussed.[20] The belief that remote islands, cliffs and springs were favoured habitations for British hermits and scholars was reinforced by these researches, which also added snippets of information on British kings, and on King Arthur in particular. With so much work under way it is perhaps not surprising that Geoffrey of Monmouth returned to the fray in about 1150 with a new work which in some ways paralleled the Lives of British saints produced by William and Caradoc. This is the *Vita Merlini*, or *Life of Merlin*.[21]

Dating the *Life of Merlin* is difficult, but it is likely to have been written before 1151, when Geoffrey was finally promoted and elected as next bishop of St Asaph's, North Wales. It is tempting to wonder whether his *Life of Merlin* represented a part of Geoffrey's campaign for promotion within the Church, as it has a Prologue addressed to Robert, the new bishop of Lincoln, asking him to be a more generous patron than Bishop Alexander had been. Even though this cannot be proved, the very fact that Geoffrey troubled to produce a long work in complex Latin verse suggests that the level of interest in Merlin was very high. The new *Life* also establishes Geoffrey once again as the expert on Merlin, since it presents a considerable amount of new information. Here Merlin appears as a magician/prophet, a British prince and a learned hermit; in other words, a figure at home in the world of post-Roman Britain as depicted by Gildas/Nennius, William and Caradoc. Like the saintly hermits, including Gildas himself, Merlin in this version wants nothing more than to leave human society and devote himself to study. What is more surprising is that the study in question is that of astrology and natural philosophy, and that Merlin's life story is both long and disturbing. This may have been troubling for readers. Certainly the *Life of Merlin* seems never to have been anything like as popular as the prophecies, or the *History of the Kings of Britain*. Nevertheless, it is possible to show that it made a gradual impact on the image of Merlin in the later twelfth century.[22]

The *Life of Merlin* not only gives a much fuller version of Merlin's life, it also offers stories of sexual scandal, adultery and bigamy to add to the established view of Merlin as the child of a demon and a nun. Assuming that readers will already know of Merlin the Prophet, and of his role in the history of Britain, the opening of the *Life* simply says: 'Now, many years and many kings had come and gone. Merlin the Briton was famous throughout the world as king and prophet. He was law-giver to the proud South Welsh, and he prophesied the future for those who governed them.' This new, princely Merlin was a war leader, who supported Peredur, prince of the North Welsh, against Gwenddolau, ruler of the Scots. We also discover that Merlin had a wife, Guendoloena, and that his sister, Ganieda, was married to King Rodarch of Cumbria.

In a battle against King Gwenddolau, in which Merlin took part, three brothers dear to Merlin were killed. Such was Merlin's grief that he 'crept away and fled into the woods. . . . He stayed hidden in the woods, discovered by none, forgetting who he was, hiding like a wild animal.'[23] His favourite companion was a wolf, to whom he addressed poems about their sufferings. Merlin's sister sent out messengers, and they tracked him down to a mountaintop spring in the Forest of Calidon. A minstrel's song brought him back to awareness of himself, but Merlin, when brought to court, could not bear the crowds. He was so desperate to escape that he agreed to reveal 'secrets' to the king in exchange for his freedom. The king may have hoped for prophecies, but the revelations he received were rather different. Cruelly, one was that his wife (Merlin's sister and rescuer) was having an affair. However Ganieda was a worthy rival to Merlin, and easily fooled her husband into rejecting this. Merlin even rejected his own wife, declaring that she was free to remarry. With this, he disappeared again.

After several years, Merlin, although still mad and distant from human contact, realized from observing the stars that Conan had seized the crown as high king, and that his ex-wife Guendoloena was about to remarry. He assembled herds of wild animals and, riding bareback on a stag, drove them to the wedding, to the astonishment of Guendoloena. But the bridegroom made the mistake of laughing, at which Merlin's generous intentions were replaced by something much more savage. 'When the prophet saw him, he wrenched off the horns of the stag he was riding, whirled them around his head, and threw them at the bridegroom. He smashed the bridegroom's head and killed him immediately, driving his spirit to the winds.' Once more captured, Merlin again bought his freedom with secrets and prophecies. This time he also allowed his sister to supply him with a princely house in the forest, which had an observatory, and secretaries to write down his observations and prophecies, thus preserving them. These facilities enabled Merlin to make a series of new political prophecies about the future of the Britons and the arrival of recognisable Danes and Normans, wars with the French and the conquest of the Irish. Emerging from his full prophetic state, Merlin then became aware that King Rodarch was dying, and that the scholarly bard Taliesin had returned from studying in Brittany with Gildas the Wise.

The most immediate of these revelations rapidly proved true, and Merlin was joined by Taliesin in his study of magic and science. The learned discussions that ensued, according to the poetic *Life*, revealed secrets and marvels of the earth and even the heavens, including a list of magical islands. Prominent amongst these is Avalon, an island to which the Britons are able to travel, and which is dominated by nine magical sisters. Taliesin gives Merlin an account of the powers of Morgen, the chief of the sisters, saying that she has 'learned the uses of all plants . . . and knows the art of changing her shape, as well as the skill of flying through the air on strange wings, like Daedalus . . . and she taught astrology to her sisters.' He goes on: 'It was to her Island of Apples that we took Arthur after the battle of Camlan. . . . Morgen placed the king on a golden bed, uncovered his wound with her own hand, and studied it deeply. At length she said he could be cured, but only if he stayed with her for a long time.' When Taliesin heard from Merlin about the troubles of the British he wanted to send a fast ship to bring Arthur back. But Merlin rejected this, saying that the British must endure a long period of defeat, and could be saved only by an alliance. The shift to politics led Merlin to recount the stories of kings whose reigns he had seen, demonstrating his supernaturally long lifetime. However, these political discussions were interrupted by news that a wonderful spring had suddenly appeared at the foot of a mountain nearby. When the sages went to study it, Merlin's madness was cured by its healing waters, leading to long exchanges about the powers of springs, rivers and lakes. Merlin was thus sane when messengers reached him, begging him to return to his people and to govern them once more. This Merlin refused, due partly to his extreme age, and partly to his wish to pursue further study of miraculous phenomena such as healing springs. The *Life* clearly establishes here that Merlin was a Christian, and his discussions of the marvels of creation are shown as deeply learned blends of classical poetry and science with mediaeval theology.

However, Merlin's adventures were still not over, as Maeldin, a soldier who had once fought alongside Merlin, suddenly appeared – but roaring and foaming at the mouth in madness. We now learn that Merlin had had not only a wife but also a lover, whom he had scorned. The rejected woman had some magical power of her own, and prepared poisoned apples intended to inflict sickness and madness on Merlin. Maeldin ate them instead, and suffered in Merlin's place, but Merlin's healing spring was able to cure him. In the conclusion to the poem, Queen Ganieda retires to the spring and takes up Merlin's spirit of prophecy. Her prophecies are still more ominous than those of her brother (they are described in the poem as 'dark words from a dark heart'). What she foretells is a long period of suffering in Britain, when nothing can save the people from war and from the Normans.

This account is starkly different from the tone of the *History of the Kings of Britain*, and even seems to present a different version of

Merlin himself. He is neither the child-prophet nor the master of magical technology, but rather an adult Welsh prince with magical and political powers. No attempt is made to fit this in with the accounts in the *History*, nor is the relationship between King Rodarch and any king of Britain from the *History* discussed. The events narrated in the *Life* appear to have taken place after Merlin's disappearance from the *History*. But Taliesin's statement that he has been to Avalon with Arthur makes the historical relationship between the two books still more confusing, when it is juxtaposed with Merlin's review of how much time has passed since Arthur's reign. However, the repeated, vague mentions of 'many years' and long periods work to place the *Life* both within and outside the relatively clear and concrete world of the *History*. Instead, the *Life* combines a sensational new personal and sexual history for Merlin with a series of extremely advanced and learned expositions of magical science and natural magic. These learned discussions make the dedication of the *Life* to a prominent churchman less surprising. But the new information about Merlin's personal life, and his insanity, is shocking, as also is its source. For churchmen and historians may well have recognized that Geoffrey had gone to a questionable set of sources. To turn Merlin the Magician into a hermit-magus was one thing; to combine this with sexual scandals and other themes derived from Welsh-language poems on Myrddin, the bard driven mad at the Battle of Arfderydd, was extraordinary.[24] This may explain why the *Life* did not circulate widely, and why it had far less of an impact on the writing of history than did the *History of the Kings of Britain*.

The sensation caused by that work, and by Merlin's appearance in it, can be seen immediately by looking further at the work of Alfred, sacrist and treasurer of Beverley Minster in Yorkshire. Alfred had reached his position of seniority at Beverley by about 1135, when he began to witness charters there, and probably died about 1157, when a new sacrist appears in the records. He records in his own *Annales* that he first became interested in history as a result of reading the *History of the Kings of Britain*, and he then seems to have worked hard to collect and read as much as he could on the history of Britain. His enthusiasm was so great that he produced a history of his own in nine 'books', following Geoffrey of Monmouth from the Fall of Troy to the end of Arthur's reign, then drawing on more 'modern' histories to bring his story up to 1129.[25] Alfred attempted to create a unified history, aimed at those who could read Latin but were not specialists. He succeeded in producing a compact, one-volume 'school history', uniting the old history of Britain with the new and providing comments on his sources. His work met a need, and copies are known to have belonged to monastic and cathedral libraries in England during the later Middle Ages.[26]

Merlin's history forms a key part of Book Five of Alfred's work, which opens with the stories of King Constantine, and the brothers Constans, Aurelius Ambrosius and Uther Pendragon. Here, as elsewhere, Alfred does his best to reconcile Gildas/Nennius, Bede and the *History of the Kings of Britain*, as well as citing the *Roman History* (Eutropius). The story of Vortigern's attempt to build a fortress is told at some length (given that the whole of Book Five is only twenty-nine pages long), with the court magicians once again called *magi*. The account of Merlin's spirit-father is handled still more fully, with Merlin's mother once again recounting how, secluded with her female companions, she was visited by 'a being in the form of a beautiful young man' who could come to her at will, and who finally slept with her 'in the form of a man'. Merlin himself is called *vates* or prophet, and Alfred does not reject his prophecies. He says that Merlin prophesied many things which were to come in Britain, but they are too long to insert into his own *Annales*.[27]

Alfred also repeats the explanation that Merlin's father was a type of sublunary spirit called an incubus, as given in the *History of the Kings of Britain*, before going on to recount how Merlin prophesied the downfall of Vortigern and the triumph of Aurelius Ambrosius and Uther Pendragon. This ends rather abruptly with the forth-coming victory of the 'Boar of Cornwall', and this oracular utter-ance is given no explanation or comment, demonstrating that Alfred assumed that all his readers would already know that this signified Arthur.

Merlin's magical transportation of the 'Giants' Dance' to Salisbury Plain is not of interest to Alfred, and is given no mention. However, Merlin's ability to interpret the 'star of wonderful magnitude' for Uther is told at some length, including the details of how Merlin, inspired, 'burst into tears and cried out' before predicting Uther's succession to the kingdom and the birth of his children. This leads on to the story of Uther's love for Ygerna, and Alfred handles the themes of seduction and adultery very carefully. He says that Uther married 'Ugerna' after the death of her first husband, Gorlois, although he had already slept with her whilst Gorlois was alive 'through the wonderful magic [*miro praestigio*] of Merlin the Prophet'.[28] Once again, Arthur is effectively Merlin's creation, and even though Alfred is at some pains to show that he is aware that Arthur, unlike Aurelius Ambrosius, appears only in the 'British History', Alfred expresses no doubts at all as to Merlin's real histor-ical existence. Another interesting aspect is the hierarchy of Alfred's interests in the supernatural. Like signs and wonders in the form of stars, both prophets and incubi are real; magic can create illusions like the deception of Ygerna, but feats of magical engineering, such as the creation of Stonehenge, are excluded from Alfred's account. It is perhaps not surprising that no mention is made of the *Life of Merlin*.

Further evidence that the *Life of Merlin* was less popular than the *History of the Kings of Britain* is that the translators and poets who prepared new versions for less learned audiences incorporated this potentially controversial material only in very small doses. Geoffrey Gaimar was writing before the appearance of the *Life of Merlin*, so it is hardly surprising that it is not mentioned amongst his sources.[29] But a Jersey man, Master Wace, made a new translation of the *History* into French poetry, for none other than Eleanor of Aquitaine in the 1150s, and thus after the appearance of the *Life*.[30] Wace may well have known the *Life*, since he has Taliesin come to court (in the time of Cymbeline), and Taliesin does not appear in the *History*.[31] Nevertheless, his Merlin is entirely the 'prose' figure. Wace may be turning prose history into French poetry, but at the beginning of his work he declares that he is simply a translator of the historical truth: 'Maistre Wace l'ad translaté, Ki en conte la verité' (Master Wace translated it, and tells it truthfully). However, Wace also makes it clear that he was writing for an audience that had already heard about Merlin and wanted a serious account of his exploits. When Wace has told of Merlin's magical challenge against Vortigern's evil *magi*, and how Merlin revealed the dragons imprisoned in the subterranean lake, he reaches Merlin's great sequence of prophecies. Here he breaks off the story and addresses his audience directly. He says that they will already have heard Merlin's prophecies, and that he himself is unwilling to translate 'Merlin's book', since that would require 'interpretation' and he does not wish to make a mistake.[32] However, this clearly left many patrons discontented, since several of the surviving mediaeval copies of Wace's *Roman de Brut* insert versions of Merlin's prophecies here. The demand for genuine information on Merlin and his prophecies was clearly high by the middle of the twelfth century – and it was to remain so.

Wace's anxiety about interpreting the prophecies may be surprising in one who writes of his studies in Normandy and Paris, and calls himself a 'Master'. Yet it is the case that the writing of commentaries on the prophecies of Merlin was a growing and specialized area for the learned. Wace, like all other commentators, is clear that the king called by Merlin the 'Boar of Cornwall' is Uther's son, Arthur, but that is as far as his handling of the prophecies goes. As a serious translation of an important work should, Wace's version stays very close to the original. He tells of Merlin's moving of the stone circle, commenting that it is called Stonehenge in English. He also describes Merlin's ability to interpret the dragon star, and the magician's role in the begetting of Arthur. Like the *History*, Wace links Merlin's prophecies to the classical Books of the Sibyl. However, Wace is cautious as to whether Merlin prophesied for Arthur, although he does emphasize that Merlin was a great prophet.

When the English priest Layamon translated the *History of the Kings of Britain* into Middle English at the end of the twelfth century, he also made little mention of the *Life of Merlin*. Layamon seems to have written, rather like Alfred of Beverley, for love of his subject. He writes that he lived and studied by the Severn, and that he travelled to get books in the three languages of twelfth-century England (Latin, French and English). His English book was Bede's *Ecclesiastical History*, his Latin book was associated with saints Augustine and Albin, and his French book was Wace's translation of the *History of the Kings of Britain*. Seeing himself as telling the story of 'the noble deeds of the English', Layamon says he used all these books, but his work is heavily dominated by Wace.[33] The 'new' history thus passed into the least learned of the three languages, but was still presented as a serious work intended to give its audience a sense of their own history in which they could take pride.

Layamon suggests what aspects of Merlin's prophecies were of most interest to an unlearned audience. He depicts Vortigern as full of wonder that Merlin could see the lake and the dragons, when no other magician or seer could see them. Immediately, the tyrant has his chief 'sage', Joram, beheaded – along with his seven assistants – and makes much of Merlin. 'The king went to his dwelling, taking Merlin with him, and addressed him affectionately. He made Merlin his guest, and offered everything he could desire in land and treasure. . . . The king asked his "dear friend" Merlin to interpret the water, the stones, the dragons, and their fight, and afterwards to give counsel on how to win the whole kingdom . . .'[34] Merlin, however, saw through Vortigern as he saw through the earth, and he 'gladly' predicted the tyrant's imminent death, and the kings who would follow him:

> Flee, flee away, and try to save your life – but wherever you flee, Aurelius and Uther will pursue you. Aurelius shall first have this kingdom; and when poison takes his life, then Uther will succeed him. Your kin will kill him, but he will have a son, a wild boar out of Cornwall, bristling with steel. The boar shall be the bravest of men, and most noble in thought; he shall rule over Rome and fell all his foes. Sooth have I said to you, though it is not sweet for you to hear.[35]

Layamon concludes, 'Then Merlin the Wise ceased his words, the king caused thirteen trumpets to be blown, and marched forth with his army, as quickly as he could.' Nothing, of course, could save Vortigern – Merlin's prophecies may have been reduced to the bare essentials, but it was impossible to escape them.

Layamon's brief handling of the prophecies does not mean that he was uncertain about Merlin's powers or his supernatural origin, as his version of the story of Merlin's conception shows. Geoffrey of Monmouth put the story into the mouth of Merlin's (nameless) mother, who explained to Vortigern that: 'I knew no man who begot this child. All I know is that, when I was with my fellow nuns in our chambers, a being would appear to me in the form of a beautiful young man, who held me tightly in his arms and kissed me. . . . He would also talk to me without becoming visible, and he made love to me in the form of a man, leaving this child in my womb.'[36] This was, as shown above, followed carefully by Alfred of Beverley. Wace's version was calculated to emphasize the nun's innocence, and there she says that she never saw the 'phantom' who came to her, spoke to her, kissed her and lay with her 'like a man', finally making her pregnant.[37] But Layamon has her recount how, at fifteen, she grew 'wondrously fair', and dwelt in a royal bower with her maidens, in the mansion of her father, King Conaan.

> And when I was slumbering in bed, softly sleeping, then came to me the most beautiful being that ever was born, in the form of a knight, arrayed all in gold. This I saw every night, and the thing glided before me, glistening gold. It kissed me, caressed me, held me and embraced me. When I looked at my own limbs, my flesh was foul to me – I marvelled at my strangeness, and wondered what was happening to me. Eventually I found that I was with child. But I know not who or what begot this boy, whether an evil being or a creature from God.[38]

Merlin's supernatural conception is here a visual and physical experience – and one which is separated from his mother's entry into a nunnery.

One thing on which both Wace and Layamon agree (and which did not interest Alfred) is that Merlin was associated with Wales.

This is hardly surprising, although it goes slightly beyond what is actually stated in the *History of the Kings of Britain*. Wace describes Merlin as liking to spend time at a Well of Labenes, deep in Wales, where Wace has never been.[39] Layamon has the bishop of Caerleon refer to Merlin as 'our' prophet, as well as having Merlin dwell by the Well of Alaban, in Wales.[40] Merlin's dwelling place is mysterious. According to Layamon, only one British courtier was in contact with a hermit who knew a great, wild wood, far to the west, in which Merlin could be found. This mention of the hermit and the forest suggests an infiltration into Layamon's work of some of the themes of the *Life*, as – more strongly – does Layamon's reference to the 'wood of Calidon' as a place of flight.[41] In Layamon's version, Merlin's knowledge of the future is emphasized repeatedly. What is striking, however, is that whereas Wace referred to 'Merlin's book' Layamon emphasizes the oral nature of the prophecies. There are repeated references to what Merlin *said* long ago, as in the comment on Arthur's passing: 'Once there was a sage called Merlin, whose sayings were true, who said that an Arthur should yet come to help the English.'[42] At the end of the book, when King Cadwalader receives his vision of an angel, Merlin's prophecies are again reinforced. But here, Cadwalader reflects on how Merlin *spoke* the future while the wise Sibyl put it into books. Both are now equally perceived as figures of 'ancient times'.[43]

The closeness with which Wace and Layamon follow the *History of the Kings of Britain* emphasizes that they each aimed to produce a popular but reliable version of that historical discovery. They draw upon the *Life of Merlin*, but to a very limited extent. However, Layamon does add non-human figures from Anglo-Saxon tradition, such as elves. For his English-speaking audience, the details of the reigns of ancient British kings were apparently of less interest than the idea that Arthur could be a hero for the English, and that the great prophet Merlin spoke of the English future as well as that of the other inhabitants of Britain. Thus did the images of Merlin multiply, and by the end of the twelfth century he could be a hermit living primarily in Wales, an ancient prophet equal to the sibyls of the Mediterranean world, and a figure for the English. By this time he was so well known that writers producing new versions of the *History* could assume that their audiences already knew of Merlin and his marvels and prophecies. He also seems to have been so universally attractive that he was becoming a figure for non-British political and nationalistic affiliations. Nevertheless, the story of Merlin was not yet considered closed, and historians made new discoveries, even at the end of the twelfth century.

Foremost amongst these was an ambitious and aristocratic churchman now known as Gerald of Wales, who came from a well-connected Cambro-Norman family.[44] On his mother's side he was descended from Gerald of Windsor (who held Pembroke from the Norman kings) and the Welsh princess Nest (who was the daughter of Rhys ap Tewdwr, Prince of South Wales). He was both well connected and highly educated. When he returned from his studies in Paris in about 1174, he was given a set of appointments, including posts at Hereford and St David's. Gerald believed firmly that St David's had once had archbishops of its own, just as the *History of the Kings of Britain* and the 'new' Saints' Lives said that it had.[45] Moreover, he had exceptional access to oral tales of the history of the princes of South Wales, since the Lord Rhys, grandson of Rhys ap Tewdwr and ruler of Deheubarth as well as Henry II's justiciar in South Wales, was his cousin. Such were Gerald's connections that he liaised between Henry II and the Welsh princes. His royal appointments continued in 1185, when he was sent with Prince John to Ireland, as he was related to the early Anglo-Norman conquerors of part of Ireland. Gerald made use of the experience to write an account of his discoveries, the *Topography of Ireland*.

Of all his possessions, Gerald seems to have prized most his books (and perhaps his own numerous works highest of all). If Gerald's estimation of his own learning can be at all trusted, it is not impossible that he even had a copy of the extremely rare work of Gildas. In one of his historical accounts of his own times Gerald certainly claimed that he intended to follow Gildas, and he was jokingly (but very effectively) rude about Geoffrey of Monmouth's untruthfulness as a historian. However, Gerald did in fact accept much of the *History of the Kings of Britain* and its version of history, including the account of the reign of Arthur. In 1188 Gerald had an excellent opportunity to increase his knowledge by visiting libraries across Wales and listening to stories of local wonders and marvels. He accompanied Archbishop Baldwin of Canterbury on an extraordinary tour through Wales, intended to raise a crusading army. Gerald gives an account of the tour in his book *The Journey through Wales*. A second book, *The Description of Wales*, adds further information on the Welsh people and their customs and beliefs. Such 'travellers' tales' were increasingly popular in the twelfth century.[46] Both of Gerald's books on Wales followed in the model of narrative history mixed with geographical and anthropological description that he had pioneered in his *Topography of Ireland*. It is not surprising, given Gerald's interests, that one of the themes of his books on Wales is that of his own search for new evidence on Merlin, but what is surprising is that Gerald ultimately concluded that there were in fact two Merlins.[47]

Gerald's expertise on Merlin comes out at several points in his writing on Wales. For instance, when he describes Dinas Emrys he identifies it as the 'hilltop of Ambrosius', where Merlin prophesied for Vortigern.[48] He also assumes that his readers will know enough to understand the reference. Gerald's great new discovery was that as well as Merlin Ambrosius, the incubus's son, there was a second Merlin, previously unknown to scholars. This, according to Gerald, was Merlin Celidonius, who had originated in Scotland and first prophesied in the Calidonian Forest. Provocatively, Gerald claimed that Merlin Celidonius was truly the Merlin who lived in the time of Arthur, and that he had produced more prophecies than Merlin Ambrosius. Gerald clearly knew the prophecies of Merlin as they appear in the *History of the Kings of Britain*, and provides quotations from them.

Gerald's interest in prophets and belief in the great significance of prophecy emerge strongly in several of his works. He is also analytical in handling his information, and distinguishes between the Welsh tradition of purely local prophets and the much more international figure of Merlin.[49] Perhaps the most impressive local prophet described by Gerald was Meilyr, who had been driven mad during an illicit sexual encounter with a shape-shifting supernatural being, after which he could 'explain the occult and foretell the future'. Meilyr's knowledge, in Gerald's view, was derived only from communication with evil spirits, and was thus not infallible, even though some of his revelations were very accurate. Gerald also takes the opportunity to tell a story of how Meilyr revealed the sexual misconduct of an unpopular local abbot, an anecdote which suggests the type of information that evil spirits were likely to disseminate (whilst also entertaining Gerald's readers). Thus Meilyr offers echoes of Merlin's story, even whilst being a figure of much more limited prophetic power, and without Merlin's magic.[50]

Gerald says that 'his' Merlin is also called Merlin Silvester (or 'Merlin of the woods'). He comments on the state of frenzy (or madness) in which Merlin Silvester apparently prophesied, and says that this was different from the state of inspiration in which Merlin

Ambrosius prophesied. According to Gerald, Merlin Silvester's madness came upon him when he looked up during a battle and saw a dreadful monster in the air above him. The similarity to the version in the *Life of Merlin* is clear, but the differences are stronger still. Gerald's great coup came when the preaching tour reached Nefyn, on the eve of Palm Sunday. For it was here that Gerald discovered a written copy of the works of Merlin Silvester.[51] He promised to make known a full version of these, although in his writings on Wales he quotes only two prophecies. Both are political prophecies, and are linked by Gerald to Henry II. One tells of a strong, 'speckled' man and a momentous crossing of a river. The other relates to a stone bridge at St David's.[52] Since Gerald's interest in prophecy seems to have been widely shared at the royal court, he also planned to write a 'Prophetic History', bringing together the themes of prophecy and history as intertwined sources of knowledge.

Gerald's expertise on the subject of Merlin seems to have become known, since it was to Gerald that the monks of Glastonbury turned in 1191–2 when they needed an expert to authenticate another sensational discovery. This was no less than the grave of Arthur and Guinevere, discovered in Glastonbury churchyard, between two of the ancient carved stones that William of Malmesbury had described. Gerald records this memorable scene in two of his books, and it is a striking story. The grave was very deep, estimated by Gerald at sixteen feet, and Arthur's skeleton was of gigantic size. The identification was helped by the discovery above the skeletons of a stone and metal cross, with an inscription recording that this was *Rex Arturius*, buried *in insula Avalonia*. Gerald also described how a lock of Guinevere's beautiful, blond hair still survived, and shone in the sun. A monk was so powerfully affected that he leapt down into the grave and seized the tress of hair, intending to kiss it – but it fell to dust in his hand, and was never seen again.[53] The link between Glastonbury and Avalon was thus proved, and, the antiquity of Glastonbury itself further demonstrated, going well beyond anything which William of Malmesbury had recorded. Equally clearly, stories that Arthur was still alive and being cared for by the Lady of Avalon were disproved. Of Merlin's whereabouts, however, nothing was discovered.

This left the idea of two Merlins, both of whose fates were unrecorded. Welsh historical sources, preserved in the *Annales Cambriae*, show how complex the story of Merlin was becoming. These Latin annals seem to be based on a ninth-century chronicle centred on St David's. Entries are extended backwards into the fifth century, and material was also drawn from North British sources and from the Annals of Clonmacnoise (in Ireland). The whole work was edited together in the tenth century.[54] The place in which the various materials were collected and compiled together is not known, although St David's is a likely candidate. The oldest surviving copy of the collection is now in the British Library (MS Harley 3859), which was copied around 1100 and also includes Welsh royal genealogies. This manuscript has attracted considerable attention, since it contains entries both for Arthur's presence at the Battle of Badon and for the Battle of Camlann 'at which Arthur and Medraut fell'. A Battle of Armterid is also recorded, and is almost certainly the same battle as that at Arfderydd, which according to Geoffrey of Monmouth's *Life of Merlin* and the Welsh poems he used caused Merlin's madness. However, in this oldest version of the *Annales Cambriae* there is no mention of Merlin's historical role. It is only in a later version, dating from the late thirteenth century and compiled at the Welsh abbey of Neath, that a piece of information is added. The Neath annalist notes that it was at the Battle of Armterid that Merlin went mad.[55] For this thirteenth-century

Neath chronicler, it seems that there was only one Merlin, and that he combined the Merlin 'Ambrosius' of the *History of the Kings of Britain* with the 'wild man' of the Welsh poems and of the *Life of Merlin*.

What the case of the *Annales Cambriae* also shows is that by the thirteenth century Merlin was being inserted into chronicles from which he was previously missing. The motives for this may have been mixed, but it certainly suggests that Merlin was accepted as a genuine 'British' historical figure. Something similar seems to have happened when a version of Merlin Silvester was incorporated into twelfth-century miracle stories about St Kentigern. A Life of this sixth-century saint was commissioned by Bishop Herbert of Glasgow in the middle of the twelfth century. A fuller version was then put together later in the century by Jocelyn, monk and hagiographer of the abbey of Furness, which was not very far from the Scottish diocese.[56] Jocelyn tells of Kentigern's exile in Wales, using materials from Welsh sources. Kentigern encounters a mysterious Welsh madman called Lailoken, who is very like the 'wild' Merlin. By the fifteenth century a copy of the *Life of St Kentigern* had a striking heading above the stories about the saint's encounters with Lailoken. This introduces the stories about Lailoken as the *Life of Merlin Silvester*. The scribe who inserted this heading also copied Geoffrey of Monmouth's *Life of Merlin* into the manuscript, which is now in the British Library (MS Cotton Titus A xix).[57] Thus, whilst the twelfth century was the great age of research amongst sources which claimed enormous antiquity, work on the history of Merlin was still continuing in the fifteenth century. However improbable it may seem, Merlin and his supernatural powers were part of the historical record.

The final proof of Merlin's historical power and reality is provided by his appearance in encyclopaedic world histories, such as the

thirteenth-century *Mirror of History* (*Speculum Historiale*) compiled
by Vincent of Beauvais under the patronage of the French royal
court.[58] This begins with the Creation, and tells the history of the
whole world (as then known) in thirty-one books. Britain is given
scant attention, apart from mentions of how it took its name from
Brutus, until its conquest by the Romans. Thereafter, the martyrdom
of St Alban, the story of how St Patrick took Christianity to Ireland
and the necessity for St Germanus to challenge the Pelagian heretics
constitute Britain's main appearances, together with a brief notice of
the coming of the Saxons. This changes with chapter 30 of Book
Twenty-One. As in all such histories, events in Rome, Constantinople
and the Mediterranean are given precedence, so it is startling to find
this chapter entitled 'Concerning Certain Incidents and about
Merlin and his Prophecies'. The text of the chapter itself consists
largely of an account of Merlin's discovery in the reign of Vortigern,
of how his father was a spirit, and of his unique powers as a seer and
a prophet. Individual prophecies are actually mentioned, and Merlin
is stated to have foretold not only Arthur but also the Norman
Conquest of England. Whilst the prophecies are described as
obscure and no attempt is made to discuss them all, there is no
doubt that Merlin was considered to be real and important. This is
reinforced when Merlin appears again, in chapter 49 of Book
Twenty-One. The 'main event' in this chapter is Merlin's interpretation of the portentous star 'of wonderful magnitude', which is then
followed by the conception of Arthur. Thus, Merlin is not only the
first British figure of world stature since Patrick in the *Mirror of
History*; his supernatural parentage and prophetic powers mean that
he turns British history into something positive – and, even more
impressively, his prophecies are accepted as a true, if obscure, version
of things yet to come. In other words, Merlin the individual may
have disappeared long ago, but he still hovers over ongoing history.

The image of Merlin as a figure of supernatural power, long vanished yet brooding over history, central to the reputation of Britain yet known across mediaeval Europe, raises one final question for this chapter: what would mediaeval readers consider to be the facts about Merlin's own story? First and foremost there is his scandalous origin in the seduction of a royal nun by an incubus. Next there is the fact that, whilst still a child, he was nearly made the victim of blood sacrifice by evil court magicians; it was in escaping from this fate that he revealed his superhuman powers. His enormous power of prophecy was revealed at the same time. A recurring theme in Merlin's story is his rejection of political control. He had no hesitation in announcing Vortigern's impending downfall to the tyrant himself, and he was also ready to chide good kings who behaved badly. Arguably, Merlin was more powerful than any king – and he was, quite literally, a king-maker, who used his magic to produce Arthur. The royal court, centre of human power, had little attraction for him; he preferred the wild springs of Wales, although he would appear when urgently needed. Finally, his death was nowhere recorded, and his tomb was never found, though those of Gawain, Guinevere and even Arthur were discovered. These are the 'facts of Merlin', and they remained so throughout the Renaissance. What follows is to look at the powers of Merlin.

CHAPTER 3

ഇറ

THE BRITISH MERLIN

THE SPEED WITH which news of Merlin spread has now been demonstrated, as has the length of time for which research into the history of Merlin continued. Merlin's powers were established as unmatched since classical times, but he was very much more than an ancient British magician suddenly rediscovered. One of the most exciting things of all was the discovery of Merlin's prophecies. No good twelfth-century Christian could doubt the reality of prophecy, since it was central to the revelation of Christ as the promised Messiah and Saviour. Theologians from the Fathers of the Church onwards had also accepted that prophecy was not only a phenomenon of biblical times, but rather that God in His grace made revelations to humanity throughout history. St Augustine had made it clear that even classical (and thus pagan) prophets could make true prophecies, although they did not necessarily understand the real source of their own inspiration. This made the status of prophecy very high – and the issue of deciding whether a prophecy was genuine very serious. Merlin's prophecies did pass the test, were established as genuine, and henceforth became a source of enormous and lasting excitement.

The 'Book of Merlin' (as the mediaeval prophecies of Merlin became known) dealt with the whole of the future, and thus revealed how current dynastic struggles and political problems would work out. Merlin the Prophet was instantly famous, and his prophecies had the advantage that, having been 'made' in the fifth century, their truth could be immediately checked. It is no wonder that copies of the prophecies were in great demand – and, since they were expressed in deeply obscure language, the rapid appearance of commentaries and interpretations is also unsurprising. Nevertheless, the demonic origin of Merlin's powers might be expected to make them deeply suspect in a strongly Christian society. Merlin's father was an incubus, and incubi were demons. So could the prophecies of a half-demon be trusted, even if his mother was a nun? Might believers in Merlin and his prophecies not be in danger of falling into heresy? After all, it was a doctrine of the Church that future events, and the timing of the end of the world, can be known only to God.

In fact, the unique origin of these prophecies helped to explain their enormous scope. They also gained status from the fact that they were rediscovered in an ancient, long-lost book, and required special expertise to be translated and interpreted. The destruction of records from the fifth and sixth centuries provided an explanation for how such great prophecies could have been lost. It also helped that the Anglo-Norman realm was a rising power which could gain in prestige if its historic identity and mission were authenticated by supernatural revelation. The appetite for prophecy was thus strong, and Merlin's prophecies offered just what was needed. Merlin provided a perspective in which the Anglo-Saxons were not God's chosen instrument for sweeping away the sinful

British (as Bede had suggested), but merely a temporary phenomenon amongst a great sequence of invasions and upheavals. It is
therefore hardly surprising that the ruling groups of the Anglo-
Norman realm welcomed Merlin's prophecies. These revelations
were far more than mere entertainment – they raised political and
theological issues of enormous importance. Thus kings, courtiers,
churchmen and scholars all paid attention; and questions of interpretation were taken very seriously.

When the great prophecies were revealed in the 1130s, no reader
could have missed the fact that Merlin was a political prophet. The
prophecies are so long that they filled a whole booklet in manuscript
form, referred to by some writers as the 'Book of Merlin'. In modern
editions and translations they fill some fifteen printed pages.[1] They
are almost entirely focused on a complex series of rulers who will
appear in Britain, from the fifth century down to the end of the
world. This has the rather counterfactual effect of giving the idea of
Britain a status far higher than that of England – even though
England existed as a political reality in the mediaeval period, and
Britain did not. Very few of the prophecies deal in any detail with
figures or events other than those that were political, and they are
strikingly secular in content. A small selection deals with natural
catastrophes, and a larger one with supernatural and marvellous
events but there is very little comment on spiritual or religious developments. As might be expected, the language used is obscure and
symbolic, with animal imagery used to denote rulers. This gives the
kings of Britain something of the status of figures in the moral fables
and legendary stories with which twelfth-century readers would have
been familiar from their school days. It was also an innovation in
prophetic language, since neither biblical nor classical prophets had
used such imagery in quite this way. The effect was very successful,
since the prophecies are precise and obscure in equal measure.

The largest and most instantly recognizable group deals with the 'Boar of Cornwall'. This ruler occurs very early in the sequence of prophecies, and thus could be immediately understood as close to Vortigern in time. He is to bring triumph for the British, and will trample the invaders (that is, the Anglo-Saxons). We are also told that he is to rule both the 'islands of the Ocean' and the 'forests of Gaul', and will terrify 'the House of Romulus' (that is, Rome). The story of the Boar will be known everywhere because of his conquests, but his death will be a mystery. No reader of the *History of the Kings of Britain* could fail to recognize King Arthur, and none did. By contrast, the Boar's successors are rather summarily dealt with: 'Six of the Boar's descendants will hold power after him, and after them the German serpent will arise. This serpent will be raised up by a Wolf from the Sea, and hold power over the forests of Africa.' That is all Merlin has to say about these rulers, though he goes on to predict that there will be major changes in the centres of the Church, before 'a preacher from Ireland is struck dumb by a child not yet born'. No indication at all is given of how long these events will take, or whether the upheaval in the Church is to happen at the same time or later.

The reigns of the six kings are to be followed by terrible and destructive wars between the Red Dragon (the British) and the White Dragon (the Saxons).

Then the Red Dragon will do as it always does, and tear itself into pieces. Next the Thunderer will take revenge, and all the farmer's fields will fail. Death will destroy the people of all the nations, and those who survive will abandon their own land. But a king who is favoured by God will construct a navy, before being welcomed as the twelfth in the court of the saints.

Again, there was no statement of how long these events would last, but they were followed by what looked remarkably like a description of the Norman Conquest. Mediaeval readers of Merlin's prophecies thus had an obvious way to test their credibility, and that was to check their historical accuracy – as soon as commentators had established some identifications. The question of whether prophecies from a possibly demonic source were to be trusted could be given a satisfactory answer if Merlin could be shown to have made true prophecies for the period from the fifth to the twelfth century.

Some of the first twelfth-century readers bold enough to set down their reactions formally in writing were those who combined historical and theological learning. Perhaps the first was the Norman monk and historian Orderic Vitalis, author of a multi-volume *Ecclesiastical History* down to 1141 and early witness to the arrival of Merlin. He obtained a copy of the Prophecies of Merlin as early as 1135, and he was excited enough to write a response to them immediately, which he then copied into Book XII of his *History*. This book covered the reigns of Henry I of England and Louis the Fat of France, and Orderic's historical narrative shows how seriously he took the issues of divine revelation and supernatural guidance. For instance, his detailed account of the unpleasant treatment which Henry I meted out to his older brother, Robert of Normandy, builds up to a description of a tragically prophetic dream. The dreamer was Robert himself, and through the dream he was led to understand that his son, William, who had been keeping up the struggle against Henry I, was dead.[2] After the story of this dream-vision, the book breaks off for half a page, before introducing Merlin's prophecies and Orderic's comments on them. As readers of Orderic's chronicle would know, Robert's dream was true, and the story shows both how God continued to reveal the truth to humans, and how important such revelations were to mediaeval thinkers. The story of the dream thus reminds the reader of all this, before Merlin's own, infinitely greater, visions are introduced.

As an expert on British history, Orderic was able to calculate that six hundred years had elapsed since Merlin prophesied for Vortigern. He also established that Merlin's career as a prophet coincided with a time of heresy amongst the British, when St Germanus of Auxerre came from France to correct the false teachings of Pelagius and to fight personally against the pagan Anglo-Saxons. Orderic had clearly read both Bede's *History* and the later historical compilation of Nennius (which in the twelfth century was confused with the historical work of Gildas). Orderic would therefore be highly aware of how scanty the historical information was for the fifth and sixth centuries. His response to Merlin's prophecies and their revelations was both enthusiastic and cautious. He accepted without question that these were major prophecies, worthy both of that name and of inclusion in a serious, religious history. Moreover, he studied them carefully, and identified, he believed, those parts which related to his own times. This acceptance was emphasized when he called Merlin *vates*, a Latin term which denoted serious prophetic gifts. But he exercised caution when he omitted all mention of Merlin's incubus father. Orderic was also silent about Geoffrey's statement that Merlin was possessed by a spirit when making his prophecies. Moreover, when describing the revelation of the subterranean pool and the dragons that it contained, Orderic said that Merlin 'showed' these things to Vortigern, using an ambiguous term which might suggest that Merlin provided a vision for Vortigern rather than bringing about the actual excavation and loosing of the dragons.

Having set the scene in this way, Orderic went on to state that the prophet Merlin gave an accurate prediction of the pre-Conquest assassination of Prince Alfred, the brother of Edward the Confessor, by treacherous Anglo-Saxons. From this he moved to direct quotation of the passage which he identified as dealing with the period from the Norman Conquest of England to his own lifetime. It begins:

> A people in wood, and in iron garments, shall come to punish this wickedness. They will restore the possessions of the original inhabitants, and shall destroy the foreigners. The foreigners will be uprooted from our soil, and their generations shall be decimated. The survivors will be reduced to everlasting slavery, and shall labour on the land.

Thus, the Anglo-Saxons are reduced to foreign interlopers in Britain, whose wickedness is punished by the arrival of the triumphant Normans, and whose reduction to serfdom is entirely merited. Like other Anglo-Norman commentators, Orderic identified the Anglo-Saxons with 'German' figures in the prophecies. William the Conqueror and his son William Rufus are seen in the two dragons who next rule Britain, and Orderic had no hesitation in identifying the dragons' successor, the Lion of Justice, as Henry I. His roar makes the towers of Gaul and the dragons of Britain alike tremble, and he extorts enormous quantities of gold and silver from his territories, even whilst his courtiers curl their hair and dress in pretty colours. If this were not recognizable enough, there are details about the savage efficiency of his justice, and about how his 'cubs' turned 'into fishes'. The latter needs little effort to be read as a prediction of the drowning of Henry I's heir and his companions. Orderic was writing just before the death of Henry I, so had now reached his own times, and was about to venture into the immediate future – exciting but dangerous territory.

The prophecies quoted by Orderic go on to give frightening details of war in Wales, of murderous rivalries amongst the powerful, of Scottish invasions, and of struggles for power amongst members of the ruling dynasty. Finally, a sixth ruler is to conquer and settle Ireland, achieving greatness despite suffering from a 'wavering tendency' at the start. He is also to make great changes for the Church, to give great gifts, and to win divine favour, although he will produce a predatory disease which will threaten ruin to the people. Orderic's quotation ends with Merlin's prediction that, after this extraordinary reign, Normandy will lose its islands and its prestige before Britain's original inhabitants return. For a reader in 1135 this might well suggest impending failure of the Norman rule over England, a very worrying prospect indeed. It was certainly frighteningly close to the dire political events which were already under way, and were eventually to unleash nineteen years of civil war and suffering upon England.

As Orderic says, he gives only a short extract from Merlin's prophecies, but his belief in their importance was such that he wished to make them known to scholars who had not yet seen them.[3] His selection can only have helped to establish Merlin's reputation as a true prophet, especially since he says that many of the prophecies have already been proved true, as anyone who knows history can see, and that future generations will find that more will come true for them. However, the task of interpreting the prophecies relating to events yet to come is left by Orderic to 'philosophers'. He himself, as a historian, returns to his task of recounting events that have already happened. As with other commentators and translators of the prophecies, this caution does not veil scepticism about the prophecies; the reverse is true, since these were accepted as genuine revelations of things to come, which could have very serious consequences if misinterpreted.

Merlin's prophecies had such an enormous impact that they were rapidly taken into historical writing not only in England and

Normandy but also in the rival kingdom of France. Henry I's contemporary Louis the Fat died in 1137, and Abbot Suger of St Denis, Louis's adviser and regent, wrote a biography of his king and patron. In itself this is unsurprising, but Suger's work makes it clear that he also knew at least part of the prophecies of Merlin, and that he identified Henry I as the Lion of Justice.[4] How Merlin and his Book of Prophecies had reached Suger and the court of France is not explained. But the level of political interest in the prophecies is further confirmed. Unlike Orderic, Suger does not give a single long extract from Merlin's prophecies. Instead, he quotes shorter passages, interpreted in his case from the point of view of the French court. This very effectively demonstrates the speed with which knowledge and copies of Merlin's utterances were being passed on amongst those in positions of power.

For Suger, Merlin was a genuine and wonderful prophet, who had foretold not just the reign of Henry I but the 'whole future of the English'. However, Suger is much more concerned with present events in France. Like Orderic he gives detailed interpretations, but Suger's comments focus on Henry I's subjugation of the Normans. As descendants of the Vikings, the Normans are identified with the kites and wolves of Merlin's prophecy, according to Suger. Henry I's seizure of Norman towers and fortifications is interpreted as fulfilling the prophecy that the Lion of Justice would cause 'the towers of France to tremble' (and this has the happy effect, for French readers, of confirming that Normandy is part of France rather than part of Henry I's kingdom). Henry's own courtiers are treated rather dismissively, since Suger declares that the English barons are to be identified with the 'island dragons' who trembled before the roaring of the Lion. Henry I's extraction of gold from his people, both clerical and secular, is accepted by Suger as a necessary part of ensuring strong government for the whole kingdom, an interesting perspective since churchmen were prone to complain at royal levies on their possessions. As a politically informed outsider whose own king is not included in the prophecies, Suger is able to conclude that: 'All the sayings of this great and ancient prophet apply so exactly to the king ... that not one word seems out of place.'

Merlin and his prophecies thus reached high places, and reached them very fast. But does this mean that they disappeared from fashion and from view with equal speed? The answer is unequivocally that they continued to be taken as a serious guide to historical events for centuries, with historians and political commentators able to assume that their readers would already know about the great 'Book of Merlin'. The prophecies were so extensive that as events moved on new prophecies could be considered relevant to current developments. By 1155 Henry I had been dead for twenty years, a nineteen-year civil war had been fought in England, and Henry II had gained control of England and Normandy, as well as his father's territory of Anjou. This made the fate of the Anglo-Norman realm still more interesting for French rulers and commentators, whilst historians continued to work hard on turning the 'mass of events' into informative narrative. It was at this point that another highly educated French monk, Richard of Poitiers, composed a history of the world which aimed to bring together the accounts of biblical, classical, early Christian and early mediaeval authors.[5] For his account of the history of Britain he used Gildas, Bede and the *History of the Kings of Britain*, as had already become standard. But he also applied the prophecies of Merlin to events well beyond Britain itself, and seems to have been the first to do so. Like most mediaeval historians, he paid special attention to prophecy as a way of understanding the meaning of events. What is more, he treated Merlin's prophecies as both genuine and a source of significant insight into God's purpose. Merlin's status as an international authority was thus already established by the middle of the twelfth century.

It is clear that mediaeval readers had two ways of knowing about Merlin and the importance of his prophecies. The first was the direct route, through acquiring either a full copy of the *History of the Kings of Britain* or (more cheaply) a copy of the Prophecies alone. The second was the indirect route, through reading about the prophecies and their ongoing fulfilment in works of history. There is overwhelming evidence of how widely known and trusted the prophecies were. The number of surviving copies is higher than that of almost any other mediaeval work, with over three hundred identified. Moreover, by the reign of Richard I writers could refer simply to the famous prophecies without giving the name of Merlin, confident that their quotation would be recognized. One of the first to do so was Ralph of Diceto, dean of St Paul's Cathedral and author of a work known as *The Images of History* that ends in 1201. In his account of Henry II's reign, Ralph interprets the rebellions and invasions of the 1170s as punishment for the martyrdom of Thomas Becket, who was murdered in his cathedral at Canterbury in 1171. But he points out that the tide turned in 1174, when the martyred archbishop was placated and a prophecy was fulfilled.[6] No name is attached to this prophecy, but the extract quoted by Ralph is from the Prophecies of Merlin, and the suggestion is that his readers would be familiar with it. As Ralph said:

That very day, when King Henry prayed that Thomas would be merciful to him, William king of Scots was delivered into custody at Richmond castle. This fulfilled the prophecy that 'a bridle forged in the bay of Brittany will be placed between his jaws', since Richmond castle has been held by Breton princes by inheritance from times long ago.

Just how widespread belief in Merlin's prophecies had already become is shown by the fact that Roger of Howden and Benedict of Peterborough, both clerical authors of chronicles dealing with English affairs, also referred to the prophecies in detail, assuming that their readers would know about Merlin and that his prophecies were important. One of Merlin's prophecies, as given by Geoffrey of Monmouth, was that: 'The cubs of the ruler will awake, leave the forests and hunt in the cities. They will kill great numbers amongst their enemies, cut out the tongues of the bulls, and load chains upon the necks of those who roar. They will renew the time of their fore-bears.' For both Roger and Benedict this was a reference to Henry II's sons, who rebelled against him and caused considerable warfare, awaking memories of the long 'anarchy' of the 1130s and 1140s.[7]

Henry II's most celebrated son, Richard I, a famous warrior and crusader, was identified by Ralph and others as another, more fortunate, figure from the same section of Merlin's prophecies. According to Merlin, after the bridling of Scotland, 'The eagle of the broken treaty shall gild this bridle, and rejoice in a third nesting.' It seemed clear that Richard was the offspring of this third nesting, who was to make his mother, 'the eagle of the broken contract', happy at last. Henry II's wife, Eleanor of Aquitaine, was thus the eagle, and Ralph points out that the fact that she had suffered 'broken contracts' in both England and France is clear fulfilment of the prophecy. Ralph provides further evidence that the prophecies were the subject of ongoing discussion when he says that this 'eagle' prophecy had 'puzzled all' by its obscurity.[8] Interpretations continued in the reign of Richard's brother, John, hand in hand with the ongoing updating of chronicles. Another Ralph, this time the abbot of the Cistercian abbey of Coggeshall (in Essex), took on the task of continuing his monastery's record of events in England. The original work covered the period 1066–1186; Ralph took up the story in 1187 and continued it down to 1224. He made no claim to be a great scholar, but he clearly knew a range of other histories, and used them in his own work. He also incorporated the statements of eyewitnesses to recent events, such as the discovery of the grave of Arthur and Guinevere at Glastonbury. King John's disastrous loss of Normandy, Brittany, Anjou and Maine was interpreted by Ralph of Coggeshall as fulfilment of Merlin's prophecy that 'the sword shall be divided from the sceptre'.[9]

Another important writer in the reign of King John was Gervase, monk and official of Canterbury Cathedral priory. Gervase had been very involved in political disputes regarding the appointment of archbishops, and had met both the pope and the king. His view of politics was therefore not simply that of an otherworldly monk, and his account of John's reign is thoughtful and informed. He knew Merlin's prophecies, and knew that the eagle was to be followed by 'the cubs of the ruler'. Then 'the sixth shall throw down the walls of the Irish cities and level its forests. . . . His beginning will be weak and uncertain, but his end shall achieve the heights.' Gervase identified John with this 'sixth king', and recorded that many people in the early thirteenth century were discussing Merlin's prophecies and making this identification.[10] To Gervase and other commentators of the time, the links between John and this king were clear. The designation 'sixth' was further proof, since John was the sixth king since the Conquest, if Stephen was ruled out as a usurper. John's unpopularity, and involvement in the disappearance of his nephew and rival, the significantly named Arthur of Brittany, can only have added to the interest of discussing his exciting end.

Perhaps most important of the chroniclers of the early thirteenth century, however, was Matthew Paris, historian of the royal abbey of St Albans. Matthew became a monk in 1217, and took over the writing of history at St Albans in 1236, almost exactly a century after the first revelation of Merlin's prophecies by Geoffrey of Monmouth. His chronicle is sometimes idiosyncratic, and sometimes irreverent, but he boasted that his historical work was so highly regarded that the king himself came to visit, in order to ensure that Matthew gave full coverage to recent royal activities. Matthew's ambition went beyond the simple writing up of his own times. His *Great Chronicle* gives a complete coverage of world history, starting with the Creation and divided into the 'six ages', which theologians such as St Augustine had explained as corresponding to the six days of God's Creation of the universe.[11] The foundation of Britain, by Brutus and his Trojans, is placed in the third age, which concluded with the reign of the biblical King Saul. All theologians and historians were agreed that the birth of Christ had initiated the sixth age of history; Matthew Paris goes further, by calculating that this was in the year 5199 from the creation of the world, and that Cymbeline was then ruling in Britain. The account of Merlin in the *Great Chronicle* is detailed, and shows just how interested Matthew was in this great British prophet.

According to Matthew's information, the boy prophet was discovered in the year 464; the story is the familiar one, based on the *History of the Kings of Britain*, with additional details from Bede. However, after giving an account of the installation of a new pope in 465, Matthew breaks off his historical narrative. The next section is headed 'Here begin the Prophecies of Merlin', and it is illustrated (in Matthew's own copy of the work, made for St Albans itself) with a painted image of Merlin in the act of prophesying to Vortigern.[12] What Matthew does here (adding to the work of his predecessor at St Albans, Roger of Wendover) is to set out Merlin's prophecies, and to add his comments and interpretations both in the margins and between the lines. The prophecies are given in full, and, together with the interpretations, take up some seventeen printed pages in modern editions.[13] Matthew followed the established identifications of figures and events up to the late twelfth century. Thus, the people in iron tunics are once again the Normans, and the Lion of Justice is once again Henry I. For Matthew, as for Ralph of Diceto, the 'eagle of the broken contract' was Eleanor of Aquitaine, and her fortunate third offspring was Richard I.[14]

Matthew commented extensively on the prophecies that he identified as dealing with Henry I and his successors, and was prepared to make independent identifications. For him, the king who 'broke down the walls of Ireland' was not John but Henry II, and the lion who was to follow this king was clearly Richard I. Boldly, Matthew identified the destructive lynx, which was to be born from the same line and cause suffering to its own people, with King Henry III.[15] Like Richard of Poitiers, Matthew Paris interpreted Merlin's prophecies to refer not only to Anglo-Norman affairs but also to international ventures. For instance, the 'old man in white on a horse white as snow . . . with a white rod in his hand', who would appear after the lynx had wrought destruction, was none other than Pope Innocent III. And the next ruler, Conan, who was to be summoned by Cadwalader and to ally with the Scots against England, is the Emperor Frederick.[16] This suggests that Matthew saw the British revival which comes next in Merlin's prophecies, fuelled by the unification of all the British peoples, as likely to happen in his own time. This was deeply troubling since 'there will be slaughter amongst those of foreign descent, the rivers will run with blood, the hills of Brittany will burst open, and the crown of Brutus will crown them'.[17] The end of England as a kingdom seemed to be imminent, since it was to become Britain once again. Events in Europe were to be equally exciting, since Conan/Emperor Frederick was to produce a 'fierce boar' as a successor; and, according to Merlin, this boar was to attack and conquer not only 'the forests of Gaul' (all or part of France) but also the Arabs and the Africans. It was to invade 'the remotest parts of Spain', though how long it would stay there was not made clear. This suggests coming developments in the Crusades, making Merlin's prophecies a source of comfort at a time when the crusading movement was experiencing major difficulties, although Matthew himself does not comment on this.

Here Matthew's identifications ceased, with rather more than half of the prophecies yet to be fulfilled. It was thus comfortingly clear that the end of the world remained a very long time in the future. The immediate future, however, was shocking in a less warlike way. The conquering boar was to be followed by the Goat of the Tower of Venus, which would produce peace and plenty. For no fewer than three generations there would be luxury and fornication, with women 'swaying like snakes' and Cupid wantonly firing arrows. However, the excesses of this period would be ended by famine and destructive loss of life, with many towns left in mourning. Just how long all this would take is uncertain, since the prophecies give no clear measurements of time. Unusually in Merlin's prophecies, the situation is to be saved not by a ruler who is politically or militarily successful but by a 'Boar of Trade', who will restore the prosperity of the people. But for Matthew, no identification of this figure could be made as the time had not yet come; that was for future generations. As might be expected, the prophecies themselves give no indication of how long any of these reigns, wars or tribulations would last. Even the prediction of 'three generations of excess' is unusual, since most sentences simply begin 'Then will come' or 'Next will come'.

By the time Matthew Paris ceased his interpretations, the process of analysing and applying the prophecies had continued enthusiastically for well over a century, and was not yet at an end. As has been seen, commentators increasingly assumed that those able to read histories in Latin prose would be familiar with Merlin's predictions. But what is even more interesting is that knowledge of Merlin and his foretelling of the future spread not only amongst chroniclers, theologians and courtiers but also more widely. Master Wace had translated the *History of the Kings of Britain* into French verse soon after its first appearance, but had not attempted to translate the prophecies, saying that this was too complex an area for him. However, by the thirteenth century at least two translations were available in Anglo-Norman French. These translations were incorporated into new copies of Wace's work, and may also have circulated separately.[18] For the less powerful and less wealthy, who knew only English, direct access to written versions of the great revelations was slow in coming. But this certainly did not mean that they would have known nothing of Merlin.

References to Merlin and his prophecies were frequent in popular literature by this time, suggesting that even the illiterate would be familiar with tales about the ancient British prophet. Moreover, from the fourteenth century onwards grammar schools began to be available in English towns for the sons of middle-class families. History formed part of their curriculum, and Merlin constituted one of the more interesting and memorable episodes in the history that was taught in such schools. Linked to this is the fact that, from the early fourteenth century, works of history were beginning to be written in English. Serious translation and interpretation of prophecies was still an elevated task, but the presence of Merlin was strong nevertheless. About 1300, one Robert of Gloucester wrote a *Metrical Chronicle* in English, incorporating free translations of Geoffrey of Monmouth, Henry of Huntingdon and William of Malmesbury.[19] The *History of the Kings of Britain* included a full text of Merlin's prophecies, but Robert quoted only a short excerpt relating to the 'Boar of Cornwall'. Like everybody else, he was confident that this was King Arthur. Beyond this, however, he did not venture, saying that the prophecies overall were 'too dark' for 'simple men'.[20] This suggests that Robert placed both himself and his readers into this modest category. The metrical chronicle itself was clearly successful, since about sixteen copies are known to survive from the late Middle Ages, which is high for a work of this sort.

From the middle of the fourteenth century, the gathering impact of the Hundred Years War ensured that political and military leaders in both England and France stood in great need of prophetic guidance. By this time, English was becoming a literary language in its own right, although still with a rather lower cultural status than French or Latin, and in the late fourteenth century the 'new' British history was finally translated into English prose. The resulting work is known as the Middle English Prose Brut. It was enormously popular in England and was updated several times in the fifteenth century. It survives in around 180 manuscripts, and in a further 65 as re-translations into French and Latin. This suggests that it rapidly became almost as popular as the History of the Kings of Britain itself, and it was actually the first English-language history to be printed.[21] It takes its account of early British history from the work of Geoffrey of Monmouth – and Merlin unsurprisingly plays a central role in this section. However, Merlin's prophecies also form a major element of the coverage of more recent history, where whole chapters are devoted to the interpretation of individual projections.

What the Prose Brut does is to follow the earlier Bruts in giving only a short version of Merlin's prophecies to Vortigern.[22] Its innovation is to take up a current political prophecy, about the 'Six Last Kings of England', and to present a long version of this as the prophecies that Merlin made for King Arthur (mentioned at the end of the

History of the Kings of Britain, but not given). Chapter 75 of the Prose *Brut* is headed, 'How Kyng Arthur asked of Merlyn the adventures of the last six kings that were to reign in England, and how the land should end.' Here Merlin's prophecy is very precise, stating that the first king in the sequence, the Lamb, will appear in 1215. His successors will be a Dragon, a Goat, a Boar, another Lamb and then 'the accursed Moldewarp'.[23] In the reign of this disastrous Mole:

> Castles shall be tumbled into the Thames, and so many dead bodies shall fall into the Severn that the river will seem dry. The four chief waters of England shall run with blood . . . and the Moldewarp shall be driven into a ship, but will be cast aground when the water retreats. . . . The Moldewarp shall die suddenly, drowned in the sea, his line will be left in a strange land for ever, this land will be parted into three parts, and be called the Land of Conquest. So shall the heirs of England end.[24]

The chronicle then moves on, until in chapter 160 the appropriate date is reached, and it is revealed that the first Lamb was King Henry III. The heading of this chapter is 'Exposition of Merlin's Prophecy about King Henry, son of King John . . .'. The exposition given is very detailed, with the harmful 'Wolf from a strange land' being identified as Simon de Montfort, Earl of Leicester, who 'was born in France and began against the king a powerful war'. Hope is introduced at the end of the chapter, for although the death of Henry III left 'the great lords of England' bereft, this was set aright by the return from the Holy Land of his son, 'Sir Edward, the best knight in the world for honour', to be crowned Edward I, and revealed as the Dragon.[25] Chapter 186 subsequently details Edward's fulfilment of the prophecies relating to the Dragon, while Edward

II is analysed as the Goat in chapter 211. The original chronicle ends in the year 1333, whilst Edward's own son, Edward III (clearly the glorious Boar) is still alive.

By this time Merlin's prophecies had become a minor industry, with numerous new ones added to the canon, even though less grandly presented than in the Prose *Brut*. The 'Prophecy of the Six Kings' itself was of early fourteenth-century origin, and was issued in French, English, Latin and Welsh versions, and in both prose and poetic forms, as well as being embedded into the *Brut*.[26] It became so famous in the fifteenth century that it was finally satirized by Shakespeare in *Henry IV, Part One*. The quotation comes in Act III, scene 1, when the Welshman Glendower is mocked for boasting of the astrological convulsions which accompanied his birth and for 'telling of the moldwarp and the ant, Of the dreamer Merlin and his prophecies . . . And such a deal of skimble-skamble stuff. . .'. Since the first of the Six Kings, the Lamb, was Henry III, the disastrous Moldewarp was ultimately identified as Henry IV. This is what made the prophecy relevant for Shakespeare's play about that king, even if it was no longer in fashion by the late sixteenth century.

Another illustration of the ubiquitous fame of Merlin the Prophet, and of his usefulness as a source of comment on contemporary events, is given by a work known as the *Prophecy of the Sibyl and Merlin*. This was recorded by the chronicler Walter of Coventry in about 1300.[27] It is a political prophecy which focuses on the rulers of England and Scotland, and the warlike relations between them. Given that war between the English and the Scots was a major issue in about 1300, this prophecy was very timely when first circulated and copied. However, it does not appear to have gained anything like the fame of the prophecy of the Six Kings. Equally significant as an indicator of the link between history, politics and prophecy in the fourteenth century is the *Scalacronica*. This was the first English history to be written by a secular knight, rather than by a churchman or 'professional' writer. Its author was Sir Thomas Gray, and he was inspired to write it by a visionary dream which he experienced whilst being held prisoner in Edinburgh in 1355.

In his dream, Sir Thomas was taken to an orchard and shown a ladder leaning against a high wall. On its rungs were four established historians whom Thomas was to emulate. All of these were churchmen, and the dream made it plain to Thomas that whilst he could follow them in giving an account of history, commenting on the future was a deep issue and not something for him to venture into. Thomas was then directly told that the great prophet Merlin had seen revelations of the future – but that only churchmen could safely and accurately interpret them. The political future is thus presented as the area of Merlin's particular expertise, and the specialist skills required for interpreting Merlin's words are again emphasized.[28] It perhaps hardly needs saying that Sir Thomas obeyed his supernaturally given instructions, and did not attempt to supply new interpretations of the prophecies. For the *Scalacronica* Merlin thus remains a rather numinous presence, a guarantor that God's plans are being worked out, yet for that very reason beyond the scope of a mere knight – even one licensed to write by a visionary dream.

A much more self-confident approach was taken by Thomas of Castleford in his metrical chronicle. This is a massive work, completed in 1327 and telling the story of British history (down to the deposition of King Edward II) in 39,437 lines of poetry.[29] Its author shows no sign of theological training or of serious interest in spiritual matters – but he does not let that inhibit him. It rapidly becomes clear to the reader that Thomas of Castleford is very interested in weapons and warfare, which he discusses in some detail.

However, he has done his homework, and uses it to bring together a collection of dramatic stories. Once again the account of early British history is based upon the *History of the Kings of Britain* – but Thomas of Castleford's interest in Merlin's prophecies was backed by sufficient military boldness (or rashness) for him to incorporate a full translation. It is not known whether Thomas was aiming for a wide distribution of his massive poem, since he gives no statement about his reason for writing or his hopes in relation to the book. Only one manuscript of Thomas's chronicle survives, suggesting that it was circulated merely amongst friends. This perhaps helps to explain the unusual boldness of his approach. But what makes the case of Thomas of Castleford so interesting is that he demonstrates that Merlin's prophecies still had enormous impact, even three centuries after their first discovery, and that their audience was becoming very wide.

By the fifteenth century, larger numbers of secular writers in English were becoming bold enough to discuss Merlin and his prophecies – though they tended to take refuge in anonymity. One of these simply reused Merlin's twelfth-century prophecy about the British alliance that would end the kingdom of England. He put a translation of it into a political poem about events in his own time, but went no further. Even so, the author was clearly wise not to sign his work, since predicting the end of his country could hardly be interpreted as a statement of confidence in its current government. Other anonymous fifteenth-century commentators on current troubles also drew upon the 'Book of Merlin', adapting established prophecies and adding new ones.[30] Thus the very fame of the prophecies made them a powerful tool for political agitators, since everybody knew that Merlin had foretold the whole of British and English history – but only a tiny minority believed they knew what he had actually said. This made it possible for more and more prophecies to be produced, and for both sides in the fifteenth-century civil wars known as the Wars of the Roses to claim that their leaders were great kings prophesied by Merlin. The name of Merlin was indeed powerful, if it could rally armies and give legitimacy to claimants to the throne.

Thus, once Merlin's reputation as the great political prophet got under way, it gathered ever greater momentum, down to the fifteenth century. But where did it begin? Was it with Geoffrey of Monmouth, or with the older tradition of Welsh poetic prophecies attributed to the princely bard Myrddin, which Geoffrey used in his *Life of Merlin*? These enjoyed considerable power amongst the Welsh during the tumults of the civil war in England and the great uprisings in Wales in the 1130s and 1140s. However, these Welsh prophecies of Myrddin referred primarily to Welsh figures, events and aspirations, making them of specific, rather than universal, relevance.[31] Their existence would thus add to the historical credentials of Merlin for historians who could read them, but their language was unfamiliar and their details of interest mostly only in Wales and Cornwall. If evidence of this is needed, it is provided by the fate of the *Prophetiae Merlini* of John of Cornwall.[32] John appears to have worked at the request of Robert Warelwast, bishop of Exeter, who died in 1155. John had expertise in the 'British' language, and was also a churchman and scholar. His researches into Merlin resulted in a collection of 139 'authentic prophecies', which he also commented on and interpreted. John was working after Geoffrey of Monmouth, and thirty-eight prophecies in his collection repeat items in Geoffrey's work. However, the other 101 focus on the rulers, battles and histories of the Celtic kingdoms. Those looking for prophecies relating to England, Normandy or Europe would find little here. And John's work survives in just one manuscript copy of the early thirteenth century. Merlin's reputation as a prophet for the 'British', therefore, cannot account for his international success.

Geoffrey of Monmouth's version of Merlin was accepted as a major historical figure, and it is Geoffrey's work which stands out as the means by which Merlin, inspired prophet and semi-demon, achieved his lasting place in European culture. This leads to the conclusion that Merlin, in the form revealed in the 1130s, was successful at least in part because his prophecies appealed to a very wide and lasting audience. Proof of the latter point is provided by the fact that the reputation of Merlin the political prophet continued for centuries. It was in 1510 that Wynkyn de Worde responded to Merlin's popularity by printing a *Lytel Treatys of the Byrth and Prophecye of Merlin*. This *Treatys* is in Middle English verse, and dwells on Merlin's supernatural origin, and on the powers he revealed whilst still a small child.[33] It makes no attempt to present the long series of kings that Merlin had foretold for Britain. Instead it draws on Geoffrey's *Life of Merlin* for stories of how Merlin, whilst being brought to Vortigern by messengers, made sardonic revelations of political and sexual scandals taking place at court. These unsettling insights are followed by the well-known story of the dragons and Merlin's prophetic interpretation of their battle. Merlin's role in the downfall of Vortigern and in the reigns of Uther and Pendragon then forms the subject of the rest of the poem.

The making of a full translation of the prophecies into English remained a specialized task. It was finally taken on in the seventeenth century by Elias Ashmole, an Oxford scholar, astrologer and alchemist.[34] Ashmole's translation was used by his friend, the very successful astrologer and self-styled 'new Merlin' William Lilly, in support of his own prognostications during and after the Civil War. Thus, although the *History of the Kings of Britain* was no longer accepted as genuine by then, the prophecies of Merlin continued to be cited as a possible source of guidance and insight in this time of renewed political upheaval and terrible insecurity. This would hardly have been effective if Merlin's reputation as a prophet was no longer accepted. Moreover, Lilly's friendly relationship with those who ordered the execution of Charles I not surprisingly caused him problems when Charles II became king, and it was to Merlin's prophecies that he turned for evidence of his own belief in the new regime. In his story of his own *Life and Times* he pauses in his account of the restoration of the monarchy to point out that 'Ambrose Merlin' prophesied these very events 'about 990 years since'. According to Lilly, '[Merlin] calls King James The Lion of Righteousness; and saith, when he died, or was dead, there would reign a noble White King; this was Charles the First. The prophet discovers all his troubles, his flying up and down, his imprisonment, his death; and calls him Aquila [the Eagle].' Lilly goes on to quote what he says are prophecies about Charles the Second, the 'Eagle's Chick', who will be a friend to all. Lilly quotes no fewer than two Latin versions of the prophecies, as well as an archaic English trans-lation, thus proving both his own scholarship and the fact that he always knew that Charles II would be a successful monarch.[35]

By this time, the number of versions of Merlin's 'Book', and the range of new prophecies fathered upon him, were so great that the fact that the prophecies supposedly concerning the Stewart monarchs did not appear in the *History of the Kings of Britain* was supremely unimportant. Merlin's name and reputation had become inde-pendent of that musty and discredited work. Antiquarians and scientists, like the public at large, believed in prophecy just as they believed in demons. Layamon's words, written at the start of the thirteenth century, could still be applied in the seventeenth century. For everybody knew that 'Once there was a Mage called Merlin, who foretold the future, and whose sayings were true'.

CHAPTER 4

ℰꙩ

THE CURIOUS CAREER OF MERLIN THE ASTROLOGER

MERLIN WAS BY far the greatest political prophet of mediaeval Britain, and even in Europe he had very few rivals, but he was much more than a seer. As a prophet he could reveal the secrets of the future, but as a magician he himself made things happen on a national and international scale. He possessed an enormous range of powers within the field of natural magic – and one of the most potentially exciting was in astrology, a 'growth area' of magic from the twelfth century onwards, despite disapproval by the Church. He demonstrated his mastery of astrology, together with his knowledge of the cosmos, in his prophetic account of the end of the world. This gave a terrifying vision of the violent end of the stars themselves, depicting them as the living beings named in astrology. The majority of Merlin's prophecies had taken the form of foretelling the coming of various supernatural animals and beings, but when he reached the end of time, his vision became one of the greatest astrological predictions made in the mediaeval period, and one which set the tone for later astrologers.

The shift is marked by the obscure statement that 'Silver will shine white all around, and will affect the wine presses. Men will be drunk with wine . . . and the stars will turn away from them, leaving their established courses.'[1] This in turn will end the fertility of the earth and its crops. What follows is a vision of the zodiac itself falling into ruin, couched in impressively technical astrological language:

The splendour of the Sun will be dimmed by the amber of Mercury, and those who see will be filled with horror. Stilbon of Arcadia will change the shield, and the helmet of Mars will entice Venus also. That great helmet will cast a shadow, and the rage of Mercury shall go beyond all bounds. Iron Orion will raise his bared sword, and the Sun itself will become watery and stir up the clouds. Jupiter will abandon his ordered course, and Venus will desert her established orbit. Saturn's star will rain down malignity and destroy humanity, cutting down mortals with its scythe. The twelve-fold houses of the stars will weep as the planets wreak this havoc. The twins of Gemini will cease to embrace one another but draw Aquarius into the water. The scales of Libra will fall out of balance and Aries will hold them upon his horns. Scorpio will hurl lightning from its tail while Cancer makes war on the Sun. Virgo will climb upon the back of Sagittarius the Centaur, ruining her virginal flowers. The chariot of the Moon will run wild in the zodiac, and the stars of the Pleiades will weep. Janus will abandon his duties as doorkeeper of time and hide in the shades of Ariadne. Responding to these rays the seas will rise, the dust of the dead will be reborn, the winds will fight with deadly blasts, and their howls will echo through the stars.

Clearly, Merlin's vision of the end does not include the Second Coming; this is not an apocalypse of the familiar type. Instead, the

self-destruction of the zodiac initiates an unmaking of God's creation. The cycle of time, signified by Janus, will end, and the seas,
the 'dust' and the winds, whose creation was described in the high
prophetic language of Genesis, will fall into chaos and anarchy.
This vision of the end is of a strikingly scientific sort, perhaps
closest to that granted to the biblical prophet Esdras when he
asked the angel Uriel for signs by which to recognize the approach
of the end of time. The first sign vouchsafed is that humanity will
increase greatly in faithlessness and iniquity. The next is that the
land will lose its fertility. The third is that the sun will shine by
night and the moon by day, that wood will bleed, stones speak,
birds flee and all the usual rules of nature be overthrown. Beyond
this stage it is not given to Esdras to know, and even so his mind is
faint with fear and foreboding, so that the angel has to hold
him up.[2]

Merlin, then, appears to see even further than Esdras, but unlike
the biblical prophet his language is scientific and astrological. Does
this mean that Merlin was an astrologer? This is much more than
just a technical question, since astrology was increasingly suspect,
and when used to foretell the future was actually forbidden. The
Merlin revealed by the *History of the Kings of Britain* does not need
to carry out astrological calculations in order to know the future.
This is further emphasized by his ability to interpret the significance of an eerie comet, which appears whilst he is on campaign
with Prince Uther. It is a star of great magnitude, emitting a single
huge beam, at the end of which is a ball of fire in the shape of a
dragon. From this dragon emerge two rays of light, one pointing
over France and the other over the Irish Sea. This star strikes
fear into all who see it.[3] The interpretation of a new star or comet
was a matter of great weight, since such phenomena were accepted
in the Middle Ages as signifying a historic change or disaster.

The best-known and most important example was the star that announced the incarnation of Christ and led the Magi to witness the miracle, and the appearance of Halley's Comet just before the Norman Conquest of England was thought by no one in the mediaeval period to be just a coincidence.[4] Even for Merlin, the interpretation of such a heavenly sign is a matter of great difficulty; he has to call upon his 'spirit', and bursts into tears, just as he did when making his great prophecies. Indeed, Merlin's interpretation of the comet is itself called a prophecy, not just in the *History of the Kings of Britain* but by almost all the writers who made use of it.

Thus, whilst Merlin clearly has knowledge of the stars rivalling that of the biblical Magi, his 'spirit' also enables him to prophesy. Why, then, would he need to make astrological computations, if he can know the future directly? The *Life of Merlin* helps to provide an answer.[5] Here, Merlin's astrological expertise is depicted in more detail. But observation of the stars, and interpretation of the results, are associated with the theme of Merlin's madness. It is when Merlin is alienated from other humans and refusing to have contact with kings and their courts that astrology plays the strongest part in his story. The first example comes when Merlin is so deeply insane that he is described as living like an animal. Even so, he is capable of watching 'the stars in their courses' and interpreting their movements. It is on a cold and frosty night, when the stars and the 'horned moon' are glittering in a sky cleared by the north wind, that Merlin sees a blood-red ray shine from Mars. At the same time, Venus, following a course close to that of the sun, is sending out a divided beam. Talking to himself, he mutters:

What does this ray from Mars signify? A king is dead, and a new king is rising. Constantine has died. His nephew, Conan, has murdered his uncle to make himself king. And Venus has joined her orbit to the path of the Sun within the Zodiac. Her ray is divided as it cuts through the ether, and the division signifies the parting of lovers.

A little later in the narrative Merlin, still mad and still refusing human society, does allow his sister, Queen Ganieda, to build him a house and an observatory. He wishes to track the movements of the sun and of Venus by day, and the stars by night, and he promises that he will learn the future of the nation from this. This is no false promise. Once the observatory, complete with seventy doors and seventy windows, is built, Merlin gazes at the stars and reads the future. He begins with the imminent death of his sister's husband, King Rodarch, and continues through a long series of defeats and disasters that will befall the British. As he himself says, much of this repeats more briefly what he had already prophesied to Vortigern; how could it not, since that prophecy covered all future time? But the first prophecies came from Merlin's 'spirit', whilst this one seems to come from the stars.[6]

Is the reading of the stars then necessarily associated with madness and alienation by the *Life*? The famous bard Taliesin, fresh from studying the nature of creation with Gildas the Wise, explains both the movements of the stars and the means by which humans can attempt to communicate with God. This suggests that astrology was safe – as long as the astrologer did not attempt to penetrate the secrets of the future. Taliesin explains that the outermost portion of the created universe is the firmament of heaven, in which the fixed stars are set. Within this is the 'ethereal heaven', a zone occupied by the sun and the wandering stars, each with its own course assigned to it. Beneath this again is the 'airy heaven', lit by the moon, and occupied by bands of spirits friendly towards humans, and willing to carry prayers up to God and to convey dreams and signs from God to humans. These spirits are to be understood as different from angels, since the latter occupy the higher zone of the ethereal heaven. Most dangerous is the sublunary zone, which is full of evil demons, bent on the deception and destruction of humanity.[7] It is they who can construct bodies for themselves out of air, and make women pregnant. Such a one, presumably, was Merlin's father.

Where does this leave Merlin the Astrologer? Nothing directly negative is said about astrology, yet unlike prophecy it does appear to be a suspect source of knowledge of the future, and one used by those alienated from ordinary society. In confirmation of this, the story's other expert in astrology is Morgen, chief of the nine magical sisters who rule the Island of Apples (or Avalon). They are described as kindly, and Morgen is expert in healing – a skill from which King Arthur benefits. Yet she is also a shape-changer, something associated with demonic illusions, and is capable of flying through the air like the sinister figure of Simon Magus, enemy of the Apostles.[8] A qualified acceptance of astrology is finally offered at the end of the *Life*. Merlin's prophetic spirit has by now been taken up by his widowed sister, Ganieda. She has left the life of the court and come to join Merlin and Taliesin in what is in effect a scholarly hermitage, where they study natural magic and the occult properties of the Creation. Ganieda's visions of future events are mixed with comments on the significance of stars, and of two moons appearing in the sky over Winchester. This is immediately followed by Geoffrey of Monmouth's appeal to his patrons that they grant him his due reward. It seems unlikely that he would make such a request on an offensive or heretical note – especially as he has dedicated the work to a bishop. Ganieda's harnessing of the interpretation of the stars within a framework provided by prophecy therefore seems to offer an acceptable role for astrology.

In accord with this, neither Merlin nor Taliesin ever says explicitly that the use of astrology to foretell the future is always wrong. Instead, a hierarchy of supernatural sources of knowledge is suggested. Genuine knowledge of the future can only come from God. Merlin has the ambiguous gift of a 'spirit', but Gildas and Taliesin confirm that God does send signs through such spirits. Most open to difficulty are signs which God sends through the stars. Comets are so important, but so difficult, that even Merlin needs the guidance of his spirit to interpret them correctly. And if the stars are to be correctly read at even a more mundane level, then technical knowledge is needed. The problem with astrology thus becomes one about technical difficulty, and the consequent likelihood of errors. Why, then, introduce astrology at all? Since Geoffrey was writing in the hope of promotion and reward, the answer must be that he believed that his educated and powerful audience would be keen to learn about it; and this is all the more likely since major new sources of knowledge about astrology were becoming available by the middle of the twelfth century.

The *Life of Merlin* offers instruction on the cosmos and the zodiac, not just from Merlin but also from Gildas via Taliesin. Merlin and Taliesin discuss how the planets and the stars were given complex, but fixed, courses by God. If observers wished to understand their movements, it would therefore be necessary to know their standard tracks across the sky. Taliesin's expertise is shown when he discourses on the path of the sun, explaining that the solstice is the term for the 'stop' that the sun makes at the furthest point of its orbit. As he says, this is the point at which the sun's rays reach their prescribed limit, since after this 'stop' the sun changes direction and swings back around the earth. Finally, at the latitude of *ultima Thule*, this is also the time at which there is 'endless night', when the withdrawal of the sun's rays causes terrible coldness and a 'hardening' of the sea. The exposition is not entirely clear – but it is well in excess of what most readers would have known in the first half of the twelfth century.[9]

The problem for Europeans interested in astrology in the early Middle Ages was that most of the Greek works, and their Latin translations, that set out the details of the art had been lost. All that remained were a few summaries, which made little sense without the textbooks of the second-century Alexandrian astrologer Claudius Ptolemy, and which were viewed with considerable mistrust as both pagan and possibly heretical. Thus, whilst belief was strong that the rays of all the planets, not only the sun, affected life on earth, detailed analysis of these effects was almost impossible. The calendar of the Church, which was based on that of the Roman Empire, preserved the names and images of the signs of the zodiac, together with the dates on which the sun transited from one sign or 'house' to another. The complexity of the calculation of the date of Easter each year also required clerics to know the dates of the equinoxes, and to keep track of the lunar calendar; thus these also appeared as standard features in the calendars that accompanied all prayer books and liturgical books (for those wealthy enough to possess them).[10] However, whilst readers of classical histories and poetry would learn of the sorts of astrology practised in the past, they would be unable to carry out any such calculations themselves. Astrological knowledge was effectively reduced to knowing which zodiac sign the sun was in; which planet was close to it; and how many days old the moon was (that is, how many days into a lunar month it was) on any particular day. Such limited data could produce only crude interpretations, largely limited to which days were fortunate or unfortunate for various undertakings.[11]

Meanwhile, however, scientists and mathematicians working in the Arab Empire, of which Alexandria had become a part, had built upon Greek astronomy, astrology, mathematics and geometry to go very much further in all these fields than the Romans had. They had built great observatories, compiled data on the movements of the planets, made discoveries on optics and the behaviour of light rays, and developed the mathematical skills to cast complex horoscopes. They had translated Claudius Ptolemy's works and made considerable additions to them, not least of which was the development of the sophisticated piece of technology known as the astrolabe. This consisted of a disc of metal, representing a formalized 'map' of the heavens, with moving pointers mounted upon it, and further data engraved on the back. Used together with an appropriate set of tables on the orbits of the planets, the astrolabe enabled an expert user to make complex calculations on the relative positions of the planets as seen from a point on earth on any chosen date. In a sense, it offered the cosmos and all its secrets in the palm of one's hand – and it is hardly surprising that it burst upon Western Europe in the twelfth century with almost as much impact as Merlin himself. The scholarly lovers Abelard and Heloise even called their son Astrolabe.[12] However, in the time of the Crusades, knowledge which came from the pagan past via the Saracens was doubly troubling, and had to be handled with extreme care.

Bad things happened to the reputations of scholars who had expertise in astrology, even if they never touched an astrolabe. A small, but telling, example is that of Archbishop Gerard of York, who died in 1108. Gerard was a learned man, who read widely and who possessed a copy of a summary of astrology known as the Matheseos Libri Octo compiled by a fourth-century Roman senator, Julius Firmicus Maternus.[13] Gerard's clergy disapproved so strongly of this reading material that, according to William of Malmesbury, they refused to have the archbishop buried in their cemetery.[14] Still worse was what happened to the reputation of Pope Sylvester II, who had been master of the cathedral school of Rheims before becoming pope at the end of the tenth century. His knowledge of mathematics and natural philosophy (including the courses of the stars) was extremely unusual for his time, especially as he had travelled to Spain to study. However, he could scarcely be criticized whilst he was pope. Once dead, he was accused of trafficking with demons by a cardinal, Benno of Osnabrück, who called Sylvester a necromancer, with a 'personal' demon. The story was repeated by Orderic Vitalis.[15] William of Malmesbury depicted Sylvester as an expert on the astrolabe and the abacus – and also as an astrologer and a necromancer, who was in possession of a bronze head capable of giving answers to questions. Sylvester had supposedly learnt all this from a Saracen in Spain – and when forced to flee for his life he had resorted to 'calling up the Devil with incantations and promising to pay him perpetual homage'.[16] William distances himself from the story, but cautiously accepts it, and he never challenges the idea that, just as in the Bible, the devil offered temporary rewards to those who entered into pacts with him. Astrological knowledge was clearly terribly dangerous, even in the hands of archbishops and popes, and it is perhaps not surprising that Merlin is never said to have used an astrolabe, or even a set of tables on the positions of the planets, even though both were becoming available by 1150. His lack of such artificial aids also helps to emphasize his innate mastery of arcane knowledge.

Merlin's astrological observations in the *Life* do become technical, however, when he comments on planetary aspects. This was a part of ancient, Arab astrology which was only newly available in twelfth-century Western Europe. It involved knowing the positions of the stars, not just individually but in relation to one another. When they were close together, they were in conjunction – and this is what Merlin suggests when he tells of how Venus is moving 'in company with the Sun'. Such relationships meant that the power of one planet affected the normal influence of the other. Thus it may be inferred that it is the sun (the more powerful body) which is splitting the beam of Venus. Since Venus had influence over love and marriage, it is logical that this signifies the separation of lovers, as Merlin says. It is therefore clear that knowledge derived from the stars could be very precise in the hands of a skilled astrologer, but the tales of Gerard and Sylvester show that the use of astrology to predict the future opened the astrologer up to the danger of demonic influence. Why, then, does Merlin use it at all, and how representative is he of mediaeval astrologers?

The twelfth-century Merlin's use of astrology is inseparable from the fact that astronomy and astrology were experiencing a great renaissance. Astrology was exciting and fashionable, and it offered enormous political advantage to those who could employ skilled astrologers. Perhaps the best surviving proof of this is provided by a set of nine horoscopes drawn up in a twelfth-century hand, and relating to events on both sides of the channel from the 1120s to about 1150 – in other words precisely the time of Merlin's first appearance. They now form part of a manuscript in the British Library (MS Royal App. 85, folio 2). They deal with issues such as the death of a count of Anjou, and whether a certain person will come to England.[17] In the context of the Civil War in England, this was politically explosive. Like all mediaeval horoscopes, they are drawn up as squares, not circles, with each square divided into twelve triangles or lozenges, relating to the zodiac signs or 'houses'. One has a smaller square at its centre, in which is written: 'On the question of the Norman army – the answer is that it will not come.' The right-hand side of this smaller square forms the base of a triangle labelled 'Aries' (the first sign of the zodiac), and the other signs follow anticlockwise. The positions of the planets are noted, with both Saturn and Venus appearing in the rather peaceful sign of Virgo, and warlike Mars in unwarlike Pisces. However, no commentary or explanation of the 'answer' is actually provided. Just how rare astrologers were at the time is demonstrated by the fact that there were probably only two men in England who could have drawn up these horoscopes. The older man, Adelard of Bath, had travelled in France, Italy, Sicily and the Holy Land to gain his knowledge, while Robert of Chester had studied in Spain.[18]

By the thirteenth century astrologers capable of such calculations could command high fees and court positions from European rulers. It was also in that century that astrology became more established as a field of formal study, since doctors and natural philosophers used it in their work on the human body and the cosmos. By then, professional astrologers could openly achieve positions of great influence at court, and became famous (or notorious) for their predictions.[19] Yet Merlin the Astrologer continued to attract far less attention than Merlin the Prophet, as attitudes to astrology as a source of information on the future continued to harden.

The historian from this period who showed greatest interest in Merlin was Matthew Paris, chronicler of the wealthy abbey of St Alban. As well as his interest in prophecy, Matthew had expertise in divination and in various 'mechanical' means of foretelling the future. He compiled a collection of works on fortune-telling, and provided diagrams and illustrations.[20] These include an astrological element, since one treatise offers to supply answers from 'the twelve signs of the zodiac' to questions asked by the person carrying out the consultation. Matthew also studied the heavens and the courses of the planets. He was expert enough to give technical accounts of two solar eclipses, complete with diagrams, in his chronicle. There is also evidence that he read on the Creation, and on the nature and structure of matter, spirits, the weather and creation. He knew enough on these issues to provide illustrative diagrams for St Alban's copy of a scholarly work entitled *Dragmaticon Philosophiae*, which deals with all this.[21] And yet Matthew showed no interest at all in the idea of Merlin as an astrologer: neither in his interpretation of Merlin's prophecies nor in his account of the ancient world and its rulers does Matthew discuss astrology, horoscopes or royal employment of astrologers. He does mention the zodiac, but only in the general sense of marking the sun's position, and thus the season, when a particular event occurred – for instance, when describing a major outbreak of 'pestilence' in 1247.

Equally striking is the absence of Merlin the Astrologer from the work of Gervase of Tilbury. Gervase was a member of the highly sophisticated courts of King William II of Sicily and of the Emperor Otto IV, and composed an informative work for the diversion of the Emperor, the *Otia Imperialia*. This shows that he was well read on the nature of spirits and demons, and their place in Creation. Book One of his 'encyclopaedia' offers an account of the nature and make-up of Creation and of time, with a whole chapter on 'The Sun, the Moon, the Stars, and the Signs of the Zodiac'.[22] Gervase's account, despite his secular, imperial audience, pays considerable attention to the Church's teaching on these subjects. Standard mediaeval interpretations of the book of Genesis are followed, and the stars, like the signs of the zodiac, are discussed as markers of seasons and of time, but definitely *not* as causes of events. Typical is the statement that 'the Sun's descent to Capricorn marks the winter solstice'. This does not mean, however, that Gervase ignores astrology. In his account, Abraham was so skilled in astrology that it was he who taught it to the Egyptians, who then taught it to the Greeks. Moses in turn learnt it from the Egyptians, and Virgil, like other Romans, practised it. And yet, Gervase's Merlin, despite the extent of his prophetic and magical powers, did not.

The explanation for this silence seems to have been not igno-
rance but fear of the growing reaction of the Church as the impact
of astrology itself grew. Gervase was writing during the time when
one of the most famous astrologers of the Middle Ages, Michael
Scot, was issuing translations of key astrological works. For the
guidance of beginners, Scot also wrote an Introduction to astrology.
He had begun his career under the patronage of the French royal
dynasty, and his scientific studies gained him the favour of popes
Honorius III and Gregory IX. His reputation became suspect when
he became the court astrologer of the Emperor Frederick II (an
enemy of the papal claims to political and territorial power).[23] For
Scot, as for other practitioners, astrology was not a magical art but
part of natural philosophy (the mediaeval term for science). He
argued that actual magic, or 'magia', involved the invocation of
demons, whereas study of the stars was a way to find out about the
hidden forces of nature. His expositions were presumably strengthened when the sultan of Damascus, al-Ashraf, sent Frederick a
marvellous planetarium, worth no less than 20,000 marks. This had
images of the sun and the moon, which followed their courses
across the sky and marked out intervals of time, but sadly, like the
Emperor Charlemagne's silver 'table' of the cosmos, it no longer
exists.

Scot himself, then, practised astrology but argued that it was for
the scientific benefit of humanity. In his textbooks on astrology he
emphasized that heavenly bodies do not *cause* events on earth; they
offer signs to the educated observer, who can deduce the best times
for, and likely outcomes of, action. Such scientific deduction, he
argued, was very different from the forbidden arts of divination. He
nevertheless boasted of how the emperor had consulted him both
on medical treatments and on questions such as the likely outcomes
of military actions against rebels within the empire. Like the

anonymous English astrologer, he provided diagrams of his horo-scopes – but Scot also provided explanations of his interpretations. He clearly took care to stay within Church law, both in writing on astrology and on natural philosophy, even though he could not resist boasting of how the emperor consulted him on the latter also. Here, Scot's knowledge surpassed that of Geoffrey's Merlin, since he was able to discourse not only on the spheres of heaven and the location of hell but also on the fact that the earth is spherical and that the oceans are kept in place around it by divine dispensation.[24]

For all this, Scot's negative reputation as a practitioner of forbidden arts grew. Later thirteenth-century Italian chroniclers, such as Salimbene, already depicted him as so powerful that the emperor supposedly consulted him about the future of all key issues.[25] Nor was Scot alone. Guido Bonatti was equally famous, both as a writer on astrology and as a consultant to the powerful. Whilst employed by Guido of Montefeltro he gave such precise directions on how that leader should conduct his affairs that he even gave signals on army manoeuvres. He himself claimed to have uncovered a conspiracy against the emperor in 1246, through astro-logical observations, and to have forewarned Frederick. The *Annals of Forli* called him a 'most eminent astrologer' and stated that whilst working for Guido of Montefeltro he had saved the town from the army of Pope Martin IV. He did this by forecasting the future and giving instructions on the times at which the citizens should carry out certain actions.[26] Bonatti, like Scot, believed that he avoided the forbidden territory of foretelling the future, but his own admirers clearly thought otherwise.

This supposed knowledge of the future was what raised the anger of the Church (though political opposition to the papacy scarcely helped). Not only was such knowledge the preserve of God; there were also the problems of just what role astrologers were ascribing to the stars, and whether they were (knowingly or unknowingly) opening channels of communication with demons. Such anxieties made the status of astrologers more and more problematic. For Dante, writing in the fourteenth century, both Scot and Bonatti clearly belonged in the Inferno. They are placed in its Eighth Circle, which is next to the very lowest pit. Like the other inhabitants, they are accused of deception by magical means and of trying to see what is forbidden; for this reason, their heads are twisted on their necks, so that they can only see backwards.

When it came to astrology, even those who showed knowledge only by criticizing astrological arguments were at an increased risk of being perceived as suspect themselves. But did this make writers afraid of discussing Merlin the Astrologer? The thirteenth-century Italian *Prophesies de Merlin* offers interesting evidence.[27] This strange, hybrid work gave a large range of 'newly discovered' prophecies by Merlin, set within a fictionalized narrative. The prophecies themselves are primarily of thirteenth-century interest, and relate to the great political upheavals of the time. More will be said about them when discussing Merlin's fame as an international magician and prophet. But besides prophecies, the book has narrative sections offering exciting accounts of magical feats, love affairs and battles. As the opening words put it: 'Here begin the prophecies of Merlin, with his works, and the marvels which he wrought.' How, then, is astrology handled?

For a book of nearly three hundred pages in its modern, printed edition, and giving much space to Merlin's magic, the remarkable thing is that astrology appears hardly at all. Merlin does demonstrate that he has knowledge of the orbit and history of the sun, which is shown particularly in a prophecy about the recapture of Jerusalem by Christians. On that day, says Merlin, the sun will shine as brightly as it did on the day God created it, and on only one other day – the day of Solomon's coronation. This Merlin also has mastery of the powers of the moon, since chapter 119 consists of a list of all thirty days in a full lunar month, with Merlin's comments on the power of the moon on each day. Having dictated the whole list, Merlin claims that this in itself is the 'art of the stars', and explains its links to the calendar of the Church. This would be perfectly uncontroversial, since such 'lunaries' or 'moonbooks' had been copied along with works on the Church calendar for centuries. They can be found at least as early as the eleventh century, and had become part of the common stock of astrological and scientific knowledge. If anything, they make Merlin look oddly old-fashioned.[28]

Merlin's mastery of the heavens is stressed in the *Prophesies*; but he never carries out any astrological observations or calculations – and in chapter 160 we are told why. At this stage of the story a learned cleric is introduced who tries to check Merlin's prophecies, using his knowledge of astrology. The attempt, however, fails to reproduce anything like the accuracy of Merlin's revelations – and the cleric undertakes further studies. These lead him to the sad understanding that, whilst the 'subtle science' of astrology can deal with the courses of the heavens, and the times of their changing, it can never grasp truly celestial things. Merlin's prophecies are here said, for the first time, to have been inspired by the Holy Spirit – making the role of Merlin's incubus father marginal, and putting them into an entirely different category from astrological predictions. To make the point still more emphatic, the cleric himself is described as using necromancy, a term that is not applied to Merlin's magic.

The authors of the growing number of popular versions of the history of Britain, written from the end of the thirteenth century onwards, were also faced with the problem of how to handle Merlin the Astrologer. These *Bruts* offered the complete story of Britain, from the arrival of Brutus up to a point close to the writer/editor's own time, in an approachable form. The first seems to have been produced at the end of the thirteenth century, in the aristocratic language of Anglo-Norman, with continuations taking it to 1333.[29] Anglo-Norman versions survive in forty-nine known copies, which is an impressive number in itself. However, the *Brut* was soon translated into Middle English – and this version was the one which placed heavy emphasis on Merlin's prophecies about the last kings of England. It was enormously popular, and new versions were issued, taking the story through the fifteenth century. Moreover, for scholars and clerics who preferred to read their history in Latin, a Latin *Brut* was produced, which went up to 1367. This, too, was later expanded, with a new translation going up to 1437.[30] It is clear that the *Brut* was enormously popular – at least in mediaeval England. There are pocket-sized editions in amateur handwriting, there are professional volumes made for university scholars and there are luxuriously illuminated gift copies.

All versions of the *Brut* gave an account of the early history of Britain that was almost completely unchanging, including the depiction of Merlin and his magic. Moreover, the chapters covering Merlin and Arthur are, in almost every case, the ones that show the largest number of marks, annotations and comments by readers. In other words, this was the material in which late mediaeval readers were most interested, and the lack of variation is due to the acceptance of this part of British history. It is therefore significant that no version of the *Brut* has any mention of Merlin as an astrologer. Even in the Middle English *Brut*, issues relating to astrology appear only when Merlin is asked to interpret the comet for Uther. In all cases, this is shown as a very serious undertaking. The Anglo-Norman *Brut* simply has him sigh deeply and weep, thus signalling both the effort involved and the bad news announced by the comet. The Middle English *Brut* goes further, and has Merlin shaking and weeping, before giving an interpretation inspired by his spirit.[31] Merlin's expertise in interpreting the stars is thus clear, but his ability comes from his prophetic gift, not from astrological skills. Merlin is a great prophet who also has a superhuman range of magical abilities, but who has no connection with astrology.

If such a popular work as this shows no interest in astrology, it might be concluded that the interpretation of the heavens was of no interest in the fourteenth and fifteenth centuries – but there is an enormous amount of evidence to show that this was not the case. Astrology was by this time firmly established as a necessary part of the study of medicine as well as of time and the calendar, and was being taught at prominent universities in these contexts. Predictive astrology was in theory outlawed, but was in fact offered on a commercial basis by practitioners with varying expertise, and kings of France were as interested as Holy Roman emperors in employing good astrologers. Some were recruited from Italy, but others, such as Pierre d'Ailly, found it perfectly possible to study astrology in France.[32] Pierre received his theology doctorate from the University of Paris in 1381. It was his concern about the state of the Church, and particularly the upheaval of the Great Schism, which led him to study astrology, prophecy and the nature of revelation. After twenty years of work in this field, he became convinced that astrology and theology could be complementary to one another. Only divine revelation, whether in the form of new prophecies or of inspired interpretation of scriptural ones, could give knowledge of the future – the role of astrology was simply to calculate the dates on which the events foretold would take place. Pierre's beliefs and skills reached a wide audience when he predicted in 1414 that the Council of Constance would be able to end the Schism, as indeed it did. His further prediction, that the Antichrist would not arrive until 1789, was also reassuring for those who believed that the division of the Church was a sign that the last times were beginning.

The work of Pierre d'Ailly shows that astrology could, if handled with care, be applied even to the affairs of the Church itself. The employment of astrologers as royal advisers continued into the fifteenth century and beyond. So the absence of Merlin the Astrologer from the *Brut* cannot be owing to lack of belief in astrology. Moreover, at least one fifteenth-century writer compiled a book listing *The Most Famous Astrologers* in the whole history of the world, and included Merlin. This was Simon de Phares, who openly practised predictive astrology and made ambitious claims for his art.[33] He was supported by King Charles VIII of France, who called him 'our dear and beloved astrologer', but he was forbidden to practise by the archbishop of Lyon. He and his books were scrutinized by the theologians of Paris in 1491, and they agreed with the archbishop. Simon's response was his book, addressed to the king and written in French. It set out to show how great astrologers had predicted each key event in world history, and started (logically enough) with Adam, whose unique knowledge and grasp of Creation included astrology. Merlin is included as a figure from the Sixth Age of the world, and is called an astrologer, prophet and philosopher.[34] His prophecy of the end of the world is quoted at length, in Latin, and is declared to prove that he was expert in the science of the stars. But even Simon does not go further than this.

Merlin, then, both was and was not an astrologer. He was an astrologer in the sense that he possessed both far greater than normal knowledge of 'the courses of the heavens' and the ability to interpret these movements better than anyone else. Yet he was not an astrologer in the technical sense since he never practised astrology, and never needed to – his prophetic powers rendered this beneath his dignity. From the thirteenth century on, writers about Merlin were, on the whole, happy to avoid the combination of scientific complexity and theological peril that the subject of astrology raised. This had the paradoxical effect that, as the practice of scientific astrology grew in late mediaeval society, Merlin's association with it was progressively reduced. But what Merlin the Astrologer lost in impact, Merlin the Prophet gained – and without undercurrents of forbidden practices.

Arguably, a precedent was provided for Merlin's range of knowledge in the biblical Book of the Wisdom of Solomon. This contains numerous paeans of praise to the figure of Wisdom, sent by God to the poet as a 'spirit'. By this means God has given the visionary author:

Unerring knowledge of the things that are, to know the constitution of the World, the operation of the elements, the beginning and end and middle of times, the alternation of solstices and changes of seasons, the circuits of years and the positions of stars, the natures of living creatures and the ragings of wild beasts, the violence of winds and the thoughts of man, the diversities of plants and the virtues of roots. All things both secret and manifest I have learnt, for she that is the artificer of all things, even Wisdom, taught me. . . She knoweth the things of old, and divineth the things to come; She understandeth subtleties of speech and interpretations of dark sayings; She foreseeth signs and wonders, and the issue of seasons and times.

(Wisdom of Solomon, 7: 17–22; and 8, 8)

All these things Merlin also knew, or at least studied, and this range of knowledge set him apart from ordinary practitioners of astrology, however skilled.

Merlin, then, stood aloof from the sensations and long-running disputes that marked Europe's reception of scientific astrology in the twelfth and thirteenth centuries. This also meant that he was not affected by the fear of a potentially demonic element in astrology, which took increasing hold in the fourteenth and fifteenth centuries. However, Merlin was also expert in brewing powerful potions, in changing people's appearance, and in manipulating natural objects such as stones. As a prophet and cosmologist he had the skills needed to provide accurate interpretations of dreams. He was clearly unparalleled in the erection of everlasting structures, like Stonehenge, just as he had knowledge of all the peoples, as well as all the creatures and all the natural phenomena, of the world. Merlin therefore emerges as the magus of the twelfth-century renaissance. But was all of this covered by the biblical gifts of Wisdom, or would some of it make him a necromancer? Just what kind of magician was Merlin?

ᴤↄ⳹

MERLIN'S MAGIC

THE IDEA OF Merlin the Magician has been increasingly dominated by fictional portrayals of Merlin as a member of the court
of King Arthur, which began to be developed in the thirteenth
century. But from the twelfth to the sixteenth century Merlin was a
real historical figure first and foremost, whose magic and prophecy
were both also real. This, however, did not make him unproblematic.
The reality of magic might be established by the Bible, as well as by
law, but those same authorities treated it as something very dangerous.
To take just one example, the account of Pharaoh's magicians,
sorcerers and *magi* in the biblical Book of Exodus (7: 8–12) shows
that they had real powers, even whilst condemning their magic and
the ways they used it. Still more troubling was the story of the Witch
of Endor in 1 Samuel (28: 3–20). This tells how King Saul, after
Samuel's death, had no one to bring him signs and messages from
God, and tracked down a woman with a familiar spirit, in order to
call up Samuel from the dead. The summoning is effective, though
the terrified king is angrily rebuked by Samuel, who prophesies

imminent death for Saul. Christian commentators, from St Augustine onwards, identified such practices as 'the fraudulent rites of demons', and condemned those who indulged in them.[1] Was Merlin to be classified with such as these? The answer could easily have been yes, but both the skill of Geoffrey of Monmouth and the timing of Merlin's discovery in fact produced a positive reception for the great magician.

Merlin the Magician, like Merlin the Astrologer, had appeared at a critical moment. Announcements of new discoveries in medicine, mathematics, geography, veterinary science and plant science helped to create an excited audience for the magical feats that Merlin had performed. But at the same time, fear that all contact with forces beyond human comprehension posed dangers to orthodox belief and to the soul was also growing. By the middle of the twelfth century, William of Conches, a grammarian and natural philosopher who achieved great fame for his study of the cosmos, and who seems to have taught at the cathedral school of Chartres, had fallen out with his bishop and taken refuge at the court of Geoffrey Plantagenet, then duke of Normandy. He wrote a textbook on philosophy and cosmology in the form of a dialogue between a scholar and the duke of Normandy that set out his beliefs.[2] In his *Philosophy of the World* (Book 1, chapter 23), William turned on those who had attacked him:

> Ignorant themselves of the powers of nature, and wanting everyone to share their ignorance, they are against anyone who looks into the nature of anything. They want everyone to believe like rustics and never ask the reasons behind how things appear. ... And if they hear that anyone is conducting such enquiries, they accuse him of being a heretic.[3]

The threat of such accusations made the nature of Merlin's magic a critical issue. As well as having been the intended victim of

Vortigern's bloodthirsty *magi*, was Merlin himself a practitioner of the forbidden arts? For this latter question timing was again crucial, since Merlin appeared just as interest in natural magic and occult powers was growing, but before Church law and theology had been systematized and updated in ways very hostile to magic. He thus entered the historical record just in time to be received positively. The fact that his magical feats were real, and that he could perform them without making use of talismans, summoning rituals or idolatrous offerings, were of key importance in making Merlin a universally recognized figurehead for the 'scientific' aspects of magic. The historical sources on Merlin powerfully suggested that he was not a sorcerer but a gifted practitioner of 'natural magic', the fashionable experimentation with the occult powers of the earth itself.[4] But what magic did Merlin actually perform?

Setting aside prophecy and astrology, Merlin's magic, as recorded in the *History of the Kings of Britain*, focused on two great displays of magical power: the creation of Stonehenge and the bringing into being of Arthur. The actual forms of magic used were complex in themselves, as well as enormous in their historical significance, and it is hardly surprising that mediaeval readers showed strong and lasting interest. Merlin's magic was witnessed by the landscape, as well as the political history, of Britain – but did it fall into the categories of sorcery, necromancy or 'heretical depravity' that Church and state laws increasingly defined and condemned? Even if it was 'natural magic', how acceptable and widespread was that idea?

Merlin's terrifying prophecies were made at the court of the tyrant Vortigern, whose death he foretold just as Samuel had Saul's. But, for the new regime of the brothers Aurelius and Uther Pendragon, Merlin was prepared to draw upon the forces of natural magic. He now showed himself as a magician who could manipulate the powers of stones, waters, words and potions. Worryingly, though, he could also read minds, and his potions were so powerful that they temporarily changed the shapes of three people (including Merlin himself) into the likenesses of others. For mediaeval readers excited and worried by the revelations of Arab medicine, astrology, mathematics, alchemy and natural philosophy, this put Merlin right at the cutting edge between what was acceptable and what was to be condemned. It is hardly surprising that Merlin was a sensation, but it is also understandable that Geoffrey of Monmouth, the cleric looking for promotion in the Church, emphasized that Merlin was a prophet and a natural philosopher, not a practitioner of forbidden magic, in the *Life of Merlin*.

Here Merlin expounds on the powers of birds, fish, stones, air and water. He is confident that these powers, with the ability to manipulate them, are gifts of God, and thus free from connections to demons. This is emphasized by the fact that much of this esoteric knowledge has been imparted by the saintly hermit Gildas the Wise. Nevertheless, the forces made available by tapping into the powers of the natural world are shown to be both occult and, literally, marvellous. They are so exciting, both for themselves and for their revelation of God's Creation, that Merlin and Taliesin propose to devote the remainder of their lives to researching them. However, the programme of study expounded in the *Life* was for a much more specialized audience than the exciting narrative of the *History of the Kings of Britain*. Readers of the historical work would simply be shown a Merlin who was a master of magic, but who offered no theoretical commentary upon it.

The first of Merlin's historic feats of magic, the creation of Stonehenge, involved an extraordinary combination of knowledge of the distant past, medical skill and use of verbal spells to render massive stones weightless.[5] In the course of it he also demonstrated

1 This folio from an English, thirteenth-century manuscript contains the opening of the Prophecies of Merlin, as revealed by Geoffrey of Monmouth in the 1130s. The text is accompanied by a twelfth-century commentary. This illumination is the earliest known depiction of the boy-prophet saving himself from death by revealing the secrets of the earth and of the future to Vortigern. The manuscript later belonged to the Elizabethan scholar and 'magus' John Dee.

2 This watercolour by J.M.W. Turner shows Dinas Emrys, identified by medieval readers of the *History of the Kings of Britain* as the place in which Merlin prophesied for Vortigern. As Gerald of Wales recorded in his *Journey Through Wales*, the name means 'hilltop of Ambrosius' and this is where Merlin Ambrosius first revealed his powers.

3 Another easily identifiable location was the 'Giants' Dance', erected by Merlin after he had brought the great stones from Ireland. Wace explains that the stones are called the Giants' Dance by the British, Stonehenge in English and the Hanging Stones in French.

Merlini Anglici Ephemeris:

Or, Aſtrological Judgments for the year 1680.

By **WILLIAM LILLY** *Student in Aſtrology.*

Invigilate Viri, tacito nam Tempora greſſu
Diffugiunt, nullóque ſono convertitur Annus.

Thomas Croſs ſculpt.

London, Printed by *J. Macock* for the Company of
Stationers. 1 6 8 0.

4 William Lilly published a series of successful almanacs and prognostications under the heading
'Merlinus Anglicus'. To please Charles II he claimed that Merlin had prophesied the career of James VI
and I, calling him a 'Lion of Righteousness', whose successor, a 'White King' (Charles I) would suffer great
troubles. Lilly's friend, the Oxford scholar Elias Ashmole, also worked on Merlin's Prophecies.

5 Astrolabes made possible rapid and accurate calculations of planetary positions. This fourteenth-century example has a plate calculated for Oxford and is very similar to the type of astrolabe described by Chaucer. The exoticism of astrolabes is shown by the fact that this one also has a plate for Babylon, whilst the fact that astrolabes could be used for astrological predictions was troubling. It is a sign of Merlin's status as a prophet that no medieval writer thought he needed to use such an instrument.

6 This horoscope is one of ten, possibly cast by the English astrologer and scientist Adelard of Bath, which survive on a single sheet of vellum in the British Library. It is drawn up for late August 1151, and the astrologer predicts that the Norman army will not come (presumably to England). The position of Jupiter, planet of good fortune, on the Ascendant is important, as is that of Venus in the House of Friendship. The political significance of astrology is shown by horoscopes in the same group which deal with the death of the Count of Anjou and whether the king will secure the obedience of his barons.

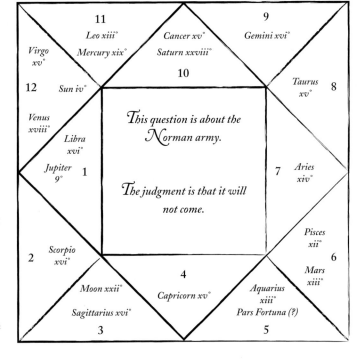

out fu iries li anemys · quant
nostre sires oc este en infer ·
et il en oc iete eue et adam

7 This illumination from a
French manuscript of *c.*1280–90
accompanies the opening of
the fictional version of Merlin's
story, as first proposed by Robert
de Boron. The demons are
shown plotting in the upper
section; and in the lower the
appointed demon seduces a
pious girl while she sleeps, in
order to beget Merlin.

8 This folio from a French
manuscript of *c.*1320 is part of a
luxury copy of the *Prophesies de
Merlin.* The manuscript has 13
miniatures, all on gold grounds,
accompanying the complete text
of the *Prophesies.* Here Merlin
confounds the disguised cardinals
who have travelled from Rome
to Wales in order to test him.
The tables are turned when
Merlin reveals the truth both to
and about them, while his scribe
writes down his revelations.

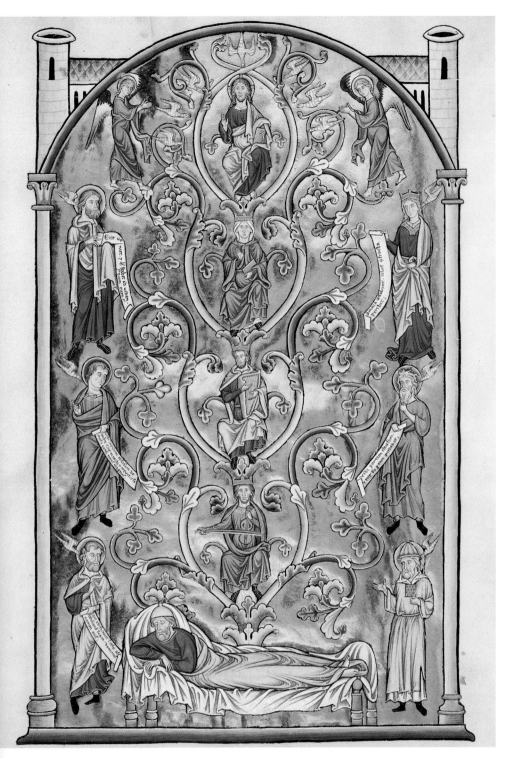

This miniature emphasises the importance of prophets and prophecy in the early thirteenth century. It is part of a luxurious psalter, believed to have been made c.1200 for Ingeborg of Denmark (queen of France). The miniature depicts Isaiah's prophecy of the 'tree' that would stem from Jesse, and shows Christ as its flower. To either side of the tree are key prophets, with the Sibyl at top right, inspired by the Holy Spirit and holding a prophetic scroll like the biblical prophets whom she accompanies.

10 This photograph of Vivien and Merlin is one of a set of twelve innovative illustrations that Tennyson commissioned in 1874 from Julia Margaret Cameron. They were later published by Cameron herself, with accompanying extracts from Tennyson's poems. This is the moment when Vivien 'put forth the charm of woven paces and of waving hands' leaving Merlin 'lost to life and use, and name and fame'.

his distance from ordinary humans when he refused to show due respect to the king and laughed at the discomfiture of soldiers and engineers with whom he was working. The context for this event is that Merlin, after his prophetic revelations to Vortigern, withdrew alone to the depths of the wilderness. Here he was later tracked down by royal messengers and conducted to King Aurelius, who had been told of Merlin as a prophet and wonder-working engineer. Asked to help in the construction of a great monument to the British war dead, Merlin told the king of the circle of massive stones, known as the Giants' Ring, which stood on a hilltop in Ireland. Paradoxically he both recommended that the stones should be brought to Salisbury Plain, but said that they were so huge and so heavy that they were beyond human strength. This made Aurelius laugh and ask whether his own kingdom had a scarcity of stones. Thus challenged, Merlin proved that indeed Britain had no such stones as these:

> The stones have mystic powers and can work medical cures. Giants brought them long ago from distant African shores to Ireland, in order to construct baths for treating illnesses. They would pour water over the stones and channel it into the baths, and thus they would work cures. For the healing of wounds they would add herbal preparations. Each stone has its medicinal power.

Such stones were so powerfully desirable that the British immediately resolved to send an army of fifteen thousand soldiers to Ireland under the command of the king's brother, Uther, who would himself be advised by Merlin.

Each individual stone thus had its own powers, which Merlin already knew. And he knew far more than this – he had the crucial skills needed to unlock those powers and to make use of them. He knew how the giants constructed baths, and how they ran water over the stones in order to create healing treatments of great power. Even more than this, by mixing the water which had taken on the powers of the stones with carefully chosen plant substances, cures for physical injuries could be created. Merlin's revelations here come close to being a manifesto for natural magic. The stones possess powers as part of their very nature – yet these powers can be released only through the application of other powerful elements, guided by secret knowledge. A masterful touch is that Merlin knows about the giants' 'secret religious rites' – but there is no suggestion that he or the British under his direction will indulge in such things. Instead, the mysterious knowledge of ancient religions can be blamelessly harnessed by the great magician. The key lies in making natural powers act upon one another. Something new and powerful is then unleashed – and by knowledge, not by demons.

This message was emphasized by the contrast between Merlin and Bladud, necromancer-king and creator of the thermal baths at Bath. Bladud is one of the characters in the *History of the Kings of Britain* who attracted most interest among later mediaeval historians. He was a contemporary of the prophet Elijah, and the father of King Lear.[6] His grandfather was a contemporary of Solomon the Wise, and Bladud's father (Rud Hud Hudibras) was a great builder. Bladud's construction of Bath is thus potentially positive, and could have rivalled Solomon's achievement in creating the great temple. However, a negative tone is introduced when Bladud creates fires which never go out, and which produce mysterious balls of stone instead of ash. Even more worryingly, Bladud was not only a great 'experimenter' in mysterious arts but also a patron of necromancy throughout Britain. It was these experiments which brought about his death. He constructed wings and succeeded in flying with them – but he tried to ascend into the upper air, a zone forbidden to human bodies, and crashed to his death. Unlike Merlin, Bladud strayed into the evils of necromancy and exceeded the bounds imposed upon humanity by God; his fall is an unmistakable contrast to Merlin's success.

Twelfth-century readers were strongly alert to such messages – but they would also have noticed that the experiments of both Merlin and Bladud offered information on topics of great interest to natural philosophers. The powers locked into stones, water and fire attracted excitement throughout the mediaeval period, so much so that bishops and royal physicians, under royal patronage, were involved in developing new (or newly restored) complexes of medicinal baths. In England, for example, this effort started at Bath, but it was not a mere revival of Roman practice. Mediaeval commentators on Ancient Rome listed baths, along with gates, triumphal arches and temples, as major achievements of the Romans, and places of interest for 'modern' visitors. However, such baths were generally described as part of the pleasures of Roman civilization, rather than as examples of magical or medical knowledge. There was a distinction between bathing as part of sophisticated Roman culture and bathing as a magical-medical practice. It was the latter which excited mediaeval natural philosophers, and on which Merlin was an expert.

Evidence of this is provided, once again, by Gervase of Tilbury. He listed nine sets of baths amongst the wonders of Rome – but did not treat them as magical or curative.[7] Other mediaeval writers contemplated such baths simply as examples of the transitory nature of earthly power and fame. In England, an Anglo-Saxon poem now known as 'The Ruin' shows this attitude being applied to a site which is probably the remains of Roman Bath.[8] This poem evokes long-lost kings as great fighters and great builders, with the skill to channel hot streams into refreshing baths, located in the heart of a fallen palace complex. Once again, there is no suggestion that magic was involved in either their construction or their use. The point of such descriptions is that the splendour of the past has faded. But from the twelfth century onwards antiquarians and experimenters were concerned to rival or exceed the pagan world in their own unlocking of the secrets of God's creation. Merlin's status as a prophet and master of natural magic thus made him very powerful as an example of what could be achieved.

The level of interest in the powers of stone and hot water is demonstrated by the post-Conquest redevelopment of the baths at Bath, begun before the discovery of Merlin and his powers. Bath was a wealthy town, with Roman carvings embedded in its mediaeval walls and Roman remains still visible – but it was far from the haunted ruin of the poem.[9] What made it unique in England was its combination of ancient baths and naturally hot springs. And it seems to have been these which brought John of Tours, physician to William the Conqueror and William Rufus, to Bath. The chronicler Henry of Huntingdon recalled how John had been famous as a physician before being made bishop of Wells by Rufus.[10] In 1089–90 John also gained control of Bath Abbey, moved his see from Wells to Bath, and paid the king the impressive sum of 500 marks for the royal rights and properties in the town. His next moves were the building of a great new church, excavation of the hot springs and the construction of two baths. These baths were 'health-giving and pleasant', filled with 'wondrous jets' of water heated without human intervention. According to a chronicler of the reign of Stephen they were frequented by sick people from all over England who treated their infirmities by bathing.[11]

The success of the hot baths of Bath, like Merlin's, continued throughout the twelfth century. In 1174 Bishop Reginald founded

St John's Hospital for the support of visitors to the baths, and three baths seem to have been in use at Bath in the late Middle Ages. However, this is not the only evidence of a twelfth-century fashion for water treatments. Something similar, if on a smaller scale, seems to have happened at St Winifred's Well in North Wales at much the same time.[12] In 1115 no lesser a personage than Earl Richard of Chester is said to have made a pilgrimage there, and in the 1130s a monk of Shrewsbury Abbey received a cure, also bathing in the water. Encouraged by the power of the spring and the jets of water which it occasionally produced, Richard I paid a special visit to St Winifred's Well in 1189, shortly before going on crusade. The belief that bathing was rejected by the mediaeval Church is thus clearly mistaken; but there was an important distinction between leisure bathing and medicinal bathing. No less a Christian authority than Cassiodorus, sixth-century founder of the monastery of Vivarium, had vouched for the spa baths of Baia, in language echoed during the high Middle Ages. Such baths, Cassiodorus says, are heated by nature, not by human means or by 'smoky balls of fire', and nature was the origin of their health-giving powers.[13] These dubious 'balls of fire' were, of course, used by Bladud. Mediaeval readers would note that in Solinus' *Polyhistor* a key feature of Roman Britain was said to be its possession of hot springs, under the patronage of Minerva. The hot springs were surrounded by a temple containing a marvellous fire which burnt perpetually, and produced not ash but lumps of curious stone.[14] Geoffrey of Monmouth's description of Bladud's Bath is so close to this that it cannot be coincidental. Once again, the distinction between dubious pagan practices and legitimate exploration of natural forces is a very important one. Merlin's magic trod this tightrope in an exciting and successful way.

Classical sources such as Solinus were being studied by a large number of scholars in the twelfth and thirteenth centuries, and the attention which Merlin and his powers attracted makes sense in this context. Gervase of Tilbury describes the healing baths at Baia and Pozzuoli, fed by naturally hot springs, in very different terms from the public baths of Rome. He also makes the healing baths the work of Virgil, here represented as a benign and powerful magician rather than simply as a poet.[15] The desire to have access to such sources of enormous power is well recorded in the case of mediaeval emperors, but it was not restricted to them. At the time when Geoffrey of Monmouth was writing about Merlin in the *History of the Kings of Britain*, Henry I of England was employing experts on natural magic, medicine and astrology. These men provide further examples of the sort of skills for which an ambitious ruler was prepared to pay highly, and are worth brief analysis as analogues of Merlin.

Located not too far from Bishop Roger's Bath (or from Stonehenge) was Prior Walcher of Malvern, who had links to the royal court and the royal abbey of Westminster. Walcher's main expertise was in astrology and the use of the astrolabe, and he wrote a treatise on the 'dragon' or the 'nodes' of the moon.[16] This entailed the calculation of the points at which the orbit of the moon crosses over that of the sun. The appointment of such a rare scholar to the small priory of Malvern may seem surprising, but it brought him to a place already known for its natural springs, and for the exceptional clarity of their water. The oldest well, St Walm's Well, is located outside Malvern, near a hilltop fort and mediaeval castle. However, the monks invested in the development of other springs, and constructed underground collection tanks for the water from the Prior's Vineyard spring (which were discovered in 1999).[17] Merlin's constant association with springs, and his expertise in magical, healing baths, thus makes him an exponent of natural, not negative, magic.

Merlin's expertise in the still greater powers to be unlocked when water and stone were brought into operation on one another offered further knowledge of the same sort. His skill in this field is emphasized in the *Life of Merlin*. Here Merlin and Taliesin explain phenomena such as the 'freezing sea' and its production of precious gemstones when its beaches are affected by stellar rays under the influence of Pisces. As would be expected, these stones have healing properties, and they were believed to have been studied by the Arabs, but Merlin emphasizes that all such curative stones are the products of God's creation.[18] This is entirely in line with mediaeval theology and natural philosophy, as reflected both in scientific works on the powers of stones (Lapidaries) and in accounts of the collections of curative stones owned by monarchs such as Henry II of England.[19] Returning to the subject of healing springs, he adds the information that the waters at Bath are especially good for 'women's diseases'. He then goes on to discuss with Taliesin the scientific problem of how new springs can appear out of mountains and how they can bring about medical cures.

The explanation is that spring waters first run underground 'through lightless caverns' where their courses bring them into contact with stones and earth. The latter imbue the water with special properties. As evidence, Merlin and Taliesin list the famous wells and springs known to classical geographers, such as the spring of Idumaea, which changes its colour four times a year, and the springs of the Garamantes, which change temperature. These evoke the especially impressive explanation that hot springs acquire their heat as they pass over alum or sulphur, stones that contain a 'principle of fire'. Lest anyone should doubt, it is immediately stressed that all such properties, although varying, were assigned to the individual springs by God, both to help the sick and to demonstrate his own power.[20] Nevertheless, to possess knowledge of the works of God, and skill to use them, is clearly appropriate for God's rational creature, the human. Thus, the health-giving properties of the medicinal spring which Merlin himself discovers are manifested for those who understand such things by the exceptional clarity of the water (just as at Malvern). Once again, it seems that the *Life of Merlin* works to prove that Merlin's magic is entirely respectable.

Returning to the *History of the Kings of Britain*, however, Merlin's skill in rendering the massive stones of the Giants' Ring weightless, and in transporting them, does raise very difficult issues. Here Merlin appears almost as an 'experimenter' or 'artificer'. These are terms applied to Bladud the necromancer, and they carry very sinister connotations. The point is demonstrated in Layamon's Middle English version of the *History of the Kings of Britain*. Here Bladud is a practitioner of 'evil craft', who converses with a devil from whom he receives secret knowledge. This knowledge he puts into practice when he places a great stone into a 'stream', thus producing the famous hot spring at Bath.[21] William of Malmesbury's description of Pope Sylvester also shows how negative the connotations of the term 'artificer' were. Having described Sylvester's studies with Saracens, William proceeds to make accusations about the summoning of spirits and entering into a pact with the devil. Sylvester's achievements as an artificer are also impressive, consisting of a complex mechanical clock, organs that can produce sound using hydraulic power and a bronze head which can speak when animated by a demon.[22] That such things led the experimenter into the power of demons is emphasized by the fact that in the late twelfth century Walter Map, described Sylvester as the lover of a succubus demon named Meridiana.[23]

Both Geoffrey and Layamon work to suggest that Merlin's skills in moving stones are not of demonic origin. He simply produces 'gear' and dismantles the stones 'with unbelievable ease', before transporting and re-erecting them. All we are told is that he achieves it through his 'artistry'. But is Merlin's artistry as suspect as Bladud's craft? Geoffrey is carefully vague. Layamon is bolder, since Merlin's method here is to walk three times through and around the stones, while moving his mouth as if praying. This reduces the stones to featherweights, easily lifted by the soldiers.[24] The use of muttered words is worrying, since demons can be invoked by the correct words, but the suggestion of prayer is reassuring. Layamon also repeatedly emphasizes Merlin's unique wisdom, as well as his possession of the more dubious 'craft'. Moreover, King Aurelius next holds a feast to celebrate both Merlin's work and Whitsun, and this is happily attended by senior churchmen. Once again, Merlin's power is emphasized but made safe at the same time. Indeed, compared with Pope Sylvester, Merlin is a model of virtue.

Nevertheless, Merlin did share with Sylvester and other magicians an interest in both the courses of the stars and the flight of birds. William of Malmesbury believed that Sylvester had studied the flight of birds, and its occult meaning, with the Saracens.[25] This is explicable, since the Arabs were known to have unusual power over hawks and other hunting birds. In the twelfth century Adelard of Bath composed a treatise on birds after his own travels in the East, and in the thirteenth the notorious Emperor Frederick II sought to gain Arab wisdom on the subject.[26] However, William of Malmesbury goes so far as to link it with Sylvester's lessons on how to summon the spirits of the dead. The latter is necromancy, and a very dark art indeed.

Once again the *Life of Merlin*, is reassuring. Here Merlin himself comments that he had the greatest knowledge of 'the secrets of nature, the flight of birds, the courses of the stars and the movements of fish' when he was mad and was 'as a spirit'.[27] But when sane he can still deliver a lecture on birds, and of an unexceptionable sort. Fifteen types of bird are listed, from the everyday woodpecker to the symbolic phoenix and magical halcyons. Merlin knows the flight patterns of vultures and herons, as well as the prophetic behaviour of the diomedae and the powers of the halcyon over the weather at sea. He is able to interpret the flight of a group of cranes – but only because the flight of birds is another element of nature which God has imbued with special significance. It is thus a suitable and safe topic of study for the natural magician.

The key difference between natural magic and necromancy is, of course, that the natural magician respects the boundaries imposed upon human knowledge by God. Humanity, as God's rational creature, is equipped to understand much of the Creation, and to use the unique tool of language in doing so. But some knowledge is forbidden, and the exploitation of such knowledge is even worse. The understanding of the flight of birds, and the powers of the winds upon which they move, raised just such a problematic frontier for mediaeval science. The *Life of Merlin* emphasizes that Taliesin and Merlin have learnt the secrets of the winds from Gildas and from their own study of nature, thus not from forbidden sources. They discuss how the winds take up 'qualities' from the zone of the air in which they were formed, and how they lift water-filled clouds into the upper air and thus produce rain, hail or snow under differing conditions. This is the combination of elements through which the birds naturally move, and their movements can thus safely tell of impending changes in weather and season. But the memnonids can show the way to the 'lost' tomb of Memnon; while the diomedae foretell sudden death or disaster. These birds are thus at the very edge of the acceptable wisdom to be derived from natural phenomena. Once again, Merlin is poised at the forefront of natural magic, but even the supernatural knowledge of memnonids and Diomedae was rendered acceptable by the parallels with the literally marvellous qualities of birds and other creatures set out in the Bestiary.

The bestiary's information on the vulture includes the following:

> The vulture is so called because of its slow flight (*a volatu tardo*) which is caused by the size and weight of its body. Vultures can scent corpses from afar, like eagles. They can fly very high and see what is hidden under the shadow of the mountains. . . . They can predict the deaths of humans from certain signs. In particular, when a terrible battle is about to be fought, a great crowd of vultures will follow the armies and show that many men are about to be killed in warfare.

Still more marvellous is the Charadrius bird, which has highly desirable qualities:

> The Charadrius is a river-dwelling bird, and is said to be entirely white, without any black markings at all. Its dung is a cure for poor eyesight, and it is sought after by kings. If someone is ill, the Charadrius bird will show whether they will live or die. If they are going to die, the bird will turn its head away as soon as it is brought near. But if the sick person is going to recover, the bird takes their illness into itself through its gaze. It then flies up to the sun, burns off the sickness, and scatters it into the air.[28]

Merlin's information on birds and their secret knowledge comes from related sources, and is thus acceptable.

Moreover, the nature of the winds and the powers of air currents were investigated in no less a place than Malmesbury Abbey, home of William the chronicler. The investigator was the eleventh-century monk Eilmer, who then undertook nothing less than the first historically attested human flight. He was also an astronomer, and an expert interpreter of the courses and significance of comets. The monks of Malmesbury were not embarrassed about this, but proudly told stories of his achievements. Eilmer studied the flight of birds and the movements of the air before constructing wings, which he fixed to his arms and legs. He climbed to the top of the church tower, waited for a suitable wind, and jumped, spreading his wings. He caught a current of air, and succeeded in flying for more than a furlong (which is roughly two hundred metres) before being caught by turbulence. Sadly, he crashed to the ground, broke both legs, and was afterwards lame, leading the abbot to forbid further experiment. Eilmer's recorded comment is that he should have made some sort of tail for himself, to increase stability. His observations of the heavens and of the flight of birds and of winds clearly went together with his experiment in the use of wings, but no one seems to have been unkind enough to accuse him of practising dark arts.[29]

It is thus clear that the world was ready for Merlin as an expert on the powers of earth, water, air and birds, even while his magical skills as an 'artificer' made him dangerous as well as exciting. This leaves Merlin's expertise in potions to be investigated. In this case, the great magician himself promised 'methods which are quite new and unheard of', and which took the form of 'drugs' or potions.[30] The suggestion is that these potions are something unique to Merlin, which only a magician of his powers could create. Their effectiveness is certainly clear, since they were the means by which Merlin brought about the conception of Arthur. To recap, Merlin proposed these drugs as a desperate remedy in a desperate situation, when King Uther Pendragon was ill, and believed that he would die if he could not consummate his love for Ygerna, wife of the duke of Cornwall. Ygerna at the time was locked inside the strongly defended castle of Tintagel, whilst the armies of her husband and the king fought one another nearby. Some magical form of transport might have seemed the obvious solution – but Merlin is never obvious. What he suggests is to change Uther and his adviser into the shapes of the duke of Cornwall and his faithful attendant, using magical drugs.

In accepting this proposal, the king placed his life in Merlin's hands. Reassuringly, Merlin also undertook to change his own appearance and to accompany Uther into Tintagel. Uther then swallowed Merlin's potion, and his appearance was duly transformed. No details at all are given in the *History* of how Merlin prepared the drugs, or of the ingredients. Indeed, he seems to have produced them instantaneously. Interestingly, Merlin is constantly referred to as either a prophet or a wise adviser – definitely not as a physician or a magician. Yet what is utterly clear is that the power and accuracy of the drugs was enormous. Even Ygerna, Gorlois's wife, was completely deceived, and trustingly slept with Uther in his disguise. Moreover, as soon as Uther wished to resume his own appearance, he changed back – safely and painlessly. Merlin's boast that such potions were 'unheard of' in Uther's time was clearly justified; the question is how the mediaeval audience regarded them. Merlin's potions were far more powerful than any drugs known in either the twelfth century or the fifth – but were they medical, magical, or both? Uther's trust is certainly notable, since his own older brother and predecessor, Aurelius Ambrosius, had been poisoned by the drugs of a fake doctor. This clearly places Merlin in a different category from that of ordinary physicians. But it is inescapable that the transformation of individuals into the likenesses of others comes very close to sorcery.

Information on the developing attitudes of mediaeval audiences is provided by the translations into French and Middle English that appeared over the next half century. First out, and aimed at a courtly audience, was the Anglo-Norman translation by Wace. This version stresses that Merlin is master of many arts, and uniquely placed to offer help and counsel. Here the potions are called 'new medicines' (*nuvels medecinemenz*), and their effect is so exciting that it is dwelt on at some length.[31] As in Geoffrey of Monmouth's *History* it is the appearance or likeness of one person that is changed into that of another, but Wace elaborates on the theme, and has Merlin say:

> I know how to change someone's face, and make one into another; the one will look just like the other, and become exactly the same as him. You shall have the looks, the body, the face, the speech, the whole appearance of the count [*sic*] of Cornwall. I need not dwell on it – I shall make you just like the count, and I shall come with you, taking the form of Bretel.[32]

The change thus appears to be physical, and effected by medicine. It is therefore clearly not a matter of glamour or deception. Importantly, this means that it is not the product of sorcery (which uses demonic power to deceive the senses of the onlooker, rather than changing anything physically). And yet the negative idea of illusion can hardly be avoided, since it is a matter of appearance or 'semblance', and the effect is to fool others. Even more dubiously, this illusion is worked in order that the king might seduce a virtuous, married woman without her knowledge or consent. Thus it is not surprising that Wace goes on to apply the word 'enchantments' (*anchantemanz*) to Merlin's actions, whilst emphasizing that the outcome was entirely positive, in that it was this adventure which led to the conception of the great King Arthur.[33]

What of the less courtly English version by Layamon? Here Merlin's status as a counsellor is repeatedly stressed, as is the purity of his motives. Merlin's unrivalled 'counsel' and 'magical power' are linked together, and his search for something far beyond earthly riches is underlined by his refusal of all 'land, silver, gold ... or possessions'. Moreover, the story of the potions is immediately preceded by an encounter between Merlin and a pious hermit, who is acting as the king's spokesman. To the hermit Merlin makes a long prophecy about the coming of Arthur.[34] This effectively justifies whatever means Merlin needs to adopt in order to bring this king into being. Once again, it is the medicinal aspect of Merlin's drugs which is underlined, since they are called 'leech-craft', and once again they have the power to change not just faces but also speech and ways of behaving.[35] Merlin says: 'If I were to seek riches then I should lose my craft. But my leech-craft shall be priceless to you, since you shall have all you wish. All your looks shall become like the earl's: your speech, your courtly actions – even your horse, your clothes and the way you ride.'[36] Unlike the other versions, however, Layamon spells out that it is Merlin who restores everyone to their own appearance and 'features' when morning comes. Readers are explicitly reassured that Merlin's 'craft' has brought about both the conception of Arthur and his birth at 'the time that was chosen':

Ygaerne was with child by Uther the king, through the wizardry of Merlin, even before they were wedded. Then came the time that was destined: Arthur was born. As soon as he came to this world, elves took him in hand; they enchanted the child with their strongest spells. They gave the prince elf-gifts ... and he grew great as they intended.[37]

Mediaeval readers and translators, then, interpreted Merlin's potions as medicinal – but they were medicines produced by a prophet and superhuman counsellor, not an ordinary doctor. The difference between Merlin and human physicians is emphasized in all versions of the story. The latter are ambitious courtiers, paid well for their services and willing to move from one employer to another. This is how the treacherous Saxon Appas is able to poison Uther's older brother Aurelius. In Wace's version, Appas is well educated, speaks several languages, knows how to behave at court and is highly trained in both medicine and surgery. But his greed and his bad faith are equally great. To make himself appear trustworthy, he disguises himself as a monk as well as advertising his skill as a doctor, and since Aurelius is already ill, Appas is ushered to the king's bedside. He checks the king's pulse, displays an effective bedside manner, and says that he has diagnosed the problem. All are convinced, and when Appas has prepared his poisoned potion the king trustingly swallows it. Appas then twists his medical skill still further, by wrapping the king warmly in a rich cover, so that the heat helps the poison to take hold.[38]

Layamon gives still more medical detail than Wace. Appas here produces a glass vessel and uses this to study the sick king's urine, as described in medical treatises. He then pronounces that he can cure Aurelius, and proceeds to make a potion. Layamon even names the poison used by the treacherous doctor – it is scamony. Appas's stock of medicaments is both professional and costly, since he gives Aurelius's 'chamber-knights' gifts of 'canel', ginger and liquorice. Convinced by all this, the king and his companions allow Appas to administer the poison drug, and to prescribe a period of resting and sweating for the king. This is to last until midnight, when Appas will return with further treatments and finish the cure. Needless to say, by midnight the treacherous doctor has fled the town, and the poisoned king is not only sweating heavily but badly swollen and close to death.[39] The assumption that kings are constantly attended by doctors occurs again in Layamon's account of Uther's seduction of Ygaerne (Ygerna). When Uther's knights wish to conceal the king's absence from the battlefield, they say (following Merlin's orders) that he has been bled, is resting in his tent, and must not be disturbed.[40]

A highly skilled, and highly paid, doctor was thus an important asset to a royal court, and able to find patrons wherever he chose to travel. In this, as in much else, the story of Merlin accords with mediaeval reality. Yet Merlin is not a mere royal physician any more than he is a royal soothsayer or a necromancer; just as he is not Bladud, he is also not Appas. But was his skill with his magical drugs as fashionable as his prowess in other areas of natural magic? The career of John of Tours has already suggested that it was. But perhaps even more famous were two of Henry I's doctors. The first, Grimbald, was so important to the king that he slept in a corner of the king's bedroom. This is how he came to witness a dramatic incident, when King Henry experienced three visionary dreams, revealing the discontent of his subjects.

Grimbald's account of these dreams was so striking that the chronicler of Worcester Cathedral, who was amongst Grimbald's audience, entered it into his account of Henry's reign.[41] Grimbald, the 'skilled doctor' who treats the king by the interpretation of dreams, is here compared with the prophet Daniel. Moreover, a semi-autograph copy of John's *Chronicle* provides the account with illustrations.[42] Like the royal physician envisaged by Layamon, Grimbald holds a glass vessel for the examination of urine, a newly fashionable tool of the medical trade. The importance of the story is emphasized by the fact that such illustrations are almost unprecedented in the context of a chronicle. Moreover, John placed this incident almost immediately after his account of a minutely observed, light-emitting UFO, which appeared in the sky over

Hereford shortly after midnight on 17 February 1130. Thus, medicine, dream interpretation and celestial marvels are closely related. We are here very much in the territory of Merlin – and it is the territory of natural magic, not of demonic magic.

Henry I's other famous European doctor was Faricius of Abingdon, who also trained in Italy before travelling to the Anglo-Norman court. Faricius's patients paid fees high enough to help rebuild much of the church and other buildings of Abingdon Abbey, showing just how much wealth Merlin could have gained. His help for Queen Matilda in her first two pregnancies led to further royal gifts, and again is reminiscent of Merlin.[43] In Geoffrey of Monmouth's *Life of Merlin*, Merlin emphasizes that the hot springs of Bath are especially helpful for women, suggesting that he has specific expertise in this field as well. Both Grimbald and Faricius made a major impact on the court of Henry, but the chroniclers give no details of their medicines. Once again, as in the story of Merlin, drugs are the stuff of mystery.

And yet classical works on the uses of both plant and animal substances for the making of medicines were known in the twelfth century. Treatises on herbs and their medical uses were available in both Latin and English, together with texts on the medical uses of animal body parts, and on specialized areas of medicine. Why, then, was Merlin's drug-making an area of such mystery? Merlin is stated in Geoffrey of Monmouth's *Life of Merlin* to have full knowledge of trees and plants. Both can be either food or poison. Complex poisons, blending plant extracts together, are the result of human magic, as in the case of the poisoned apples prepared by Merlin's rejected ex-lover, which cause insanity. But even such magical poisons can be immediately counteracted by the power of medicinal springs. As in Geoffrey's *History of the Kings of Britain*, where the use of plant substances is secondary to the application of water and

stone, there seems to be a hierarchy here. Human skill and knowledge can compound effective potions from plants – but the forces
given by God to the elements of creation are more powerful still.

Just as with astrology, however, twelfth-century pioneers were
working on the very problems with which Merlin had also dealt.
One of their products was a new edition of the herbal of 'Apuleius',
together with a treatise on the medicinal qualities of animals, with
new illustrations, innovatively drawn from life. A copy, which
belonged to the monastery of Bury St Edmunds, is now in the
Bodleian Library, Oxford (MS Bodley 130).[44] There were also
more theoretical approaches, which sought to integrate study of
plants into the growing study of natural magic. By the second half
of the twelfth century these were producing results which were
being incorporated into encyclopaedic bestiaries. One of the earliest
was commissioned by a canon of Lincoln Cathedral – to whose
bishops Geoffrey of Monmouth dedicated both his *History of the
Kings of Britain* and his *Life of Merlin*. This expands the basic 37
chapters of the early bestiaries to an impressive 110 chapters,
including new entries on nature and the regions of the earth.[45]

Lincoln and Oxford, the very places that had seen the first
revelation of Merlin, were also centres for this new, integrated study
of the powers of the natural world. Geoffrey of Monmouth's associate, Henry of Huntingdon, wrote not only a *Chronicle* but also
treatises on plants, gemstones and aromatics.[46] An Augustinian
canon from Oxford, Robert of Cricklade, who was an expert on
natural philosophy, prepared a compilation of key texts and dedicated it to Henry II.[47] Like Adelard of Bath, Robert had also travelled to Italy and Sicily to further his studies. Canons of Lincoln
commissioned up-to-date bestiaries and world maps, reflecting this
expanding knowledge. This was the circle to which Merlin was first
revealed when one of the very earliest copies of his great prophecies

was sent to the bishop of Lincoln by Geoffrey of Monmouth. The endorsement of these scientists and scholars paved the way for the acceptance of Merlin and the whole *History of the Kings of Britain* by the wider, political world. Their researches amongst the rare books they were collecting would also have provided sources for Merlin's powers of natural magic, and the theological teaching they offered would help to ensure that Merlin never indulged in the 'rites of demons'.

Merlin's magic was therefore so constructed as to excite readers throughout the mediaeval period, since it brought out key problems relating to the forces of nature, the powers of demons, and the boundary between the two. For readers in Northern Europe it was all the more attractive, and all the more believable, for being an embodiment of the cutting-edge studies being undertaken there from the twelfth century onwards. Scholars in regions such as England and France drew upon the classical resources of Italy and Sicily, but had access also to translations of Arab works of magic and science. The revelation of Merlin's powers proved that Northern Europe was the rival of the old, Mediterranean world in learning and magic, just as the imperial conquests of Charlemagne and Arthur rivalled the military might of the Romans. This made it all the more important that Merlin's magic remained free from the taint of sorcery, with which 'Saracen magic' was increasingly associated in the era of the Crusades. There is, however, another serious problem, and that is the significance of Merlin's parentage. Could the son of an incubus demon really be so innocent of *magia*?

CHAPTER 6

ℰℭ

A DEMONIC HERITAGE

O NE OF THE most sensational mysteries about Merlin was the fact that his father was an incubus. This provided an explanation for his superhuman powers in both prophecy and magic – but it was also very troubling. Could the son of a demon have access to a genuine spirit of prophecy? If not, then Merlin's prophecies could not be accepted. No one in mediaeval Europe dismissed the story as a physical impossibility, since no one questioned the existence of demons or their capacity to have contact with humans. One commentator did point out that it was possible that Merlin's mother was simply lying, to cover up a more ordinary, and more sordid, story, but that was very much a minority reaction.[1] For those concerned with theology and Church law, a much more serious problem was whether a being with such a negative supernatural heritage could be trusted, especially since magic was already a very troubling issue, precisely for the reason that it was highly likely to involve contact with demons.

Once again, the timing of Merlin's presentation to the world seems to have been crucial. In the 1130s, when the *History of the Kings of Britain* first revealed Merlin to Anglo-Norman and European readers, views on demons and spirits were still relatively flexible. There was still a possibility that the *daemons* of late classical tradition were different from the demons of the Bible. It was only from the 1150s onwards that the Church began the long process of bringing order and cross referencing to theological and legal definitions of such complex issues as demons, spirits, and their roles in the various forms of magic that were recognized to exist. By that time Merlin was established as a genuine prophet, whose place in history was accepted. He still raised very troubling questions, but the possibility of his outright rejection was over. This can only have been helped by the fact that the historical Merlin was emphatically contrasted with the negative categories of *magi,* necromancers and diviners. His innocence of such forbidden activities as summoning up the dead, or making ritual sacrifices involving blood, is powerfully underlined by the fact that his first appearance in the historical record is as the planned victim of a group of just such practitioners. The account of Vortigern's *magi* stresses that they instructed their patron to have a fatherless boy sacrificed so that ritual use could be made of his blood.[2] Merlin's courage, truthfulness, refusal to fear the tyrant and genuine prophecy are in complete contrast to such wickedness.

And yet the paradox remains. For the *History of the Kings of Britain* itself, through the figures of Vortigern and his court scholar Maugantius, raise the problems of whether it was possible for a spirit to impregnate a woman – and just what sort of spirit this would be. Merlin himself remains, of course, the innocent product of such a liaison, but if Merlin's mother was telling the truth, and if his superhuman powers were real, then Merlin's father had to be some sort of demon or spirit. The great prophet-magician therefore presented a puzzle, in need of explanation. Those with knowledge of the Bible (a group that included all educated people in Western Europe at the time) would know that demons were capable of possessing humans, and that Christ's miracles had included several triumphs over such beings. However, these demons had caused illness, madness and suffering to their victims – but not pregnancy. In fact, the New Testament contains no accounts of demon-lovers who seduce human women. This absence is mirrored in the stories of miracles worked by early mediaeval saints. Triumphs over demons are certainly found, but none of these demons had engaged in sexual relationships with women.

Once again Geoffrey of Monmouth's book seems to have been at the forefront of a new trend, since by the late twelfth century such creatures are starting to appear in miracle stories. One of the earliest is in the *Life and Miracles of St William of Norwich*, written *c*.1173 by Thomas of Monmouth, a monk at the Cathedral Priory of Norwich. In this collection we read of a young woman from Dunwich, who was repeatedly tempted by a demon-knight.[3] The demon never seems to have been invisible – but was capable of appearing both by night and by day, and inside closed rooms. This young woman was saved by a vision and by St William, and no pregnancy resulted. However, her story was not an isolated one. Sexual contacts between demons and humans became a growing theme as the twelfth century continued, and appeared in accounts of heretics as well as in miracle stories. The story of the notorious heretic Eudes de Stella was retold in the last part of the twelfth century by the chronicler William of Newburgh and the moralist Walter Map. Tempted by a demon, Eudes set himself up as leader of a group of brigands who terrorized the region of Beauvais. They attacked indiscriminately, but were especially hostile to the Church.

It was clear to chroniclers that Eudes had been seduced by a demon, and tales of his sexual orgies confirmed this. In Map's version the story was a source of much information on demons and their ability to use illusions and enchantments on humans.[4]

Demons and the theme of sexual contact with humans were thus apparently a matter of growing concern for twelfth-century writers and moralists. Walter Map was writing for the amusement and edification of the Angevin court, and his work suggests that the theme of demons was felt to be especially relevant for such circles. He introduces his book by comparing the royal court to the circles of hell, and goes on to tell numerous stories of supernatural apparitions, monsters and ghosts, as well as of demons and their temptations. It must be acknowledged that most of his sexually alluring demons are succubi, adopting the female form to tempt (and even marry) human men. Perhaps unsurprisingly, the Augustinian chronicler who tells Eudes's story, William of Newburgh, indulges in fewer accounts of illicit sex. His tales of the supernatural are mostly concerned with how the bodies of the dead could be revived, and how they might come back from the grave.[5] Demonic lovers clearly achieved a growing place in the fashionable imagination, but was Merlin the cause of this phenomenon? And where did the story of Merlin's own conception originate?

The story of Merlin's demon father is not taken from the Welsh poems relating to the Celtic Myrddin. However, biblical sources from the Old Testament and the Apocrypha do offer parallels, especially in the form of the Nephilim. Perhaps most important of these sources is Genesis (chapter 6), whose opening verses tell of how humans began to multiply on the earth as the descendants of Adam reproduced. Verse 2 narrates how the 'sons of God' desired the 'daughters of men'; verse 4 goes on to say that this was the time when giants walked the earth, and that the offspring of these unions between the sons of God and the daughters of men were 'mighty men' of this heroic age. The problem was how to identify the 'sons of God'. St Augustine took the down-to-earth view that they were human, but other theologians differed.[6] The Book of Enoch was more informative, and offered evidence that the Nephilim (identified with the offspring of the 'sons of God') were the children of fallen angels. The status of the Book of Enoch was itself dubious, but what nevertheless emerges is that there were real, if difficult, scriptural authorities for Merlin's conception. Moreover, these sources made it possible to argue that such supernatural beings, capable of fathering children, might be fallen angels or the 'sons of God'. This left open the possibility that Merlin's father was something less sinister than a demon, as well as providing an explanation for the 'ancient giants' on whom Merlin was an expert. By extension, a context for Merlin himself is suggested. But these biblical passages had been known since the beginning of Christianity, and so they scarcely provide an explanation for the growing mediaeval interest in demon-lovers, and in supernatural beings more generally. The question which arises is therefore whether Merlin was the cause of this interest, or merely one of its effects.

This issue is complicated, since mediaeval beliefs about demons, magic and the supernatural were all closely interrelated. It is also important not to lose sight of the figure of Merlin himself in the mass of material on demonology, angelology and magic. Thus, the necessary starting point is the *History of the Kings of Britain* itself, in order to see just what ideas about demons, spirits and supernatural beings are offered there, and how Merlin is presented. What emerges from such a reading of the *History* is surprising, since that work presents a good deal of material on pagan deities and supernatural themes, and yet offers very little comment on religious or spiritual matters. This makes it very different from the work of moralists such as Walter Map, as well as from those of monastic chroniclers of more recent history. The *History* takes a morally neutral tone from the very start in its presentation of pagan beliefs and practices, even though the Christian Church had taken the view, almost from its earliest times, that pagan gods were not only false idols but likely to be demons in disguise. In the *History* the paganism of the Trojans and the Greeks is treated as a simple matter of fact, and it is perfectly possible for pagan rulers to be described as good and just kings.

This neutrality goes so far that when Brutus and his followers land on a deserted island in the Mediterranean and make ritual offerings to a statue of the goddess Diana, the results are wholly positive. No detail of the pagan ritual is spared, including the offering of blood from a sacrificed deer to the goddess, something which was especially rejected by Christianity, and which might suggest that Diana did indeed have the tastes of a demon. Yet Diana grants Brutus a vision in which she makes a true prophecy of his future destiny. This is then fulfilled, and the island of Britain is thus at least in part the gift of a pagan goddess.[7] However, once Brutus' descendants are established in their new country, and have become the Britons, matters of religion and belief are dropped for a very long time. They resurface with Bladud, the necromancer-king, who dedicates a temple to Minerva in his city of Bath.[8] But Bladud's paganism is treated as a separate issue from his necromancy. Overall, the worst thing that is said about the paganism of the Britons is that it was 'superstition'.

However, whilst paganism is treated very lightly, the history of Britain has its complement of marvels and wonders. As with the pagan deities, many of the monsters and marvels will have been familiar to readers of classical works (and of the Bible). When Brutus and his Trojans first arrived at the island then called Albion, they found it inhabited only by giants, who were especially numerous in Cornwall. The leader of the Cornish giants was Gogmagog (or Goemagog), who could uproot oak trees with his bare hands. However, Gogmagog's weakness was his lack of skill at wrestling, which enabled a British leader, Corineus, to throw him over a cliff and kill him.[9] Sea monsters were fewer, but did include the Sirens, one of the last perils to be encountered by Brutus before reaching Albion/Britain. The ships had sailed along the coast of Africa, passing a great salt lake and the 'mountains of Azara', before coming to the Pillars of Hercules. Here the Sirens surrounded them, swimming around the ships and nearly sinking them, but were defeated by the seamanship of the exiles. Later, a sea monster appeared off the coast of Britain itself, and preyed upon the local inhabitants before killing King Morvidus.[10] In general, however, Britain is a land of benign and natural marvels. Only one plague is narrated, in the reign of King Rivallo. This takes the form of a rain of blood, which lasts for three days and leads to swarms of flies, which cause widespread human deaths.[11] The dragons of the subterranean lake beneath the mountains of the west were awe-inspiring, but attacked only one another, not human beings.

Another surprise is that ghosts and spirits, of the kinds which occur frequently in twelfth-century chronicles of recent events, are scarce in the *History of the Kings of Britain*. The Yorkshire chronicler William of Newburgh included several stories of ghosts, such as that of a man from Buckinghamshire who left his grave on the very night after his burial and terrified his wife by climbing into bed with her. He had become so heavy that he nearly crushed her with his 'insupportable weight' before going on to disturb his brothers and neighbours. This ghost was made quiet when the bishop of Lincoln had the grave opened, and a letter of absolution placed on the body.[12] Still more frightening were stories such as one in

Geoffrey of Burton's account of the recent miracles of St Modwenna. This told of two discontented tenants, who stirred up trouble between the abbot and monks of Burton Abbey and Count Roger the Poitevin, before being suddenly struck dead. They were buried in a churchyard, but reappeared that same evening, carrying their own coffins, and changing into animal shapes. They also brought an outbreak of pestilence down upon the village, killing nearly all the inhabitants. Once again, the bishop was appealed to, and in this case he gave permission for the graves to be opened. When the bodies were found intact but with faces smeared with blood, 'they cut off the men's heads and placed them between their legs, then they tore out their hearts and took them to a ford. There the hearts were burnt, and they burst with a great noise, after which an evil spirit in the form of a crow was seen to fly out of the flames.'[13] This seems to be a tale of demonic possession as well as of shape-shifting and possible vampirism.

In the *History of the Kings of Britain* it is noteworthy that spirits appear only from the reign of Vortigern (in Book Six) onwards, and thus within the account of the Christian period of British history. This is, of course, precisely the time at which Merlin himself appears. Vortigern, like other British characters of the period, is described as a Christian, despite being a tyrant and employing murderous magicians. However, he is perfectly willing to make treaties with pagan Saxon leaders, and even to marry the daughter of one of them. The 'tyrant' is slightly drunk when he encounters the beautiful Renwein, daughter of Hengist, at a banquet, and immediately desires her. It is Vortigern's lust for Renwein (rather than his involvement in treachery and murder) that is attributed to the direct action of the devil, who is described as 'entering his heart' only at this moment. Hints that Vortigern's Christianity left something to be desired are confirmed by the arrival of St Germanus, bishop of Auxerre, to enquire into growing problems of heresy amongst the British. However, Renwein herself is next affected by an evil spirit, which enters her heart and causes her to be envious of her stepson, Vortimer. Once the evil spirit has taken up residence, Renwein (now an enthusiastically wicked stepmother) plots to kill Vortimer, resorting to poisons and corruption in order to do so. The poisons are not described as magical, nor is the process by which Renwein administers them to Vortimer – she simply bribes a servant.[14] Thus, demons are clearly able to enter the hearts of both pagans and Christians, and are associated with sexual desire and the wiles of women. However, they do not cause political upheaval or war – that is left to the ambitions of rulers.

How does this affect the reader's view of Merlin as the son of a demon? On the one hand, the narrative, like mediaeval Christianity, leaves no room for doubting the existence of demons. But on the other hand, the negative role of demons is restricted, and pagan deities are not attacked as demons in disguise. Similarly, supernatural marvels and wonders are frequently benign, and rulers are perfectly capable of wickedness without demonic inspiration. Thus the reader is prepared to accept Merlin as supernatural, semi-demonic, and yet morally neutral. In fact, Vortigern is a far more negative character, and Merlin's condemnation of his treachery shows that he, although a half-demon, is far more moral. This can, of course, be accounted for by the fact that Merlin's mother is a nun, and that he has been brought up as a Christian child. Moreover, when Merlin's mother swears an oath upon her very soul, there is no doubt that it is to be taken seriously. And it is with this oath that she prefaces her statement that Merlin has no human father and neither has she herself ever slept with a man. Rather, she was the victim of a being who could appear and disappear at will within closed rooms, and who could both talk to her and touch her whilst invisible. Oddly, the princess appears not to have been terrified by this, and not to have told anybody what was happening to her. However, she has no doubt that this supernatural being must have been Merlin's father, since she became pregnant after having been seduced by him, and this is the only sexual experience she has had.

Vortigern does not accuse the princess of lying, and neither does he consult his humiliated *magi*. Instead, he sends for a new expert, one Maugantius, who is not part of the court.[15] Thus, Geoffrey presents a scholarly opinion from a neutral source on Merlin's father, and on Merlin's own nature. Maugantius listens attentively to the information, and then refers the king to books written by wise men and to historical narratives. He is able to assert that he has read of 'a number' of men being conceived in the same way. Lest this appear unbelievable, he goes on to cite the testimony of Apuleius, the late classical author of the *De Deo Socratis* and himself the victim of accusations of fraud by magical means. Apuleius was (rather vaguely) known in the twelfth century as the author of obscure philosophical works. More famously, he was mentioned by St Augustine, who criticized his views on spirits and demons.[16] His name was therefore one which readers with a high level of education would probably have recognized, and might well have associated with expertise on demons. At the same time it was unlikely that they would have read his works, and thus they would not have known that he actually says nothing about incubus demons fathering human children.

There is further evidence that mediaeval readers were interested in the revelation of Merlin's conception, and in the tantalizing information about spirits and demons which the *History* offered. This is that when Geoffrey of Monmouth went on to write the *Life of Merlin* in around 1150, he added a lot more information on spirits. Moreover, the *Life of Merlin* manages to give seductive spirits an ordered place in the natural world – and even one which accords with fashionable philosophical views on the structure of the universe. The earth, we learn, is surrounded by a band of 'heavy' air, filling the space between earth and the moon. This space is the realm of demons, here openly acknowledged as evil, who do not live on earth but who can tempt, cheat and deceive humans. They can make bodies for themselves out of the 'matter' of the air, and thus can have relations with women and can even make them pregnant. Beyond this zone is the 'airy heaven', through which the moon follows its orbit around the earth. This more luminous space is 'thronged with bands of spirits', who are sympathetic to humans, and act as intermediaries between humans and God. A scientific note is added when the reader is told that the air is not only what makes it possible for the light and position of the stars and planets to be visible to humans, but also what makes the production of sounds audible to human ears. The next zone is the 'ethereal heaven', through which the sun and the planets follow their courses. This is the realm of the angels, but no details are given of their nature or functions. Outermost is heaven itself, also called the firmament, and this is the zone of the fixed stars.[17]

Thus, God has created a system of multiple heavens, populated with a three-tier 'order of spirits'. Finally, a further, potentially controversial, claim is made. This is that God has ordered things so that it is the spirits who are responsible for looking after and renewing the world and all the forms and beings it contains. The result of this is a view of the world that is both scientifically modern (in twelfth-century terms) and exciting to the point of being frightening. It also has the convenient effect of creating a group of 'spirits', who are placed in the hierarchy between angels and demons and are able to be in contact with human beings. Every human being is surrounded by demons, spirits and angels, constantly engaged in attacking, defending and renewing God's creation. Communication between humans and spirits is perfectly possible, if dangerous. Moreover, the whole of the natural world becomes a terrain on which both spirits and demons exercise powers of renewal and destruction which far exceed those available to humans. Against such a backdrop, even Merlin's powers appear not just explicable but positively reassuring. Scholars across Europe were working on these challenging problems, and coming to differing conclusions. But angels and demons were amongst the topics which attracted their attention.[18] Once again, as with the subjects of medicine and marvellous technologies, Merlin was at the cutting edge of intellectual interests.

Again, it is clear that the timing of Merlin's appearance was very fortunate. There was growing interest in both angels and demons, but there was not yet a fixed view as to what was, and was not, either possible or theologically acceptable. The attention given to a work of early Christian mysticism and of Neo-Platonic philosophy, the treatise on the *Celestial Hierarchy* attributed to Dionysius the Areopagite, provides further insights into the debates. It is a discussion of the ranks of heavenly spirits and beings, and is thus scarcely concerned with demons and their works. Nevertheless, its circulation in the early twelfth century helped to focus attention on the issue of supernatural beings.[19] It was a rare work in the early Middle Ages, even though its supposed author, Dionysius the Areopagite, was (mistakenly) identified with St Denis, one of the most important saints in mediaeval France. The abbey of St Denis was given a copy of the Greek version of the work in the ninth century, and two Latin translations were subsequently made.[20] However, all this material remained obscure and little read outside St Denis and its region – until the twelfth century.

The first English scholar to show an interest was the erudite William of Malmesbury, who was responsible for the production of a copy of Eriugena's work in around 1125. Characteristically, William seems to have been interested because he believed that Eriugena had visited Malmesbury during the reign of King Alfred rather than because he was concerned with this area of philosophy.[21] However, other twelfth-century writers were more enthusiastic, and the subject of angelology began to grow. An influential exponent was Honorius of Autun, a popular theologian of the time. He studied in England as a pupil of St Anselm, archbishop of Canterbury and leading theologian. That Honorius knew Eriugena's work is clear from his compilation of a set of extracts from it. Honorius's most popular work was the *Imago Mundi*, which offered an all-in-one, simplified version of cosmology, geography and world history.[22] This was widely used for the instruction of the educated laity, and here again Honorius included selections of the 'new' material on angels and spirits, which had a considerable impact. One version of the work was dedicated to none other than the Empress Matilda, daughter of Henry I of England and mother of Henry II. The new ideas about demons and angels were thus being introduced to royal courts in England, France and possibly the empire in the first half of the twelfth century – just as Merlin made his first appearance.

Nor was Honorius alone. A number of treatises on angels appeared at this time, several showing the influence of the *Celestial Hierarchy*. Leading scholars in the developing schools of France, and Paris in particular, produced such works.[23] In England, theological study was being undertaken at both Oxford and Canterbury in the 1130s. In the case of Oxford, this teaching was offered first by Theobald of Etampes and then by Robert Pullen. Robert was a pioneer in the movement to compile a textbook on key theological subjects, and produced an eight-part guide. The second section of this work included his discussion of archangels, angels and the fate of the rebel angels.[24] This School of Oxford was small and short-lived, but it appeared in the 1130s under the authority of Archdeacon Walter Calenius, who was also provost of the collegiate church of St George in Oxford Castle.[25] This is the church in which Geoffrey of Monmouth is believed to have been a canon from 1129. It thus seems very possible that Geoffrey gained his own expertise on angels, spirits and demons at Oxford, and that Walter Calenius was the 'Archdeacon Walter' who Geoffrey says provided the ancient British book that was the basis of the *History of the Kings of Britain*.

However, from around 1140 until almost 1190 the embryonic School of Oxford disappeared, for reasons that remain unclear. And from 1150 onwards, Robert Pullen's textbook was increasingly displaced by the magisterial work of Peter Lombard, who was based at the much larger and more influential School of Paris. This work was *The Sentences*, and it provided the groundwork for the development of theology across the rest of the mediaeval period. The second book was on 'The Creation and Formation of Things Corporeal and Spiritual', and was largely dedicated to assembling the key doctrinal statements of theological authorities on the subjects of angels and fallen angels.[26] This once again emphasizes the importance of these subjects for twelfth-century intellectuals – but it was also the beginning of a powerful movement to reduce areas of uncertainty within Christian teaching on supernatural beings. For Peter Lombard effectively rules out the possibility of there being categories of spirits who could interact with humans and yet were morally ambiguous.

First, he says, the angels were created by God before the forma-tion of the earth and its firmament. The angels were all created good, but some chose evil and followed Lucifer into rebellion.

Their punishment was to be barred from the Empyrean, and to have their very being weighed down and solidified by their malice. They thus became demons, and were principally condemned to occupy either hell or the gloomy and turbulent aery zone close to the earth. They are not allowed permanently to inhabit the earth, and they cannot actually make or grant anything real. They can be defeated by saints, as well as by angels. Nevertheless, they can tempt humans. Part of what makes them so dangerous is that they have knowledge of the cosmos, of angels and of time – and they can use this to deceive and tempt. They also have greater power over created matter than do mere humans. Peter Lombard says quite definitively that magical arts can work only through the actions of these demons.[27] Thus the magi of Pharaoh, mentioned in the Bible, achieved their results through the operations of demons. Peter Lombard does use the alternative terms 'spirits' and 'aery powers'; however, these appear to be synonyms for angels and demons, rather than intermediate categories of supernatural beings. Finally, he is definite that demons can take possession of humans, but does accept that humans also have guardian angels to protect them.[28]

In a world view based upon Peter Lombard's great theological textbook, there is thus no longer any real space for an incubus demon that can impregnate a woman without the involvement of maleficent powers. Moreover, there is also no space for a magician who is not himself (at best) deceived by a demon. Merlin, as described in the *History of the Kings of Britain*, thus becomes a very difficult figure. However, the new theological doctrine on spirits did not mean that Merlin had to be written out of history; rather, that his powers had to be rethought. After all, it was established that both demons and magicians certainly existed, and stories of sexual contact between demons and humans were told (in ever-increasing numbers) by perfectly orthodox churchmen.

This material became, however, fraught with danger for anyone who was not an expert in the theology of the topic.

The problems relating to Merlin's magic and its nature became even greater. If magic could work only by collusion with demons, and if the magician himself was the son of a demon, where did this leave Merlin's feats of magic? This question cannot be given a short answer, since the theological and legal status of magic was undergoing rapid development in the twelfth century before hardening into a clearer form in the thirteenth. If the dangerous allure of Merlin's magic and the increasing care with which it had to be handled by serious writers are to be understood, then some attention also needs to be paid to theories of magic – and the starting point needs to be those works that were influential at the time when Merlin first appeared.

The most fundamental of these was a sort of encyclopaedia, called the *Etymologies*, put together by Bishop Isidore of Seville in the seventh century. This was a handy, one-volume reference work, which offered brief extracts from classical texts and traditions on matters of religion, science, history and geography.[29] It gives an extensive, though not altogether clear, coverage of magic and its practitioners in Book Eight, using terminology that suggests very strongly that this is where Geoffrey of Monmouth got a lot of the material for Merlin. The 'art' of magic originated with Zoroaster, king of the Bactrians, and was taken up by the Greeks, though the experts were the Assyrians. They excelled in reading entrails, and interpreting birds, lightning and stars – two of which were also practised by Merlin. Here Isidore also discusses demons, who are rebel angels who have changed after their fall, so that they are now confined by aerial bodies to the murky zone between earth and the moon.[30] Subsequent chapters discuss the pagan gods of the dead, who have power between the earth and the moon, an expert on whom being none other than Apuleius (also cited by Geoffrey of Monmouth). This leads on to the subjects of ghosts, lamiae (female creatures who steal and murder children), and incubi (who are related to classical satyrs, and also to the god Pan, who copulate with animals and women, of whom at least one is a demon).[31] The source material for Merlin's father is clear.

Human practitioners of magic, according to Isidore, are many, and their skills divide roughly into divination, reading auguries, giving oracles and necromancy. All these arts are of demonic origin and are used to tempt and deceive humanity. However, it seems that the most wicked magicians are the *malefici* and the necromancers. The former use spells to disturb the elements, affect people's minds and cause death, drawing upon the power of demons and making use of the bodies of the dead. The latter use incantations to summon the dead, as well as using the blood of corpses to attract demons, and from both they attempt to get answers to questions.[32] These are obviously very dark arts, but those who try to discern the future are all, whether they know it or not, receiving answers from demons. Such practitioners are 'diviners', and if their 'craft' uses incantations then they are also 'enchanters'. Similarly, the *arioli*, who offer prayers and sacrifices at the altars of idols, are actually contacting demons. Less strongly condemned are the *haruspices* who advise on the best times for specific actions, and the augurs and auspice readers who examine in particular the flights and calls of birds. However, casters of horoscopes, those who tell fortunes by casting lots and makers of amulets are also to be repudiated as users of the 'craft of demons'.[33] It seems from this that Merlin's magic, whilst highly dangerous, was carefully chosen to avoid the most clearly demonic practices. Moreover, Isidore's handling of his terms and categories is complex in structure and hard to follow at key points. There is thus considerable scope for interpretation, and space for Merlin's magic to be separated from demonic magic.

As concern about angels and demons grew in the high Middle Ages, anxiety about the associated subject of magic grew too, and it is scarcely surprising that attempts were made to organize and interpret Isidore's information. Inevitably, such work had the effect of reducing the area of uncertainty within which Merlin, as a positive figure, fitted. In the 1120s the growing School of Paris produced one of its first authoritative textbooks, in the form of *The Didascalicon* by Hugh of St Victor, a very influential guide to the basic nature and contents of Christian philosophy and theology. Hugh added a final section to this textbook, on the subject of magic and its component parts, showing his own growing concern.[34] His argument that magic is not genuine philosophy, but is false and malicious, suggests that he was worried by an increasing popularity of the subject amongst his pupils. All of magic, according to Hugh, seduces men into 'the cults of demons', and all of its five parts are to be rejected as sorcery.[35] Hugh's information is still largely taken from Isidore, although he reflects the growing power of astrology in having far more detail on that subject than the *Etymologies* provides. For Hugh, there are five main parts of magic, which can be broken up into eleven types of magical practice. Astrology is placed under 'false mathematics', along with soothsaying and making auguries from the flight and sounds of birds. Necromancy has become a category all of its own, and is generalized to any divination that involves offering blood in order to gain information from demons. Enchantments also form a category of their own, and all who offer these are wicked sorcerers whose incantations are demonic. Even makers of illusions use demonic arts in order to fool human senses, and to pretend to turn one thing into another. Merlin's magic could clearly not escape condemnation at Hugh's hands.

These anxieties, coupled with a sense that magic is gaining increasing recognition in secular society, recur in the work of John of Salisbury. John was an adviser to successive archbishops of Canterbury, including Thomas Becket, and ended his career as bishop of Chartres. He had considerable experience of courts, both secular and ecclesiastical, and wrote his *Policraticus* as a book of advice for those in power.[36] The very first book deals with fashionable amusements and occupations, such as hunting, gambling and music – and close upon their heels comes magic, discussed in no fewer than four chapters.[37] Sorcerers and creators of illusions first appear amongst the mimics, comics, wrestlers and jesters who entertain those with time to waste, which does not seem too sinister. That magic was popular is demonstrated by the sheer range of professional practitioners included by John. Some are still listed under the terms used by Isidore, making their reality in the twelfth century questionable. But the details given – including material on makers of entertaining illusions, those who make wax or clay images in order to affect selected people, those who harness spirits to images and amulets, palmists, astrologers, fortune-tellers, scryers and readers of omens (especially birds) – suggest considerable experience of actual practice. John is also deeply negative about magic, and adopts two main strategies towards it. The first is to emphasize that all forms of magic are in reality demonic, and the second is to devote a very long, sarcastic (and derivative) chapter to pointing out how ridiculous, and hampering, observance of omens can be.

This might suggest that good Christians increasingly had no option but to condemn Merlin as a seductive agent of the devil. However, the situation was not so simple, since there were also defenders of the new, scientific learning, who included at least parts of what Hugh and John dismissed as magic under the heading of natural philosophy. A leading figure in this movement was the English Franciscan Roger Bacon whose work became so famous that Pope Clement IV (1265–68) requested copies of it. Bacon's most important book was his *Opus Majus*, which provides a summary of all the new scientific learning, and argues for its positive contribution to the work of the Church. Part IV makes the case for mathematics as wholly necessary for a Christian understanding of the world, pointing out that it is needed for theology, time-keeping, the calendar, optics, astrology and astronomy.[38] Nevertheless, Bacon takes a negative view of what he calls 'false mathematics', which is also the 'art of magic'. This includes forecasting the future, making charms, illusions and fortune-telling. That he has also had exposure to 'modern magic' is demonstrated by his lists of the false methods used by magicians, which have expanded to include 'characters' and 'circles' as well as conjurations and sacrifices, all intended to summon 'demons of celestial natures'. True mathematicians make no use of such dangerous rubbish, and all (including Roman and Arab scholars) are strong in their refutation of any claim that the heavenly bodies can make anything happen, or override free will.[39]

Sadly, Bacon was nothing like as good a politician as he was a philosopher, and his attacks on the problems of the Church, and the errors which he believed were being made in the universities, led to his trial and imprisonment. European society in the thirteenth century was in the grip of a rising moral panic, with the University of Paris a key battleground. William of Auvergne was bishop of Paris and responsible for the university from 1228 to 1249. Aware that he and his friends had themselves been interested in magic as students, William condemned belief in the power of the stars in particular, calling it idolatry, and gave a list of magical paraphernalia very like that of Roger Bacon.[40] He said that magicians created combinations of letters and numbers, which they linked to parts of the body, and which were also used to summon 'planetary intelligences'. These were passed on in books of astrology as well as in volumes written by *magi* and necromancers, and they are involved in the making of illusions and the casting of horoscopes. William agrees that all such practices work by the power of demons – but he takes the negative argument a crucial step further when he links together the ideas of demons, idolatry, obscenity and injury to humanity. In 1277 another bishop of Paris, reinforced by Pope John XXI, issued a list of portions of the new philosophy and science that were to be condemned. Notoriously this included a list of banned books, and amongst these were works on geomancy, necromancy, casting lots, demon summoning and enchantments.[41] Magicians were very real – but they were also demon-worshipping enemies of society, and that would appear to include Merlin (who was, of course, safely dead).

It was thus inevitable that a sense of self-preservation increasingly affected depictions of Merlin created by writers of serious historical and philosophical works. It is scarcely surprising that historians stayed close to the *History of the Kings of Britain*, and continued to retell the same events right down to the sixteenth century – comment and deviation had become dangerous. What is perhaps more surprising is that none attempted to write Merlin out of history, as a stain upon the reputation of the British. The crucial work for transmitting knowledge of British history, as revealed by the the *History of the Kings of Britain*, to those who preferred to read in English, was the chronicle of Robert of Gloucester. He seems to have been writing in the reign of Edward I, was well educated, and drew on a range of chronicles and saints' lives. His decision to write a chronicle in English poetry, rather than in learned Latin prose, is surprising. However, since the chronicle makes flattering mentions of the prowess of one Sir Warin of Bassingbourn at several points, it seems that the work was originally commissioned by that knight. Two versions of the chronicle rapidly began to circulate, which survive in at least fourteen mediaeval manuscripts, and two new prose adaptations of it were written in the fifteenth century.[42] Clearly, this was a story that was in demand, and which was accepted as a true history of Britain. What image of Merlin did it transmit?

Its account is closely based on the *History of the Kings of Britain*, and the early translations into French and English. The boy Merlin is brought with his mother to the court of the tyrant Vortigern, who consults his 'clerks' about the story of demonic seduction told by Merlin's mother. This is clearly an important matter and is treated at some length. The learned experts explain that 'philosophie' states that there is a category of beings, or 'gostes', who inhabit the upper air but can take on the form of men in order to seduce women. These 'gostes' are also known as 'elven'; and it is thus in accordance with theology and science that one of them could have made Merlin's mother pregnant. Merlin's existence and nature are both supported by this account, which also proceeds to establish that Merlin was a great prophet. The prophecies, however, are not given in full. Instead, only the part relevant to early British history is recounted, with the explanation (if anybody needed it) that the 'Boar of Cornwall' who appears in the prophecies is King Arthur. Robert then explains that he does not feel competent to translate the rest of the prophecies for 'symple men', since he himself does not have sufficient knowledge. Nevertheless he stresses the extent of Merlin's knowledge. Merlin the son of a demon and Merlin the great prophet are thus both passed on to serious readers in a way which shows that this is an important, but potentially dangerous, topic.[43]

The same can also be said of Merlin the magical artificer and Merlin the master of magical appearances. Once again we are told of how Merlin is summoned to the court of Aurelius Ambrosius, and how he discusses his spirit of prophecy with that king before going on to use his esoteric knowledge, or 'quoyntyse', to bring the great medicinal stones from Ireland to Stonehenge. To do this, Merlin uses a combination of magical 'engines', 'quoyntyse' and (troublingly) 'enchantery'.[44] Merlin's ability to 'read' the meaning of the comet is described at some length, and he is made to give a detailed prophecy to Uther Pendragon. There is even a play on the reader's belief in Merlin here, since Uther does not immediately believe Merlin – something which is shortly proved to be a mistake. Robert's handling of Merlin departs from the established version in only one important area, and that is the transformation of Uther into the likeness of Duke Gorlois. In Robert's account, Merlin effects this (and thus the conception of Arthur) not by potions but by 'art'.[45] No explanation is given, and the reader is left with an impression of the sheer power of Merlin's magic – but the dangerous word 'enchantery' hangs over it. However, once again it is Merlin the prophet who is most strongly endorsed. The truth of Merlin's prophecies is several times mentioned, and once again no less a witness than an angel confirms that the British future was set out by Merlin's revelations.

Much less ambitious than the chronicle of Robert of Gloucester, and probably intended for a younger audience, was a short version of the *Brut* in English poetry.[46] This seems to have been produced in the early decades of the fourteenth century, and survives in seven versions. Each concentrates on exciting events, narrated in easily memorized, rhyming verse. This therefore seems to have been a 'school history', and it is interesting that it assumes that the reader will already have heard of Merlin. Its educational purpose is also suggested by the fact that it spends little time on the reign of Arthur, stating that readers will already know that king's 'aventures'; instead, it dwells at length on the necromantic engineering feats of Bladud at Bath, that were presumably less well known.

Similarly, the great prophecies made to the British kings are briefly and anonymously mentioned.[47] Oddly, Stonehenge is mentioned, but Merlin is not named as the creator of that monument. In this version, Merlin's most important role is that of an infallible prophet, who foretold the downfall of Vortigern.[48] No explanation of Merlin's identity is given – presumably the basics were known even to school pupils, while the issue of demons was too complex for such a work.

That Merlin was indeed a standard historical figure, in fourteenth-century England at least, is proved by the work known as *Castleford's Chronicle*. This is also in verse, and was written in around 1327, in a northern dialect of English. It now survives only in one fifteenth-century manuscript; the point here is not its readership but its testimony on the general view of Merlin.[49] This version of the familiar story seems to devote most attention to the parts that its author found most interesting – and Arthur and Merlin are at the top of the list. Unusually, Thomas Castelford (if he was the author) was unafraid of handling Merlin's prophecies, and translates them in full.[50] This follows the usual account of Vortigern and the discovery of Merlin and his mother. Thomas's lack of fear around theological complexity is apparent in his handling of the problematic issue of Merlin's father. 'Doctour Mangans' once again appears, to expound on 'philosophy' and to explain that there are spirits, known to the English as devils and 'fendes', which are part man and part angel, although hostile to both. They are capable of making women pregnant, in the same way as men, and one of these must have been Merlin's father.[51]

This bold revision of theological doctrine on demons is in no way a suggestion that Merlin himself is a negative figure, since he is strongly contrasted with Vortigern's wicked 'mages'. In fact, Merlin functions as a voice of truth, and great stress is laid on the importance of his prophecies. The whole sequence of prophecies is given here, carefully translated, and including even the final darkening of the sun and disruption of the planets. Only the very end is truncated when, following the dire prediction of the destructive influence of Saturn, the reader is abruptly told 'thereof no more to learn'. Similarly full accounts are given of Merlin's creation of Stonehenge (here called the Giants' Carol) and interpretation of the comet, with the usual emphases on his powers in 'craft', wonders and medicine.[52] Medicine is again the term used when Merlin transforms Uther into the semblance of Gorlois.[53] It is significant, however, that all mention of astrology is removed. Instead, heavy emphasis is placed on Merlin's 'spirit', which enables him both to prophesy and to understand the meaning of the comet.

Castleford's Chronicle appears to have been the work of an amateur. The latter fact makes it all the more important as evidence of the views about Merlin held by the 'middling sort' in the later Middle Ages. Clearly, whilst demons and political prophecies were unsuitable for school pupils, the appetite for Merlin had in no way decreased amongst adult readers, despite the growing attack on magic. Another chronicle which testifies to this is the work of Robert Mannyng of Brunne, who was also the author/translator of an influential work on penance called *Handling Synne*. He was a Cambridge-educated churchman, but wrote his chronicle in 'light language' so that a wide audience could learn of the 'chaunces bolde that here before was done and tolde'.[54] His book seems to be aimed at teachers, rather than directly at 'lewed men', since surviving manuscripts have headings and marginal notes in Latin. Its educational function is emphasized by the care with which Robert names and recommends the main sources for British history, including the work of 'Geffrye Arthure' who translated a Breton book discovered in Gloucester.[55] Again, Merlin's demonic parentage is given careful discussion, with the testimony of Merlin's mother emphasized by a Latin note, and the usual discussion of the teachings of philosophers. Mannyng gives the standard view that Merlin's father was one of the class of spirits who inhabit the upper air between the earth and the moon. They are given no fewer than three names: incubi, demons and 'fiends-in-bed'.[56]

For Robert Mannyng of Brunne, Merlin's spirit-father serves to set the prophet-magician and his powers apart from the magic of wicked humans. Terms for human magicians include masters, diviners and astronomers, and these are all negative, as is any attempt to foretell the future by casting lots. Mannyng was writing in the 1330s, and was clearly informed about the legal and theological attack on astrologers, magicians and fortune-tellers – so much so that an incubus father appears to be almost a lesser problem. In handling Merlin's prophecies, it is accepted that Merlin foretold all the future kings of Britain and their fates, and (surprisingly) that Merlin's prophecies are supported by 'Ptolemy' and other experts. On the other hand, the problems both of obscure language and fake prophecies are cited as the reasons why only a brief list of prophecies, relating to events already over, is given.[57] Merlin's powers with 'engines' are not apparently problematic – but his means of moving the giants' stones include 'conjurisouns' which he allows no human to overhear. This is sorcery, and very negative.[58] Similarly direct is the statement that Merlin transforms Uther not by scientific inventions ('engyns') but by 'queyntise' – which here implies deceit. Merlin speaks directly, making the enormous claim that he can 'turn any form that there is' into the 'likeness' of another. A Latin note uses the term 'transfiguration' for this transformation of 'likeness', and thus avoids the issue of demonic deceit. The concluding view is that Merlin used his own power or 'vertue' to bring about this effect, which sidesteps the issue of the source of that power, but emphasizes that Merlin was no demon worshipper.[59]

So far, it appears that by the middle of the fourteenth century anybody with any level of education would have effectively known the same facts about Merlin and his enormous powers. But this established history faced a serious challenge in the 1360s, when the *Polychronicon* appeared. This was a world history in Latin by Ranulph Higden, a monk of the powerful abbey of St Werburgh, Chester.[60] Book Four covers Brutus and the early kings of Britain, and Book Five opens with the coming of the Saxons and the downfall of Vortigern. Unlike most of his contemporaries, Higden expresses concerns about the fact that the *History of the Kings of Britain* is the sole and unsupported source for so much of early British history.[61] Moreover, he does not even try to deal with the philosophical problems raised by Merlin's demon father. Instead, he notes that only one source tells of Merlin's parentage – and condemns the account as 'fantastic'. A similar approach is taken to Merlin's other appearances. The prophecies are described as very obscure, and both they and the story of Stonehenge are weakened by the fact that only the 'British Book' includes them. Equally radically, the story of Arthur's conception is here stripped of all magic, and his conquests are actually rejected, on the grounds that other works of history would have included them if they had really happened.[62] However, Arthur's burial with Guinevere at Glastonbury is accepted, since Gerald of Wales independently vouched for it. Gerald's figure of Merlin Silvester is also accepted, and is said to have prophesied in a clearer style than Geoffrey's Merlin.[63]

How was this rewriting of the history of Britain received? It was in demand amongst the learned, and at least a hundred manuscript copies of it survive. Moreover, it was selected for translation into English by John of Trevisa and his patron Lord Berkeley in 1382.

Trevisa's translation itself was highly popular, and was published by William Caxton as an authoritative world history. Trevisa faithfully follows Higden most of the way, including the dismissal of the idea of Merlin's demon father. But his account of Merlin's creation of Stonehenge is slightly less sceptical than Higden's, and the rejection of so much of the story of Arthur is too much for him. He feels so strongly about this that he inserts a long rejoinder into his translation. This starts with a downright assertion that Higden's argument is false, since much of Christian doctrine rests upon the testimony of single writers, but is not rejected for that reason. No stronger statement of faith could be made – but Trevisa backs it up with the more circumstantial points that many of those writers who omitted Arthur from their histories were supporters of his enemies, and that anyway many writers actually do mention Arthur.[64] Since Higden had accepted the reality of both Merlins, even though he rejected the incubus father and criticized the obscurity of the prophecies, Trevisa had no need to defend Merlin.

In fact, neither the ever-growing attack on magic nor historical revisionism could remove Merlin from the general consciousness during the late Middle Ages. Just one example of the conviction with which English historians clung to Merlin and Arthur is provided by John Hardyng. This self-taught historian was a soldier and constable of Warkworth Castle before being employed on royal diplomatic and spying missions into Scotland. His powerful patrons recognized his interest in history, and helped him to examine chronicles and records. He finished the first version of his own *Chronicle* in around 1436, and it incorporates an emphatic return to the traditional history of Britain.[65] Hardyng's history reaches Vortigern and his encounters with the Saxons in chapter 69, and assumes that all readers will know the story of Merlin the Prophet. He appears to be aware of the criticisms made in the *Polychronicon*, and confesses that he himself cannot certify all the details of Merlin's conception and prophecies. But he immediately cites 'wise philosophers' who 'affirm well' that incubus demons do exist, and that they have begotten children on human women. Moreover, in chapters 70 and 71 he covers the stories of Stonehenge, the comet and the transformation of Uther in the traditional manner. His Merlin is both a prophet and a master of 'conjurisons', and he even makes an extra appearance in the story when he is said to have foretold the career of Galahad.[66]

Merlin, then, reached the end of the mediaeval period still established as a historical, if excitingly controversial, figure. If anything, as belief in the involvement of demons in magic hardened, it was Higden's scepticism about Merlin's incubus father that was out of line. The great magician still had a place in histories of the world, as well as being a 'national treasure' for patriotic English historians. His feats of magic were beautifully calculated to touch upon recognizable categories, whilst at the same time having nothing to do with blood rituals or actual offerings to demons. The reality of his magic is shown by the use of terms such as 'conjurisons', with all their frightening implications, but his magic has strongly positive effects, and his acceptability to God is proved by his prophecies. Problems for Merlin in the late Middle Ages seem more likely to emerge from political rather than theological enmities. Could a figure so closely associated with English patriotism be accepted in mainland Europe during the time of the Hundred Years War?

CHAPTER 7

ഇ)രദ

MERLIN IN EUROPE

So FAR, MERLIN has appeared very much as a British figure.
Despite his enormous knowledge and his terrifying powers, his
travels, as reported in both the *History of the Kings of Britain* and the
Life of Merlin, were very limited. Merlin may have known about the
gigantic peoples and the distant lands of ancient history, and he may
have seen the very heavens fall into chaos in the distant future, but he
physically left Britain only once. This was on the expedition to Ireland
which captured the stones for Stonehenge, when Merlin seems to have
been able to lead Uther to the Giants' Dance, even though he seems
not to have been to Ireland before.[1] Merlin's knowledge was clearly
international, but as a historical prophet and magician he was located
very much in the British past. He thus appears to be of only limited
relevance for European readers, who had little to do with Britain and
its inhabitants. After all, even his famous Book of Prophecies was first
and foremost an account of the future of Britain, not of Europe.

Despite this, Merlin achieved great fame in mainland Europe
both as magician and as prophet. In fact, this fame was so great, and

so lasting, that Merlin was turned into a European prophet, who was found to have foretold events in France and Italy down to the end of the Middle Ages. He also became the central figure in a series of widely read fictional romances, which made him both a key figure in the history of Christianity and a tragic lover, doomed to a living death by a wicked woman.[2] For historians and political commentators it was Merlin the international prophet who was of most interest, whilst for poets it was Merlin the magician. While both traditions demonstrate the sheer scale of Merlin's fame, and the level of public interest in him, their coexistence shows that he was becoming an ever more complex figure. His impact upon European politics depended upon the maintenance of belief in his reality as a great prophet, even whilst his status as a magical figure of whom everybody had heard also made it possible for poets to expand greatly on the more sensational aspects of his story.

For modern readers, Merlin the European prophet is the more unfamiliar figure, and it is this story which now needs to be told. His fame has already been demonstrated, but the speed of its spread across Europe bears repeating. Geoffrey of Monmouth claimed in the 1130s that there was already a public clamour, at least in Oxford and Lincoln, for the publication of Merlin's prophecies.[3] Geoffrey was an unreliable witness, and no statement of his can be accepted without supporting evidence. But the Norman chronicler Orderic Vitalis was entirely trustworthy, and he had a copy of the prophecies by 1135.[4] Soon after, the news of Merlin had spread to Mont St Michel, also in Normandy, on an occasion attended by delegates from Canterbury who were on their way to the papal court in Rome.[5] By 1140 Merlin and his prophecies were famous in Paris and the French royal court, and thereafter they can be tracked into Germany and Italy.[6]

What this shows is that Merlin was seen as more than a figure from the remote British past. Prophets transcended such boundaries, and offered knowledge not otherwise available to humanity – and Merlin was accepted as a prophet. It must have helped that his prophecies, as published by Geoffrey of Monmouth, offered insight into twelfth-century developments in Europe as well as in Britain. The recognition of the Lion of Justice as Henry I seems to have been almost as universal as the perception that the Boar of Cornwall was King Arthur. This gave readers an immediate method of locating their own time, and to see what came next. Readers of around 1150 would thus find that a king of 'Britain' was about to make conquests in Ireland (a prophecy that was shortly proved true) and that this same king would give rise to a She-Lynx, who would bring down Normandy and cause it to lose control of the Channel Isles. That would be followed by a reunification of Britain and Brittany. According to Merlin: 'Armorica shall wear the crown of Brutus, Wales shall rejoice, and the oaks of Cornwall shall grow strong. The island shall again be called by the name of Brutus.'[7] When Henry II married his son Geoffrey to Constance, heiress to Brittany, and the couple called their son Arthur, this prophecy must have appeared likely to come true. And when the childless Richard I of England made Arthur his heir, the prophesied unification must have seemed imminent – although what actually followed was Arthur's disappearance at the hands of John. Finally, crusaders can only have been encouraged by reading that a new boar would appear, who would attack France and win victories across Spain, terrifying the Arabs and Africans.

Geoffrey's version of Merlin's prophecies thus offered much of relevance for Europeans, for at least a century after their publication. By that time, Merlin's reputation as a prophet was fully established, and further prophecies were being 'discovered'. On its own, however, this is no more than proof that nothing succeeds like success, and it does not answer the question of what it was that made Merlin's 'original' prophecies so immediately convincing. Of course, a desire to believe in something so wonderful was part of the answer; but Merlin's prophecies were scrutinized by theologians and experts in textual commentary, and they passed that very technical test also, raising a more complex problem. One popular explanation for the convincing nature of Merlin's prophecies could be called the 'Celtic theory', since it draws on the fact that Geoffrey of Monmouth was using Welsh poems and prophecies as raw material. Historians of Welsh prophetic tradition point out that prophecy was particularly well established in Britain, and that Celtic prophecies were especially likely to use animal imagery. It has even been suggested that animal metaphors were 'unknown outside of Celtic vaticination' until Merlin made them part of the mainstream.[8] This suggests that Merlin was accepted largely on the basis of being historically convincing. However, it raises the question of how theologians in France and Italy would have known about Welsh forms of prophecy which even Gerald of Wales had to search out in Wales itself.

There is another, and much better known, precedent for Merlin's prophecies in the prophetic books of the Bible. It is true that not all of these use animal imagery, but it is equally true that two of the most important do. These are the Book of Daniel and the Book of Revelations, both the subject of considerable analysis and commentary in the Middle Ages. They set out large-scale sequences of events leading into the last times and the end of the world – and they both make use of animal imagery in doing so. Of the two, by far the closer to Merlin's story and prophetic style is the Book of Daniel. Isidore of Seville's encyclopaedic *Etymologies* provides the information that 'prophet' is a Christian term for those whom the Bible calls seers and pagans called *vates* and sibyls.[9] Of the biblical prophets, Daniel is one of the greatest, and Isidore says of him that he uses 'clear speech' to 'proclaim the kingdoms of the world and designate the time of Christ's advent'. Daniel, like Merlin, began his prophetic career as a child, when he was taken from his home to the court of Nebuchadnezzar, and trained for three years amongst the Chaldeans, astrologers, magicians and soothsayers of the king. When Nebuchadnezzar experiences a prophetic dream of a great 'image' (described in Daniel 2, verses 31–45), only the young Daniel can expound it, thus triumphing over the court magicians and saving his own life. Later, Daniel alone can interpret the king's next visionary dream, which is of a great tree, giving shelter to all beasts and birds, but doomed to be cut down to a stump (Daniel 4, verses 10–26).

Daniel's own dream-vision, when it comes, is much more expansive than these (Daniel 7). It begins when 'the four winds of heaven strove upon the great sea. And four great beasts came up from the sea, diverse one from another.' They have the likenesses of a lion, a bear, a leopard and a nameless beast with iron teeth and ten horns. Amongst the horns appears a smaller horn, with eyes and a mouth speaking great things. This signifies a king, who will rule for 'a time and times and the dividing of time', changing times and laws, until he is destroyed by the Ancient of Days, and replaced with the everlasting kingdom of the saints. Merlin's visions of the future were strictly limited to worldly events – he had nothing to say on the Second Coming or the Last Judgement – but his vision of a tree bears comparison with Nebuchadnezzar's:

A tree will grow above the Tower of London, with three branches to overshadow the whole of Britain. The north wind shall be its enemy, and shall blow down the third branch. Of the surviving branches, one will grow and choke the other with its foliage. It will attract birds from foreign lands but put fear of its shadow into native birds, who will be unable to fly freely. The tree will be followed by an Ass of Wickedness, swift to pounce upon those who make gold but slow to take action against rapacious wolves.[10]

Chapter 8 of the Book of Daniel is not a dream but a vision, in which the prophet sees a huge ram challenged by a goat with a large horn between its eyes. The vision is interpreted by Gabriel, who explains that the creatures signify the kings of the Medes, the Persians and the Greeks, and that the details of the dream foretell a sequence of kings and kingdoms. At the end of the visions of Daniel, in chapter 12, comes an account of the end of the world, when Michael will appear, 'and many of them that sleep in the dust of the earth shall awake . . . and they that be wise shall shine as the brightness of the firmament'. Merlin's sequence of animal and mythical figures signifying kings, and ending in a cataclysm involving the rising of the seas, the battle of the winds and the dust of the dead being reborn, gains credibility from its subtle echoes of this established account of the coming end.

Other biblical books provide further models and hints. Joel uses locusts as images of destruction (1: 4–6), while Zechariah makes symbolic use of horses of varying colours, which are to bear riders and pull chariots (1: 7–13). Ezekiel's visions use the images of an eagle, a cedar branch and a grapevine, and in chapter 19: 2 Israel's rulers are described as lions with a brave lioness as their mother. In chapters 29: 3 and 31: 3–9 the king of Egypt is a crocodile and a giant cedar. Chapter 38 tells of King Gog and the Land of Magog, while chapter 40 deals with a vision of a city, being measured by a man of polished bronze. The prophecies of Isaiah include that of the Tree of Jesse (11: 1), which was much commented on in the twelfth century. In the same chapter peace and justice are described through the imagery of leopards lying down with young goats, and calves and lions eating together. The desolation of fallen Babylon and Edom is evoked by reference to creatures with negative connotations (13: 19–22), such as owls, ostriches, goats, hyenas, wolves, wildcats and vultures (although these are overshadowed by the screams of demons and creatures of the night). Esdras's prophecies include a vision of an eagle with twelve wings and three heads, which foretell the sequence of human rulers yet to come, and whose cruelty is to be ended by an avenging lion (II Esdras, 11). A further vision adds the idea of nations being represented as dragons who ride hissing in chariots, and as 'wild boars of the wood' (II Esdras, 15: 28–32). Merlin's language comes close to this as his prophecies reach their end, and Esdras, like Merlin, is described as having a 'spirit' who inspires him.

The prophecies of Merlin thus skilfully combine originality with faithfulness to biblical precedent. To those expert in the languages of biblical prophecy they would feel familiar, and those expert in Celtic prophecy, such as John of Cornwall and Gerald of Wales, found related sets of prophecies, thus making them more acceptable still.[11] Merlin's success also built on that of his already established forerunner, the sibyl. Unlike Merlin, the sibyl has fallen almost completely from modern fashion, but admirers of the Sistine Ceiling will be familiar with this now obscure figure, since Michelangelo incorporated a series of sibyls into his paintings of the great prophets of the pre-Christian world.[12] In the twelfth century the sibyl attained fame and acclaim just before Merlin himself, when her great prophecies, also long lost, were revealed.[13] The two prophets were thus twin voices of revelation, whose visions came from an ancient past and offered supernatural guidance for the future.

It may seem surprising that pagan prophetesses were accepted so eagerly by twelfth-century Christian scholars. However, the sibyl came with the approval of St Augustine himself, and her status as a prophet of Christ to the pagan world was thus unquestionable.[14] Even the confusion over whether 'the Sibyl' was one person or many only added to her mystique. Plato, a philosopher very much in fashion in the twelfth century, had written of a single sibyl. Later Greek writers speak of sibyls, in the plural, and Roman writers, such as Varro, could list ten. Isidore devoted a whole section of Book Eight of his *Etymologies* to the sibyls, who he said were the female equivalent of the pagan male seers or *vates*. He provides a list of ten, though he cites no sources or authorities. Their importance is that they prophesied to pagans about the coming of Christ. Isidore says that 'songs' by all of them are in circulation, even though the Erythraean Sibyl is the most honoured.[15] However, both Virgil and St Augustine, the two most important authorities, spoke only of one. More importantly, they established the sibyl as a major prophet in both political and religious affairs.

Virgil's sibyl played a literally fateful part in the *Aeneid*, and through that in European history. Aeneas encountered her at the entrance to her cave near Lake Avernus, in southern Italy, and she led him into the Underworld. Here he was given prophecies of the future greatness of his descendants, the Romans.[16] This made her a major political prophet for the new kingdoms of mediaeval Europe which also claimed Trojan origins. 'Prophecies of the Sibyl' are referred to at several points within the *History of the Kings of Britain* in a way which suggests that they were highly regarded across Europe.[17] And the sibyl excelled even Merlin in the mystery and supernatural length of her life. Roman historians, whose works were studied in the twelfth century, told of how the sibyl had come to Tarquin, king of Rome, many centuries after the time of Aeneas. Tarquin bought her books of oracles, at fabulous expense. The emperors Augustus, Nero and Julian the Apostate all consulted these Sibylline oracles, which were stored in the Temple of Apollo. However, they were almost entirely destroyed when Rome was sacked in the early fifth century.[18]

Meanwhile, the sibyl had become a surprisingly popular source of religious prophecy for both Jewish and Christian writers from the second century onwards. A place in biblical history was created for her by an oracular text in which she claimed to have lived through the Flood, and to have been one of Noah's daughters-in-law.[19] Virgil wrote of the Sibyl again in his fourth *Eclogue*, and her prophecy here was the one known and quoted by St Augustine. For Augustine this was a prophecy of the coming of a future saviour, who would transform history. By the mediaeval period, it was accepted that Augustine had identified the sibyl as the main prophet of Christ to the gentiles. Her attested oracles were so important that they were even incorporated into the liturgy. No fewer than four of the greatest twelfth-century philosophers and theologians referred approvingly to the sibyl and her prophecies, and the idea that pagans and gentiles also received divine revelations was accepted doctrine. The Legend of the Sibyl even became a part of the tourist attractions of Rome, as listed in the *Marvels of Rome*.[20] Whilst Merlin's secular prophecies were never going to become part of the liturgy, the idea of Merlin the Prophet as a more recent addition to the prophetic tradition was highly attractive.

The sibyl's reputation rose even higher when a Latin text, known as the *Sibylla Tiburtina*, began to spread – just before Merlin and his prophecies were revealed. This was not a bestseller on the same scale as the prophecies of Merlin, but nevertheless 112 mediaeval copies are known to survive. The prophecy has been traced back to the early centuries of the Christian era, and identified as a Christian production. It appeared in Western Europe before the year 1000, and the most popular version came equipped with a learned prologue, summarizing the classical information on the sibyls.[21] The Sibylla Tiburtina (or Tiburtine Sibyl) herself was linked by her very name to Rome, and her prophecy took the form of an elaborate interpretation of a mysterious dream, which haunted one hundred Roman senators on the same night. So terrifying was this dream that, in biblical fashion, the Emperor Trajan summoned the sibyl to Rome to interpret it.

What the prophecy offered was an outline for the shape of world history down to the Second Coming and the Last Judgement. In the ninth (and last) generation, kings from Syria and Egypt would wage war, and a Last Emperor would make his way to Jerusalem. The End of History would be marked by his defeat of pagans and conversion of the Jews, as well as his epic struggle against the tribes of Gog and Magog. During the reign of this Last Emperor, Antichrist would be born of the tribe of Dan, and the killing of Antichrist by the Archangel Michael would initiate the Day of Judgement. The *Sibylla Tiburtina* then ends triumphantly with the poem quoted by Augustine in Book Eighteen of his *City of God*. All this dovetailed neatly with the visions of the end provided by the Bible – and had a sensational impact in the age of the Crusades. The appetite for prophecy was strong, and reached the very highest levels.[22]

The revelations of the sibyl were clearly of interest to aristocratic as well as ecclesiastical readers, since they were translated into Anglo-Norman verse as the *Livre de Sibile*, probably by 1140.[23] Twelfth-century scholars lost no time in comparing the sibyl's prophecies with those of Merlin, and in bringing their stories and visions together. Twenty-three copies of the *Tiburtina* were produced in mediaeval Britain alone, and nine of these also contain Geoffrey of Monmouth's *History of the Kings of Britain* (with the prophecies of Merlin). Moreover, six of these nine also contain another historical work – a supposed eyewitness account of the Trojan War.[24] Volumes produced for monastic libraries added reflections on the transitory nature of earthly power and glory, but not all readers were so far above secular concerns.

In the early thirteenth century, the sibyl's prophecies about Syria, Egypt, Jerusalem, Rome and a great emperor appeared to be being fulfilled – to deeply exciting effect. In the years following 1229, when the Emperor Frederick II had recaptured the city of Jerusalem, European chroniclers frequently identified him with the long-foretold Last Emperor.[25] This led logically to the conclusion that the reign of the Antichrist was imminent, and thus contemporaries could reflect that they lived in times that were not so much interesting as downright terrifying. What is surprising, however, is that whilst European commentators continued to reinterpret the sibyl even after Frederick II's death and throughout the thirteenth century, this did not happen in England. Even Matthew Paris, who was strongly interested in prophecy and who wrote when the majority of European historians were fascinated by the sibyl's 'Last Emperor', placed much more emphasis on Merlin.

What made such a difference for English readers and interpreters? Part of the answer appears to be that the sibyl's account of world empires and of Syria, Egypt and Jerusalem, did not directly affect Britain – at least, not before Richard I embarked on the Crusades. However, English readers will also have known that the arrival of the Last Age would be signalled by the reign of the Antichrist. Why, then, were they less prepared to accept that the Last Age had already begun? One answer is that Merlin's prophecies showed that Britain had a lot of history yet to experience. If the Lion of Justice was accepted as Henry I, and the Eagle of the Broken Covenant was Eleanor of Aquitaine, then the twelfth century had been reached less than one-third of the way through

Merlin's prophecies. Moreover, if John was the ruler who was to 'throw down the walls of Ireland', then the thirteenth century followed in the next section. The conqueror of Ireland was to be succeeded by a She-Lynx, and then by Cadwallader and Conanus, by a fierce Boar and a Ram, by another Boar and an Ass. These seven figures still only brought the prophecies to their midpoint. Thus, if Merlin's account of the history of Britain is correct, then the Emperor Frederick II could not be the Last Emperor. And those who trusted Merlin were proved correct as the thirteenth century wore on.

The ferment caused by competing prophets and competing rulers was increased in the late twelfth century by the presence of living prophets, whose divine inspiration was accepted by a series of popes and learned theologians. The first to appear was a woman, Hildegard of Bingen, a child of an aristocratic family in what is now Germany, who began her visionary career as a child. Her parents committed her to the religious life in 1106, when she was aged eight, and she took full vows when she was about sixteen. She only began to write about her visionary experiences in the 1130s, when she became abbess of the convent of Disibodenberg. The first collection of her visions, the *Scivias*, was given papal approval in 1147–8, and was well known by the 1150s. The visions made Hildegard famous, and kings, emperors and churchmen wrote to consult her on both religious and political issues. Despite her gender, and despite her relative lack of formal education, Hildegard also was accepted as a prophet.[26] This status only increased when she published further great visions as the *Book of Divine Works* in 1173.[27] By this stage her visions encompassed images of the whole structure of the cosmos, as well as of God's relationship with the Church and the events to come in the time of the Antichrist. However, Hildegard was aware of her lack of higher education, and emphasized in all her visionary works that, as well as seeing the visions themselves, she also heard a great voice explaining them to her. Thus neither the visions nor their interpretation were her own inventions.

Hildegard rapidly became known as a new sibyl, the Sibyl of the Rhine, whose prophecies could be searched, just like Merlin's, for insight into ongoing events. It was in this spirit that John of Salisbury, adviser to archbishops of Canterbury and himself bishop of Chartres, asked his contact in Cologne to look in Hildegard's writings for visions relating to the troubles in the Church.[28] After her death in 1179, the nuns of Hildegard's convent helpfully compiled a 'giant book' of all her works, but this was difficult to consult. It was therefore very welcome when, in about 1220, Gebeno of Eberbach, prior of this of the powerful Cistercian abbey, compiled a selection of Hildegard's most important prophecies, especially those relating to the end of the world. This became known as the *Pentachronon* (or Book of the Five Ages), and it was in demand throughout the rest of the mediaeval period, with over one hundred manuscripts still known to survive.[29] Hildegard's visionary works openly quoted from, and echoed, prophetic books of the Bible, and were thus different from Merlin's. Nevertheless, she offered further proof that the age of prophecy did not end with the Revelation of St John, and that it was perfectly possible for new prophecies to appear.

If further evidence were needed, it was provided by another living prophet, whose career overlapped with that of Hildegard's. This was Joachim (of Fiore), who was born in Norman Sicily in the 1130s and educated for a political career, before experiencing a religious conversion in the Holy Land. Returning to Italy, he became a Cistercian monk and a biblical scholar. It was in the 1180s that his writings on the interpretation of biblical prophecy became the focus of much discussion and excitement, and popes Urban III and

Clement III expressed support for his findings. Joachim himself refused to assert that he was a prophet, arguing that he was a mere interpreter of the Bible – but his acclaim as a prophet began in his own lifetime and lasted until the end of the Middle Ages.[30]

Joachim's fame and influence were greatest of all in Italy itself, where his writings were eagerly applied to contemporary events. As with Hildegard in Germany, a living prophet, available for consultation, was extremely exciting. He himself believed that the hidden meaning of the Bible had been revealed to him, and the holiness of his life and miracles attributed to him all helped to support this. His studies led him to the belief that world history was to pass through three great epochs. The Age of the Father had ended with the coming of Christ; the Age of the Son was already drawing to its close; and the Age of the Holy Spirit would soon begin. Joachim believed that the second age would last for forty-two generations, each of thirty years, and that it had begun with the incarnation of Christ. His followers therefore expected that this age would end in 1260, and that the reign of the Antichrist – with its literally apocalyptic struggles – must be imminent. The excitement peaked as 1260 drew closer, but what is more surprising is that a core of devotees remained loyal after that year was past.

The initial excitement about Joachim's prophecies had been strongly linked to the enthusiasm aroused by the early stages of the Third Crusade in the late twelfth century. The times were clearly out of joint, as Jerusalem had been taken by Saladin's army, and in 1187 the Christian kingdom in the Holy Land seemed doomed. A concerted response was agreed to be urgently needed: the pope and the emperor negotiated, and kings were faced with difficult decisions about how much of the resources of their kingdoms to commit to the struggle. It was clear that this was an age in which prophecies about fated emperors and climactic struggles in the East were being fulfilled. The English lands were drawn into the fight by Richard I, who set off to the Holy Land, joining Philip Augustus of France. The two kings stayed in Sicily during the winter of 1190, and Richard decided that Joachim's insights into the great struggle for Jerusalem would be of great value. The *Deeds of King Richard* describes how Joachim was reputed to be 'filled with the spirit of prophecy' and to 'interpret the visions . . . in the Apocalypse as if he had written the book himself'. In response to Richard's invitation, Joachim agreed to come to Sicily.[31]

The scene is striking: the crusader king was holding court, 'surrounded by many of his people', when the prophet was escorted in. His text was Revelation 12: 1–6, about 'A woman clothed with the sun and with the moon under her feet and on her head a crown of twelve stars, who was in the pangs of childbirth', and the 'great red dragon with seven heads' who waits to devour her child. Joachim identified the woman as the Church, the dragon as the Devil, and the seven heads of the Devil as seven great persecutors of the Church, ending with Saladin and the Antichrist.

> Then going to King Richard, the prophet said: 'God has revealed all this, and He will give you victory over all your enemies . . . But one will come soon, and that is the Antichrist. He has already been born, and fifteen years have passed since that time.' Then many cried out about these things, and the king asked the abbot where Antichrist had been born and where he was to reign. Joachim replied that he believed the Antichrist had been born in Rome, and that he would hold the Apostolic See.[32]

However, Richard and his advisers seem to have regarded Joachim's prophecies with some scepticism, pointing out that the biblical prophets showed that the Antichrist would be born in Babylon or

Antioch and of the tribe of Dan (with which the sibyl also agreed).

It appears that Joachim's prophecies were more widely accepted in Italy and the Mediterranean lands than in England. Nevertheless, the craze for Joachim was so strong that new prophecies and commentaries were issued under his name, even after his death in 1202. The idea that the current age was experiencing the reign of the Antichrist was a major political topic in the thirteenth century. It gave an additional force to the disruption and fear generated by the great struggle between the Emperor Frederick II and Pope Innocent III. Thus the prophecies of Hildegard, Joachim and the sibyl concerning the imminence of the last days and the age of the Antichrist were of great importance. Equally, Joachim and the sibyl were clearly the prophets of the Third Crusade and of the war between papacy and empire. But did this mean that Merlin faded from fashion in Europe, and that his prophecies were too parochial to compete with these ongoing revelations? The answer is that the reverse was the case: Merlin too became a prophet for the stage of international politics.

His earliest occupation of this role is perhaps his 'guest appearance' in William of Tudela's *Chanson de la Croisade contre les Albigeois* of around 1213. As the title suggests, this is an account of the 'crusade' against the heretical Albigensians, or Cathars, in the south of France. Here we are told of a prophecy by Merlin which foretold the manner and timing of the death of Simon IV de Montfort (who died in battle in 1218), leader of the crusading army. What is more, the poet sees no need to introduce or explain Merlin; readers already know about Merlin and his 'Book'.[33] The process is further illustrated by Fra Salimbene, a contemporary Italian Franciscan friar and chronicler who recorded his own early excitement about Joachim and the impact of his prophecies in Italy.

Salimbene was another highly educated diplomat, who encountered many of the great political leaders of the time. He himself knew prophecies of Merlin, and he also told a story of a scholarly hermit, Hugues de Digne, who could quote further prophecies by Merlin. Indeed, Hugues interpreted Merlin's prophecies almost as Joachim interpreted Revelation itself. Hugues showed that Merlin, like Joachim, had predicted the clash between Frederick II and the pope. Moreover, he defended Merlin against a consequent charge of heresy, and placed Merlin together with Joachim and the sibyl as the great prophets of the age.[34] Salimbene later became disenchanted with Joachim, when the year 1260 came and went in uneventful fashion. This did nothing to discredit Merlin, however.

Merlin's international status is demonstrated further by the work of an Englishman known as Gervase of Tilbury, who was employed by the Emperor Otto IV (grandson of Henry II and friend of Richard I). Gervase was an aristocrat, who studied canon law, was employed at the Sicilian court, and then became an adviser to Otto IV in 1209. Despite being known to posterity as Gervase 'of Tilbury' he spent most of his career away from England, and was a minor member of the highest sphere of politics. For Otto IV he wrote an encyclopaedic book, the *Otia Imperialia*, which provides a busy world ruler with an up-to-date survey of world history, geography and science. This was a popular source of information on what anybody who was anybody should know from Gervase's own time up to the fifteenth century, and it shows Merlin as superhuman in both origin and power.

In Book One of Gervase's encyclopaedia, Merlin appears in relation to discussions of demons and giants.[35] Gervase recounts the standard view that the sublunary air is inhabited by unclean spirits, such as incubi, who can afflict humans during sleep. Worryingly, 'Merlin is said to have been fathered by an incubus', and the

Antichrist will be begotten in the same way. The handling of Merlin in the discussion of giants is more positive. Gervase clearly knows the 'new' British history well, and is proud of how the stones of the giants were brought from Ireland by Merlin.[36] In Book Two, which deals with history, Gervase places Merlin in his account of the ancient world. Gervase recounts Merlin's prophecies to Vortigern, his interpretation of the mysterious comet for Uther and his magical role in the conception of Arthur. When he moves on to modern history, he refers to Henry II and his sons as lions and cubs, following the terminology of Merlin's prophecies. These were clearly familiar, since he feels no need to explain them.[37] In Book Three, Gervase discusses natural magic and says that, whilst Merlin was not such a great master as Solomon, he had great skill with stones and rings.[38] Gervase's Merlin is the equal of the sibyl. The latter also appears in the account of the ancient world, as prophetess for the Emperor Augustus. But in Book Three Gervase displays his classical education, showing that he knows that there was more than one sybil, and that at least two of them made prophecies about Christ.[39]

Prophecy, in accordance with the words of the biblical Book of the Wisdom of Solomon, was increasingly considered to be not only central to understanding God's unfolding relationship with humanity, but also something which contributed to scientific knowledge. This is what made Merlin so important as both prophet and natural philosopher. The English Franciscan Roger Bacon corresponded with the pope about his *Opus Majus* (roughly, his *Great Work*) in the 1260s. In both his letter and his book Bacon wrote passionately about the importance of prophets such as Joachim and 'the Eagle' (mentioned also in the *History of the Kings of Britain*), and he went on to argue, 'If only the Church would examine the prophecies of the Bible, the sayings of the saints, the sentences of the Sibyl and Merlin, and other pagan prophets, and would add the evidence of astrology and experimental knowledge, it would without doubt be able to provide usefully against the coming of Antichrist.'[40] The case could hardly be stronger: Merlin's prophecies are part of humanity's treasury of knowledge, and part of its hope to survive the coming of the Antichrist.

The fateful year of 1260 may have passed safely, but Merlin's status as a great prophet, unlike Joachim's, did not depend upon that year. Indeed, as Joachim fell from favour, Merlin and the sibyl emerged as the greatest prophets outside the Bible. Further evidence of this comes from a curious work known as the *Prophecies de Merlin*. This takes the form of a collection of groups of prophecies, linked by brief narrative sections based upon the fictional romances of Merlin, which had become extremely popular in the first half of the thirteenth century.[41] Despite this blending of 'fact' and fiction, it purports to be a genuine testament to newly found prophecies of Merlin, collected by one Master Richard of Ireland for the Emperor Frederick II and compiled in the 1220s. Analysis shows very rapidly that it is a fake, and that it was written in the Veneto, by a Venetian (although in French) in the 1270s. And yet it was read with interest by contemporaries in Italy, was translated into Italian in the fourteenth century, and was incorporated into Italian chronicles from 1278 onwards. It is possible that it helped to inspire the undoubted fashion for 'Prophecies of Merlin', which replaced those of Joachim in Italy in the late thirteenth and fourteenth centuries.

What would Italian readers in the late thirteenth century discover about Merlin? For a start, he prophesied, as all serious prophets should, in Latin, but he also occupied the realms of *courtoisie*. He was to be found in Wales, but he prophesied the career of Charlemagne before concerning himself greatly with the upheavals of Italy. Finally, despite being a shape-shifter and only partially human, he was a good and orthodox Christian. This is emphasized by a long section in the *Prophecies de Merlin* when three of the wisest cardinals of the papal court are sent to Wales to test Merlin's beliefs on the Trinity and the sacraments. Not only does Merlin hold unimpeachable views; he also uses his shape-shifting powers and his supernatural knowledge to prove that the cardinals are corrupt. After this humiliation, they duly accept the truth of the prophecies which he goes on to make for them.

A similar picture of Merlin emerges from the late thirteenth-century *Verses of Merlin*, which relate to the future of the cities of Lombardy and Tuscany. These were respected enough to be quoted by Salimbene and fourteenth-century Italian chroniclers. They follow the time-honoured technique of narrating recent events under the heading of 'prophecies' made by Merlin in the distant past, and they cover some of the same events as the *Prophecies de Merlin* and related works. Despite their evident focus on events of the thirteenth century, these works were still being used and quoted by historians in the fourteenth century and later. Indeed, political commentators in the late fourteenth century still saw Merlin as a figure offering hope for a way out of the ongoing struggles and crises in Italy. In 1386 a learned hermit, Telesforo da Cosenza, was called by a vision to collect prophecies relating to the future of Italy. The vision reassured him that study of these would provide guidance for his very troubled times. Telesforo then spent many arduous years travelling and collecting prophetic works, and the result is a long and (understandably) complicated book. The future of Italy looks dark, but prophecies attributed to Merlin formed a major part of Telesforo's collection and offered some hope.[42] Outside Italy, full-scale collections of new prophecies of Merlin are rarer, but one survives from Catalonia. This is the Catalan *Profecia de Merlin*, which was composed in the 1370s and deals with the successors to

Alfonso X.[43] Merlin also contributed to the ongoing interpretation of events in both northern France and Spain. In the early fourteenth century the chronicler Godfrey of Paris cited a prophecy of Merlin relating to the region of Tours, and in 1476 Merlin appeared in Pedro Azamar's *Derecho Militar*. This gives a six-line prophecy of 'Merlin of Britain', concerning a 'Son of the Eagle' who will defeat 'Moorish' power and rally great forces. It is taken as a clear prophecy of the career of Ferdinand the Catholic.[44]

By the end of the thirteenth century, then, Merlin was part of the common stock of European knowledge, and had apparently fore-known and foretold everything. A particularly telling example of his power as a political weapon comes in Christine de Pisan's *Ditie de Jehanne d'Arc*, written in 1429. Christine herself was born in Venice (in 1365), and educated largely by her father who was astrologer to the king of France. She was fluent in Italian, French and Latin, and gained powerful patrons as a professional writer, not only at the French court but also amongst the leaders of the English side in the ongoing war. Emphasizing Joan of Arc's importance, Christine says: 'More than 500 years ago Merlin, the Sibyl and Bede foresaw Joan in their minds and put her into their writings and made proph-ecies about her as the remedy for France. They said she would carry the banner in French wars, and exactly predicted her deeds.' Christine wrote this at the very time when the English and their allies were accusing Joan of being in league with the devil. The British prophet is thus utilized, together with the great English historian and the classical figure of the sibyl, to overwhelm English political propaganda.[45]

Thus, once Merlin's reputation as the great political prophet got under way, it gathered ever-greater momentum down to the fifteenth century. Moreover, this was no matter of 'popular superstition'; prophecy was a matter of the highest seriousness, and a direct source of knowledge on both human affairs and the nature of God's universe. Further proof of the status of Merlin's prophecies is provided by the survival of numerous learned commentaries and interpretations which began to appear as early as the 1150s. That it was Geoffrey of Monmouth's skill in producing his version of Merlin's 'Book' which launched this great career is proved by the fate of the rival *Prophetiae Merlini* of John of Cornwall. John appears to have worked at the request of Robert Warelwast, bishop of Exeter, who died in 1155. John had expertise in the 'British' language, and was also a churchman and scholar. His researches resulted in a collection of 139 of Merlin's prophecies, which he also commented on. John was working after Geoffrey of Monmouth, and thirty-eight prophecies in his collection repeat items in Geoffrey's work. However, all the rest focus on the rulers, battles and histories of the Celtic kingdoms. The apparant unpopularity of John of Cornwall's work does suggest that prophecies on purely Celtic matters were of more restricted interest than Geoffrey's broader version.[46] There is no doubt that Merlin's power derived partly from his identity as a liminal, semi-demonic, supernatural figure from the ancient British past, but the 'Celtic' nature of his prophecies was not their main point. The Latin prophecies revealed in the 1130s were uncannily successful in their apparent prediction of major political events in the thirteenth century, and were also strongly rooted in biblical prophetic style. It was these prophecies that made Merlin one of the greatest European prophets – and a figure of political power during the Renaissance as well as the mediaeval period.

CHAPTER 8

ഇാൽ

LOVE AND DEATH

FROM THE 1130S on, the name of Merlin spread fast across mediaeval Europe as that of one of the greatest ever prophets and magicians. It is scarcely surprising that he became also a hero of romance, but what is much less known is that Merlin in mediaeval fiction was much more than simply a major figure in stories about King Arthur. Merlin was the hero in a cycle of romances of his own, in which his connection to demons and his supernatural powers made him a major figure in the legendary history of Christianity. This evolution took a certain amount of time, and it was Merlin's creation, King Arthur, who dominated the early romances, focused as they were on human emotions and knightly combat. Nevertheless, as the new genre of 'courtly' or chivalric romance, written in French vernacular poetry and telling stories of love and adventure, grew ever more popular with consciously sophisticated, aristocratic audiences, it absorbed more and more famous names and stories. Figures not only from the French and Breton past but also from classical and

British history were all transformed into heroes and heroines of romance.

The Old French of northern France, the dominant language of these romances, was spreading. The post-Conquest ruling class of England spoke Anglo-Norman, and many scholars from across Europe spent years studying in the University of Paris, learning at least some French. The outpouring of both new works and translations in this rising language was unprecedented in mediaeval Europe, and the excitement of the time is expressed by one of the pioneers of the chivalric romance genre, Chrétien de Troyes. According to Chrétien: 'Greece was once foremost in chivalry and learning. . . . Chivalry and the highest learning passed on to Rome; and now they have come to France.'[1] The historical Merlin was, of course, neither a lover nor a knight, and yet was far too powerful to be a mere court entertainer or royal physician. The roles played by Merlin in romances, from the twelfth century down to the fifteenth, can thus shed further light on his fame across mediaeval Europe. Questions of whether fictional versions of Merlin were adapted for different audiences, as Merlin's prophecies were, are also important. By the late Middle Ages, if not before, nationalism had become an issue in the writing of history, as Ranulph Higden affirmed. French historians, he said, over-praised Charlemagne, Greeks did the same for Alexander, English chroniclers made a hero of Richard the Lionheart, and the British exaggerated Arthur.[2] But was Merlin similarly appropriated?

The answer is that the power of Merlin's magic, together with his semi-supernatural status, meant that he could move on to an international stage. After all, his demon father gave him access to experience from beyond this world, whilst his prophetic visions gave him knowledge that came from beyond human perceptions of time. Thus it was possible for Merlin the Prophet-Magician to be given a central part in the story of the Holy Grail, the great story which increasingly dominated mediaeval romance and which infused stories of love and war with struggles for spiritual achievement and glory. It was Chrétien de Troyes, a poet now credited with having virtually invented the genre of the Arthurian romance, who took the first step in bringing Merlin into the world of Old French poetry. His influence is shown by the fact that his romance *The Knight of the Cart* was the main basis for the ever-growing story of Lancelot and Guinevere's love affair. Equally influential was his *Story of the Grail*, which was reworked in at least four versions within fifty years, each new version making its own contribution to the increasing mingling of 'romance' and religious themes.[3] It was Chrétien who firmly established the reign of King Arthur as the setting for socially disruptive love affairs and spiritual struggles of equal intensity. He sketched the historical setting only very lightly, but he followed the *History of the Kings of Britain* in making the time of Merlin and the time of Arthur two different periods.

The name of Merlin appears only once in the surviving works of Chrétien, and this is as part of an already exotic past. Like the writers of British history and of international, political prophecies, Chrétien could assume that his sophisticated readers would already have heard of Merlin. In fact, he assumed a fairly detailed knowledge. The reference comes in the romance of *Erec and Enide*, which editors have identified as an early work and have dated to around 1170. The story is tightly focused on the adventures of the eponymous lovers, and yet Chrétien flatters his readers by making reference to a wide range of characters and stories from classical and Christian history. The range of such characters shows the confidence with which the substance of other cultures was being assimilated into the courtly (and French-speaking) culture of the twelfth century. The figure of Erec has been linked with a character in the

Welsh *Mabinogion*, although Chrétien does not name this tale – he simply says that the story will be known to a courtly audience. More explicit is the reference to the tragic figure of Dido, and her betrayed love for Aeneas (their story is retold on an ivory carving given to Enide). Helen of Troy is already used as a shorthand for outstanding beauty (though, of course, she is surpassed by ladies in the romance).

Given that this romance is dated to around 1170, and the *History of the Kings of Britain* appeared in the 1130s, the knowledge of early Britain that Chrétien assumes in his audience is striking. Not only is Erec a knight of Arthur's court; he is also a member of the Round Table fellowship (an addition made by Wace in his French translation). Both the Isle of Glass and the Isle of Avalon are mentioned (as separate places).[4] Avalon is referred to as a place of magic in both the *History of the Kings of Britain* and the *Life of Merlin*, and in the latter work Morgan, the supernatural enchantress is said to rule it together with her eight sisters. In the world of *Erec and Enide*, female figures (even supernatural ones) do not rule territories. Knowledge of the *Life of Merlin* is suggested, yet one Guingomar is lord of the Isle of Avalon. Morgan le Fay still appears, but as his lover, though her medicine is still so powerful that a salve made by her can cure any wound within a week.

What, then, is Merlin's place in this new world? He is not the creator of any of the magical objects or places that occur in the tale. Indeed, actual magic here is something negative, and is ruled out as any part of Erec's military triumphs or of Enide's unadorned beauty. Magic seems to have played a part in the creation of King Evrain's island-castle of Brandigant, and it has certainly been used, in a dishonest way, to create the enchanted garden within that castle which holds a knight captive.[5] Erec, however, needs nothing but his strength and valour to defeat the knight and free him from the magic. The source and nature of this magic are never discussed, but it appears to be different from the 'natural' marvels of the Isle of Glass (which never suffers from storms, bad weather, toads or snakes) and from Morgan le Fay's medicines. It is also separate from the power of Merlin, who appears simply as a famous figure from the British past. His lifetime is stated to have been the time when the coins still used by Arthur, 'sterlings', were first adopted as the currency of Britain, but it is as vaguely in the past as the careers of Julius Caesar and Alexander, whose riches are compared with Arthur's.[6] Merlin thus appears as a figure of power, whose name will be recognized as a part of ancient history.

In the early thirteenth century the writing of romances loosely located in the time of King Arthur took a new turn, with more emphasis placed on the ever-growing story of the Holy Grail. This theme had also been started by Chrétien, in his unfinished *Perceval* or *Story of the Grail* of about 1180. It was another poet, Robert de Boron, who seems to have taken deeply important further steps. In his hands the Grail was firmly identified as the vessel that Christ had used at the Last Supper and in which Joseph of Arimathea had caught the blood of Christ. He composed a whole verse romance to tell the story of the Grail, which necessarily covered the period from the life of Christ to somewhere near the time of Arthur (though the latter was by no means clearly dated).[7] The story was presented through a vision, miraculously revealed to a narrator and then passed on further. The vision is described in terms reminiscent of the prophetic books of the Bible, and includes a description of how the Grail was brought west to the 'vaus d'Avaron'. With one leap, therefore, the new literature has gone well beyond translation of older, high-status texts, and is engaging with the creative rewriting not only of national history but also of salvation history. And paradoxically it is this new turn that places the prophetic and semi-demonic figure of Merlin at the centre of an ever more complex structure of narrative and revelation. It is perhaps not surprising that Merlin's 'real', historical story is forgotten as he undergoes this transmogrification to fictional magus.

The new Merlin, and the romances in which he played a dominant role, took off like rockets in the first two decades of the thirteenth century. Once again, it appears to have been Robert de Boron who was the first to create a romance of *Merlin* (of which only some 500 lines of poetry survive). Prose versions of the tale were almost instantly produced, and were circulated, along with the new story of the Grail, as prequels to the expanded accounts of the reign of Arthur and the success of a chosen knight in the Grail quest.[8] Presumably following de Boron, Merlin now becomes not only the magician who brought about the conception of Arthur but also that king's greatest counsellor. Still more innovatively, Merlin is now also the eccentric prophet through whom God brings about the final revelation of the Grail to the knights of the Round Table. The importance of this Merlin greatly exceeds that of a figure from a purely British history. Here, the Grail has become the numinous embodiment of Chrétien's image of the cultural triumph of French-speaking Europe, and Merlin is its prophet.

Other books have been written on the proliferation and inter-relationships of the prose romances of the early thirteenth century.[9] Even to compare the details of Merlin's appearances in each romance would be to write another book. Instead, what has become known to modern editors and translators as the 'Vulgate' Cycle (and also as the Lancelot–Grail Cycle, the Pseudo-Map Cycle and the Prose *Lancelot*) will be taken as representative for the dissemination of the new, fictionalized Merlin in this first period of his creation.[10] The full cycle is made up of five romances, and its popularity is demonstrated by the fact that it survives in ninety-six manuscript copies (although only nine have anything like the complete set of stories). Merlin's popularity is shown by the fact that 'his' romance is found in fifty-five of the surviving manuscripts.[11] His appearances in the other romances within the cycle are variable, but he increasingly acts as a means to link different times and places together by virtue of his supernatural knowledge. What follows is a brief account of this new, fictional Merlin as he appears in the Vulgate Cycle.

The opening section of the romance of *Merlin* is a long and sensational account of the back story to his birth. It begins in hell, with the demons plotting to get revenge for Christ's defeat of the devil. Their plan hinges on begetting a child on a human woman, and then using this offspring as their tool. The problem of whether a demon can impregnate a woman, and if so how, requires considerable discussion (reflecting the unease over this issue found amongst chroniclers and theologians). The demons are confident that they can influence and control human behaviour with relative ease, but only one amongst their entire number is able to cause pregnancy. However, even after an elaborate campaign has enabled this unique demon to trick and impregnate their chosen victim, the girl's Christian faith makes the victory hollow. The girl places herself in the hands of a trusty priest, through whose counsel the mother's soul and the baby's life are saved. The baby is, of course, Merlin, and the romance assures the reader that God allowed Merlin to have from his father 'the devil's art of knowing things that are past, done and said'. In addition, God himself gives (as only He could) the power to know the future. It is also explained that God did this in order to balance Merlin's demonic knowledge and to allow him freedom of will and allegiance.[12]

From the outset, this Merlin is an even more all-knowing figure than the historical Merlin, and it is fitting that his powers are revealed at an even earlier stage in his life. He is able to walk, talk, hold his own in a court of law and save the life of his mother at the age of eighteen months. And as a two-year-old he discusses his situation with his mother's priest, Blaise, finally persuading Blaise to 'make a book' containing both Merlin's own experiences and all the divinely sanctioned knowledge that he can reveal. This includes not only the whole story of the Grail but also the events preceding Merlin's own conception. The fictional Merlin is both the supernatural author of his own romance, with Blaise as his editor and chronicler, and the witness to the 'truth' of the Grail story. He goes on to demonstrate his knowledge of the future by prophesying about his own enemies, and about Blaise's ultimate destiny as a member of the company of the Grail. Merlin's unique status as both human and supernatural, magician and true prophet, thus makes him a figure who can link the world of chivalric romance not just to the historic past (Arthur, Charlemagne and Alexander all did that) bus also to the future and to supernatural realms.

The next section of the romance is based upon the story of Vortigern as told in the *History of the Kings of Britain*. Its political and military narratives are shortened, but considerable emphasis is placed on Vortigern's search for reliable astrologers and how scarce this skill is. From the researches of the astrologers, once assembled, we learn that Merlin is now seven years old. His knowledge, of course, is far superior to theirs, and he now instructs Blaise to become a hermit in Northumberland. This is so that Blaise can remain a safe and trustworthy scribe for Merlin's ongoing prophecies as to the coming of Arthur and the further history of the Grail. However, whilst Merlin's revelations to Blaise relate to the superior matter of Arthur and the Grail, his disclosures to the messengers of the tyrant Vortigern are far more ambiguous. These are riddling statements, punctuated by unsettling laughter, as to imminent deaths and hidden paternities – and they are very reminiscent of the curious revelations of the 'mad' Merlin of Geoffrey of Monmouth's *Life of Merlin*.

As has already been demonstrated, Merlin the prophet of the Grail has his mind on larger issues than the future political history of Britain. The great sequence of political prophecies for Vortigern is omitted in the romance. Instead, Merlin demonstrates not only his ability to see through solid rock but also his skill with 'engines' and 'crafts' in instructing on how to drain the subterranean pool and excavate the dragons. That Merlin is also a figure of justice and destiny is shown by his knowledge of Vortigern's treachery, and his certainty as to the tyrant's fate. It is not only that prophecies relating merely to Britain are too narrow for this French romance; rather, the whole romance has become the record and unfolding of Merlin's great acts of prophecy, extending from the time of Christ to the time of the achievement of the Grail.

The fictional Merlin is like the historical Merlin in coming to court only when he is truly needed. However, he is unlike the historical Merlin in making clear statements as to his own nature. After the downfall of Vortigern, the prophet announces to the next kings that he must, by his nature, spend time away from humans. He has already amply demonstrated that he knows everything he chooses to know, and that he can change his shape at will.[13] Slightly curiously, these things inspire trust rather than anxiety in the kings to whom he offers his services. A touch of fear is added, however, when a baron who refuses to respect Merlin is punished by dying just as Merlin predicts. The well-known stories of the interpretation of the comet and the moving of the giants' stones are shortened, though included. Here Merlin builds Stonehenge alone, and simply 'by the power of magic'.[14] Having achieved this, he goes on to inform Uther Pendragon that he knows all of the past by inheritance from a devil, but that God has removed him from the devil's power and given him knowledge of things yet to come. It is after this that he reveals to Uther the history of the Grail, and instructs the king on the creation of the Round Table. Indeed, it is Merlin himself who actually constructs the table, through his 'powerful craft'.

Thus far, then, whilst Merlin's prophetic powers are represented on a very much wider scale, his mastery of both magic and 'craft' is similar to that in the historical sources. Similarly, it is by providing a 'herb' that he transforms Uther Pendragon into the appearance of the 'duke of Tintagel', thus also bringing his medical skills into his new incarnation. What is very new, however, is Merlin's extraction from the king of a promise that, when the male child conceived that night is born, he should be handed over immediately to Merlin. Ygraine (Ygerna) is given neither knowledge of this bargain nor any power to intervene. Merlin's effective creation of Arthur is illustrated by the fact that he not only arranges for the baby's hiding and fostering but also chooses his name. And further mystery is added since no explanation is given as to why all this is necessary: it is so because Merlin says it must be so, and that is enough. In a similarly absolutist fashion, Merlin uses his authority to establish the boy Arthur as king and to pick out his future wife. The magician's position in relation to the king is carried even further when Merlin reveals to the adolescent Arthur his own identity, heritage and destiny to be king. Likewise, it is the authority of this Merlin which guarantees Arthur's acceptance as king after the marvel of his extraction of the sword from the stone.[15]

It is hardly surprising that Merlin and Arthur make a pact, in which the king agrees always to accept the magician's advice and Merlin promises to come whenever he is needed. Yet some unease about Merlin's powers is reflected in the romance, when the trusted and long-established courtier Ulfin declares that Merlin is 'full of the powers of necromancy'.[16] Use of this very negative term does not seem to damage Merlin's position. Yet historians had avoided applying the concept of necromancy to Merlin. Moreover, it was becoming both broader in its meaning and more strongly associated with demon summoning in thirteenth-century theology and law.[17] In its context in the romance it has the effect of suggesting the level of fear which Merlin could inspire, and it is balanced by the way the whole narrative works to show that Merlin is no user of blood rituals or of spells to summon demons. Even so, unease is suggested by the frequency with which the fictional Merlin explains that his father was a demon but that God has favoured him.

At this point a radically new element appears in the romance. Chapter 28 begins in grand fashion, with Merlin intervening to save the world – or at least Christendom. His full, prophetic knowledge of coming events makes him an enormously powerful political 'fixer', and he now temporarily deserts Britain, knowing that its attackers can be defeated without him, in order to ensure the survival of the territory of Leonce of Palerne. This is strategically crucial, in order to defeat an enemy alliance, and Merlin's reputation means that Leonce immediately trusts him and accepts his counsel. Merlin is thus an omniscient and incorruptible international adviser, able to move across Europe at supernatural speed, and to ensure the 'right' outcome in complex international affairs. However, these acts of power, and Merlin's apparent domination of his world, are immediately followed by his prophetic revelation of his own tragic fate. He then goes, despite his foreknowledge, to seek that fate in the form of Viviane, the twelve-year-old daughter of Dyonas, the godson of Diana, 'goddess of the wood'.

It is Diana who has gifted to Dyonas and Viviane the power of control over Merlin 'through necromancy'. Dark powers are clearly rising to the surface of the romance, although at first all is innocence and harmless entertainment. The young girl is discovered at a beautiful pond by a spring, and Merlin entertains her by making a castle and a river appear. This magic is described as 'tricks', and Merlin's pact with Viviane is merely that he will teach her such tricks, in exchange for her love. A darker element is appearing in Merlin's own magic, however, since such tricks were increasingly condemned by theologians. The 'trick' of making a castle appear is one found in later mediaeval books of magic for sorcerers, and in that context it required the sacrifice of an animal or bird, and the use of the blood to write the name of a demon.[18] Moreover, once the pact is made, Merlin demonstrates magic that is more clearly necromantic. He draws a circle on the ground, and brings ladies and knights out of it, who go on to inhabit an enchanted castle and orchard. The drawing of a circle has very strong connections to demonic magic – and the actual nature of the knights and their ladies is therefore troubling. Merlin's fascination by Viviane is so strong that he next puts his divine gift of knowledge of things to come at her disposal, adding even further to the reader's awareness that the story is not going to end well.

Finally, Merlin's enchantment by Viviane leads him to dictate a book of magic, giving her both spells and instructions on how to use them. Very soon things become more sinister. Viviane is not only writing down everything Merlin reveals, but putting it into practice. This appears to include the drawing of circles and the summoning of supernatural beings through them. Still more worrying is Merlin's revelation of three names, which Viviane is to write out and keep on her person as a written amulet. The function of the amulet is the harmless one of preventing anyone (including Merlin) from sleeping with her – but it is still clear that this is an example of a type of magic strictly forbidden by St Augustine and taken increasingly seriously by the Church.[19] As Merlin's visits and lessons continue, Viviane's book comes to include 'everything the human heart could think of' – an ominous term, given the number of spells for obtaining 'love' from selected individuals, and for causing pain and illness, found in surviving texts of magic.

The powers of this necromantic magic are not described in great detail in this romance, but enough is said to show that it is not a 'safe' magic, even though Merlin never uses it do harm. When visiting the court of the Emperor Julius Caesar, Merlin quite literally makes his mark by using magic to carve great black letters over the door to the emperor's hall. These name the magician as 'Merlin of Northumberland', but cannot be read by Caesar. They are interpreted by Hadrian, emperor of Greece – whereupon they disappear.[20] Less elevated is the magic which Merlin uses when he desires the daughter of King Agravadain. The magician can control anyone he chooses with his magic so, choosing to refrain from seducing the girl himself, Merlin decides to give her to King Ban (without consulting either party). Merlin casts a spell 'with little ado' and the pair immediately find one another irresistible.[21] This is worrying for King Ban, who does not wish to wrong his wife or to insult his host King Agravadain by seducing his virgin daughter. Nevertheless, Merlin's magic cannot be denied, especially when he uses it to put the whole castle to sleep, apart from the two lovers, so that they can enjoy their tryst without interruption or discovery. The girl becomes pregnant – though all is ultimately well, since Merlin reveals that the child will be a son who will bring honour to Britain. This episode has strong echoes of the way in which Merlin used his magic to bring about the conception of Arthur, and is similarly ambivalent. Merlin's moral behaviour in refusing to use his magic for his own gain is emphasized, but his decision to force two innocent people to commit adultery can only be disturbing.

The fictional Merlin thus has even more ambiguities than the historical one, as well as much more open control over human actions. His magic includes the more acceptable and scientific powers described in the chronicles, but it also deals in necromancy and in activities that are amoral at best. This ambiguity is linked explicitly to the moral duality of mediaeval aristocrats, who were both chivalrous knights and ruthless killers. Merlin's darker magic appears only in this fictional world of romance, intertwined with warfare and seduction. The link is reinforced since the fictional Merlin is also 'full of knightly valour' himself, and capable of intervening directly in battle as well as giving infallible advice. This direct action happens on numerous occasions during Arthur's campaigns, and turns Merlin from a figure of distant knowledge into something of a man of action. The historical Merlin had travelled in company with Uther and his army, but he gave advice and magical help – he did not fight himself. In the romance, Merlin involves himself more directly in the courtly world of politics, love, magic and war, and even he cannot escape the consequences. This Merlin is even more tragically doomed than King Arthur.

The depiction of Merlin's prophetic powers in the Vulgate Cycle has been analysed by other writers, and they tend to take a rather negative view.[22] It is true, as they point out, that Merlin's great sequence of symbolic prophecies on the future of Britain is omitted. However, the argument that Merlin's Vulgate Cycle prophecies relate only to Arthur, Lancelot, the Grail or future events within the world of romance is too narrow.[23] The fictional Merlin (like his French-speaking audience) shows less interest in Britain and Ireland, but he acts as a prophet and dream interpreter for great leaders, including Queen Elaine, her husband King Ban, Julius Caesar and the Saracen ruler Flualis.[24] What is more, in each case the dreams that the rulers experience, and the prophecies that

Merlin deduces from them, are described using animal symbolism very close to that found in the British prophecies circulated by Geoffrey of Monmouth. Clearly, writers and readers knew the manner in which Merlin prophesied – further proof of how widely his prophecies had circulated.

Queen Elaine's dream takes place in the early stages of a great continental campaign fought by Arthur and his supporters, which draws in rulers from across Europe. In the dream, rival kings are symbolized by two great lions, and Elaine's own unborn son is represented by a leopard. Both creatures carried powerful religious symbolisms, as mediaeval bestiaries demonstrate. These associations are strengthened by the fact that both the account of the dream and Merlin's prophecies have echoes of biblical language. Still more memorable is the depiction of Julius Caesar (who is emperor of Rome whilst Arthur is a young king) as a prophetic dreamer. Caesar dreams of a great, supernatural sow, accompanied by twelve wolf cubs – and nobody can, or dares, interpret this. At this critical moment, Merlin arrives in the form of an enchanted stag and reveals that Caesar's wife is a serial adulteress, whose twelve 'maidens' are cross-dressed men, all of whom join her in orgies. Having thus made public the moral turpitude of the Roman court, Merlin goes on to make a series of prophecies, once again using animal symbolism, for Caesar. These involve a dragon, a lion, a dove and a bull, creatures familiar from the British prophecies.[25]

Merlin's prophetic activities have thus been moved beyond Britain to continental Europe and thence to the heart of the Roman empire itself. The next steps are even more impressive. Merlin helps Arthur to establish a time of relative peace, after the defeat of the nefarious Saxons (amongst others), and encourages the rise of the fellowship of the Round Table. He then announces that Arthur can get along without him, though he will return when the kingdom has terrible need. In great haste he rushes through forests and across the sea, making his way to the region of Jerusalem and the territory of King Flualis, 'a worthy man of great renown in Islam'.[26] The occasion for this haste is that King Flualis has also had a prophetic dream, and has assembled learned men from many lands. This dream too uses animal symbolism – in this case, that of terrifying, fire-spewing flying serpents who dismember the king and his wife before burning them and spreading ash across the kingdom. Naturally, only Merlin (having arrived just in time) can reveal the true meaning of this dream: that victorious Christian kings are about to force King Flualis and his queen to become good Christians.

These prophetic episodes stand out all the more strongly since virtually no attempt is made to weave them into the dominant narratives of Arthur's wars, of knightly adventures, and of preparation of the Round Table knights for the Grail quest. They themselves have something of the quality of dreams, since they tend to lack any clear indications of date and place. King Arthur, Julius Caesar and the Islamic Empire appear to exist at the same time, in a way which would have horrified any historian. But the effect is not to undermine the impact of Merlin's prophetic powers. Rather, he is established as a prophet for all the great powers of the world. This is less surprising than it might at first seem, given that French-language prophecies were being issued in his name by Italian political forces in the thirteenth century. Like Merlin the political prophet, Merlin the tragic hero of romance is an international figure, who exceeds chronological and geographical limitation.

We are now approaching the concluding stages of the Vulgate romance of Merlin, and it is clear that he has come a long way from his early appearances within the pre-Arthurian part of the tale. Even at that stage, however, his purely British prophecies were omitted, and his appearance at the royal court had more in common with the saturnine Merlin of the *Life* than with the innocent child of the *History of the Kings of Britain*. In the romance, as in the *Life*, the emphasis is on his sardonic revelations of impending death, hidden treasure and secret love affairs. There is no hint of the madness that went with such perceptions in the *Life*, but Merlin's lack of sympathy and his mocking laughter have an unsettling effect of their own. They suggest an inhumanity, which appears also in his tendency to tease ordinary humans by changing his shape and leading them to make idiots of themselves – just before revealing his superior knowledge and the folly of mortal ways. Merlin increasingly leaves this aspect of himself behind, as he valiantly puts his powers to use in his efforts to shape the fate of humanity, and yet the infallible prophet is still counterbalanced by the dangerous necromancer. The final element of the threefold fictional Merlin is the unlikely yet tragic figure of Merlin the doomed lover.

At first sight, the theme of Merlin's fatal attraction to Viviane appears mostly as an odd but effective way of explaining his disappearance from both history and the Grail quest. Going slightly deeper, it also integrates the unsettling figure of the (almost) all-powerful magician even more deeply into the world of courtly romance, through its key theme of love. Not even the most powerful magic in the world can resist this unstoppable force. Given that the historical Merlin made contact only with the masculine side of mediaeval life, in the forms of politics, war and scientific magic, Merlin the lover stands out as a wholly fictional creation. No effort is made to insert the story of the love affair into the parts of the romance based upon the historical sources. Instead, the concept of Merlin the lover appears only after the magician has been established as part of Arthur's court (whereas he disappeared before Arthur's birth in the 'British history'). Of course, Merlin knows from the start that his love will lead to his doom, and there is growing pathos in the fact that he cannot refuse Viviane's requests to teach her about magic, even though he knows exactly how she will use her knowledge. Still more affectingly, Merlin remains true to his love, and does not condemn his lady; he is loyal to her, even though she does not keep all the vows she makes to him. In the end, he goes willingly to his fate at her hands, stating that he himself has given her power because he loves her more than himself.[27]

A romance which began with vengeful demons attempting the destruction of humanity has thus ended with the transformation of a half-demon into a self-sacrificing lover. Merlin does not actually die; Viviane wishes to have him exclusively for herself and under her power, not to kill him. He fades from the world, hidden behind a magical mist beside a flowering hawthorn in the enchanted forest of Brocéliande. But the place of his imprisonment is not entirely cruel – he believes himself to be inside a tower, not in the subterranean tombs of later versions. He also retains his own powers, although he is cut off from the outside world. This is demonstrated when he speaks to Sir Gawainet through the mist which hides and holds him. Gawainet has been discourteous to a damsel, and has been transformed into a dwarf by her curse. Merlin is able to speak, to tell Gawainet how to break the enchantment, and to show that he still has full superhuman knowledge. His final farewell is: 'May God keep King Arthur and the kingdom of Logres and you and all the barons, for you are the best men there are in the world.' All that remains for the romance of Merlin is the birth of the next hero, Queen Elaine's son Lancelot, in whose destiny Merlin has, of course, already played a part.

This fictional Merlin, more powerful than his historical inspiration and raising emotional and moral dilemmas fascinating to thirteenth-century society, was a rapid success. Once a fictional

Merlin was current, his story could be much more freely reworked and played with than could historical narratives. The demand for stories of Merlin is reflected by the fact that a new, longer retelling of the romance version appeared within a decade of the Vulgate. Yet this rewriting is openly hostile to Merlin. His power to shape events is downplayed, and his role as the mentor in whom Arthur places absolute reliance is reduced to something closer to a chief counsellor.[28] Viviane (here Niniane) actively hates Merlin, partly because she finds his nature as the son of a demon repulsive, and experiences his desire as frightening, especially since he might use his magic (here labelled necromancy) to rape her.[29] On top of this, Viviane's cruelty to Merlin is contextualized by the story of his rejection by Morgan and by hints of his hostility to other women, including Ygraine.[30] Even so, Merlin's punishment is extreme. The besotted magician first takes Viviane, the 'virgin huntress', to the very suitable location of the 'lake of Diana', and has a magical house built for her, thus turning her into the Lady of the Lake. Discovering that the site also contains the tomb of a deluded lover, hideously killed by Diana (by being sealed in with molten lead), Viviane is inspired.[31] It is another such 'rich and beautiful', yet markedly cruel, tomb in which Merlin is doomed by Viviane's enchantment to spend eternity.[32] To emphasize that Viviane is not hostile to all men, she then replaces Merlin in saving Arthur from a poisoned cloak. Her protectiveness towards Arthur is motivated by her love for his chivalry. In this version, magic is again something powerful and glamorous but ultimately destructive, yet Merlin's betrayal of women appears to be his worst fault, and worthy of a far worse punishment than that imposed on the ultimately true lover of the Vulgate story.

Further tales appeared, developing this theme of Merlin's downfall. Increasing attention was given to his imprisonment and isolation, and to his doomed attempts to contact those who were missing his guidance. This motif had already appeared in the *Prophesies de Merlin*, where a magician contacts Merlin's ghost. But a popular *Conte du Bruit* or *Tale of Merlin's Cry* made Merlin's living fate a still more tragic theme. This tale appears to have been more popular in continental Europe than in Britain, and an early version of it is referred to in the 'negative' romance just discussed. In Spain and Portugal it was the basis for the *Baladro del Sabio Merlin*, and then for the *Merlin y Demanda*, which went into print at the end of the fifteenth century. By now, Merlin's fate has become a punishment for his (and Uther's) cruelty to Ygraine, in seducing her, deceiving her and taking her baby (Arthur) away from her.[33]

Even in England, this more hostile version of Merlin's actions and fate began to take hold. The fifteenth-century Middle English prose romance, *Merlin*, stuck with the more positive Vulgate story (as had the early fourteenth-century Middle English *Of Arthour and of Merlin*).[34] But Malory, for whom Arthur was a hero to be separated from all negative associations, gave Merlin a relatively small role, and followed the harsher 'post-Vulgate' version concerning his fate.[35] In late mediaeval England, as in Europe, the earlier optimism about the power of magic to deepen human knowledge had given way to fear of demons and their wiles. Equally, in the age of the Black Death, the Hundred Years War and the Great Schism, the relationship between politics and morality had become an increasingly troubling issue. Thus, on the one hand, the loss of the enormous insights which only Merlin could provide is now shown to have left all regions of Europe more vulnerable than before. On the other hand, Merlin's willingness to use magic in order to override morality when the fate of nations was at stake could not be seen to go unpunished, and a king who stood for a lost golden age could not be associated with such behaviour.

The story is further complicated by the fact that a new audience was developing, and demanding that new themes and attitudes be addressed by the old stories. By the later fourteenth century, tales of Merlin (like those of Arthur) were in demand beyond the world of aristocratic or ecclesiastical courts. As others have also observed, the Merlin who appears in Middle English romances is in the process of being adapted for a newly literate, prosperous, urban audience. This new readership seems to have preferred the more sympathetic, Vulgate story of the fictional Merlin. In about 1425 Henry Lovelich dedicated a translation of the Vulgate *Merlin* to Henry Barton, head of the Skinners' Guild (of which Lovelich was a member), and later mayor of London.[36] He never completed it, but he showed his allegiance to the Vulgate's depiction of both Merlin's personal heroism and his relationship with Viviane (here Nymiane). Lovelich's poetry has received almost as harsh a criticism as that of *Castleford's Chronicle*, and his incomplete version of the story of Merlin was not a success in its own time. But it is interesting in that it places great stress on Merlin as a sort of master craftsman of magic. The motif of Merlin's 'tricks', and his ability to produce elaborate and entertaining appearances, is treated at considerably greater length than in the French original. For Lovelich, this aspect of Merlin's magic is the sort of entertainment produced by a master magician for the entertainment of the elite, and is a fitting part of the world of romance.[37] The impression given is that Merlin's sheer skill as a master craftsman helps to counterbalance the darker aspects of his magic.

The fictional Merlin, then, provides a barometer of changing attitudes towards magic in a more overt way than does the historical Merlin. In the fourteenth and fifteenth centuries attitudes towards magic were hardening fast, and it is in this same period that increasing emphasis is placed upon Merlin's fate. Magic was becoming more and more closely linked to the growing concept of witchcraft, and witchcraft was being described as a hidden, international cult of devil-worshippers, dedicated to destroying decent society everywhere. By 1484 Pope Innocent VIII was so convinced of the danger posed by these enemies of society that he issued the bull *Summis desiderantes affectibus*. In this bull the pope lamented that in many German regions 'many persons of both sexes have abandoned themselves to devils, incubi and succubi, and to incantations, spells, conjurations, and other accursed charms and crafts'.[38] Such persons are a deadly danger, since they have slain infants, laid waste the earth and its produce, and brought torment to men and women. Nor was this fear restricted to German provinces. In 1501 a similar message was sent to northern Italy, when Pope Alexander VI issued his bull *Cum acceperimus*. The pope had received reports that also in Lombardy 'many people of both sexes give themselves over to diverse incantations and devilish superstitions in order to procure many wicked things by their venery and vain rites'. As in all regions affected by such fears, the inquisitors were instructed to 'seek out diligently these people of both sexes . . . and secure and punish them'.[39]

The earliest indications of this fear that Christians were under attack from within Christendom had appeared at both the French royal court and the papal court in the early fourteenth century. In 1308 the bishop of Troyes was charged with using sorcery against the queen and others. In 1314 members of the French court were accused of employing a professional magician (and his wife) to cause the death of the king; the magician Jacques Dulot was killed in prison and his wife was burned, whilst members of the aristocratic d'Enguerrand family were executed. Magical attacks were also detected against the dauphin Jean in the 1320s, and against Philippe of Valois in 1398.[40] Still more sensationally, Pope John XXII discovered that he was the subject of murderous attacks by magical practitioners. In the first trial, the bishop of Cahors, Hugues Géraud, was found guilty of using both sorcery and poison in his assassination attempts. In 1318 no less a figure than Robert Mauvoisin, the archbishop of Aix, was tried for magical practices. And in 1320 came the revelation that Galeazzo I Visconti of Milan had hired a magician to make a silver image with which to kill the pope. Also in 1320, a cardinal of John XXII's court urged the inquisitors of Carcassone and Toulouse to rid southern France of sorcerers. In case anyone was in any doubt, the cardinal's letter of instruction explained that sorcerers make pacts with demons, use sacrifices and written tokens to make contact with demons, and pervert the sacraments in order to destroy Christian society.[41]

Record after record demonstrates that there were professional magicians available in most European countries in the late Middle Ages, providing a range of services for those who could afford to pay. One of the most detailed accounts comes from fifteenth-century England, where the Duchess of Gloucester was accused of hiring a witch and two priest-magicians to clear her husband's path to the throne. One of the magicians, Roger Bolingbroke, was put on public display in London along with the magical equipment he used, in order to demonstrate the degree of danger posed by sorcerers. He had magical robes, worn when he practised his 'necro-mancie', as well as an enchanted sword, a sceptre and a painted chair. The chair had swords at each corner, from which hung images of copper and other frightening artefacts. Once a crowd had been gathered a sermon was preached, to leave no doubt as to the power and the danger of sorcery.[42] Clearly, if Merlin were still alive he would be a source of terrible danger to society as much as a protection.

Fear of magic and sorcerers grew as Renaissance studies in science and natural philosophy expanded, and would develop in the sixteenth century into the 'witch craze'. This was accompanied by a further shift in the public perception of Merlin. As chivalric romance went out of fashion in the early modern period, the theme of Merlin's relationships with women became much less compelling. But this did not mean that Merlin himself disappeared from fictional works, any more than Merlin as prophet disappeared from political discourse, or Merlin's magic disappeared from discussions of natural philosophy. Even when beliefs in witchcraft and astrology went into decline in their turn, Merlin was not rejected but simply remodelled. For the great Romantics of the nineteenth century, the ageing magician's fate at the hands of Viviane was once again a subject of tragic resonance, although necromancy and adultery are no longer the flaws that bring the great magician down. By this stage his prophecies no longer attracted anything like the old levels of interest. In nineteenth-century poetry, the same theme that had emerged in fifteenth-century London, that of Merlin as a great master and maker, is again emphasized. When Merlin goes to his doom, it is his wisdom and his practical skill that are lost to the world. A century characterized by great feats of engineering saw only positives in Merlin's superhuman achievements as an artificer, even though it could no longer accept Merlin himself as a real historical figure.

ᔡᔒᘓᘕ

THE MEASURE OF MERLIN

For some five hundred years, the existence of Merlin as an actual historical personage was not only widely accepted but also exerted a very powerful effect. No fictional, or even legendary, character could have had anything like the impact that Merlin achieved in the real world.

Along with King Arthur, Merlin made British history not only widely known but also exciting and memorable. Merlin's magic gave the story of Britain a combination of mystery and power that rivalled or even outstripped the histories of other European kingdoms, and his prophecies guaranteed the survival and the significance of Britain until the very end of time. That is why the cognoscenti were so quick to interpret – and therefore validate – Merlin's words. It also explains why 'new' prophecies of Merlin, relating to other parts of Europe, appeared over such a long period of time. He became a figure on an international stage almost immediately after his first revelation, in a way that would not have been possible had he not been accepted as a real, historical figure.

Merlin's attractiveness beyond the boundaries of Britain lay in his ability to link ancient and biblical prophecy to more recent times. He proved conclusively that prophecy did not end with the Book of Revelation, neither was it geographically restricted to the Holy Land and the Roman world. Possession of such a great prophet helped to bring the new, post-Roman peoples nearer to a position of equality with ancient Rome, just as King Arthur's military conquests did. Merlin was thus in demand well beyond Britain and England. And he was even more than a prophet. People believed that his more-than-human parentage gave him knowledge of the past and the present which no human could rival, and which did not depend upon the difficult, obscure languages of prophecy or visionary dreams. This made Merlin a more powerful source of information and understanding even than Aristotle was believed to have been for Alexander the Great. He was included, and taken seriously, in such influential world histories as the *Speculum Historiale*.

The magnitude of Merlin's magical powers also provided a link to the past, and surpassed it. Here was a magician able to achieve feats equivalent to those recorded in the Bible, even though he lived in a much more recent period. He was also master of the powers of the natural world, and understood the movements of the stars. No Greek or Roman philosopher, mathematician or astrologer achieved feats greater than the creation of Stonehenge, or the transformation of Uther Pendragon into the exact form of Gorlois of Cornwall. Merlin was a link between the old world and the new, but even more significantly he looked forward to the future rather than mourning the past. In annexing the stones of the ancient giants he showed that his knowledge reached back well before the Roman empire, and was combined with medical skills that rivalled those of the Greeks. Yet for Merlin the stones were not important merely as a testament to the lost achievements of the ancient world. They were brought to Britain to become a monument to British fighters killed in the war against the Saxons and for future use as a source of medical cures.

Merlin also brought ancient magic into a new Christian moral framework. Unlike the court magicians described in the historical and prophetic books of the Bible, he refused to accept a position as royal fixer or political adviser. Merlin preferred to live away from court, and was to be found in quiet, unfrequented settings. His preference for uninhabited woodland, close to water and away from human settlements, was comparable to that of the reforming Cistercian monks, whose form of monasticism also swept across Europe in the twelfth century. This rejection of the temptations of the court, as well as the fact that he never sought power or material reward in return for his prophecies, counsel or magic, demonstrated that he exercised his powers for the greater good and not for himself. His father may have been a 'spirit', but clearly the historical Merlin was unmoved by traditional forms of temptation. Nor did he seek disciples, or, as a half-demon, mediate between the worlds of the living and the dead, as did classical seers and the biblical 'pythoness' of Endor. Merlin was, as mediaeval commentators agreed, a Christian, and as such he rejected communication both with the dead and with demons. He also refused to engage in the very serious practice of prophecy except in response to grave need. Time and again he proved his moral strength to the mediaeval mind.

This is important, since Merlin's feats of magic are poised right on the complex boundary between science, natural magic and necromancy. They are all the more exciting for being so, but they make of Merlin a potentially troubling figure. It is thus deeply reassuring that Merlin's own morality was strong, if inscrutable, and that he used his magic for commendable purposes, in the service of good British kings who cared for their people. Merlin's magic, despite its potentially terrifying combination of reality and power, is kept safe by his own moral code. A magician who could render huge stones weightless, and manipulate them single-handed into whatever formation he chose, could wreak havoc upon human constructions and defences, but there is no sense that the historical Merlin would engage in such misuse of his powers, even if the exploits of the contemporary, fictional Merlin show that mediaeval readers were well aware of what could be done with such magic.

A world that did not believe in the reality of magic could not believe in the reality of Merlin, as his decline in the eighteenth century showed. Throughout the classical and mediaeval periods, as well as during the Renaissance and the Reformation, magic was seen as real; after all, without such an acceptance the witch trials of the fifteenth, sixteenth and seventeenth centuries would have been impossible. But a sense of the nature of magic did change, from the twelfth century's open exploration of natural magic alongside other philosophical and scientific ideas, to the fourteenth century's conviction that magic, by definition, involved traffic with demons and was hostile to true Christianity. This was what made witches so threatening, and all magic was subject to the same rule. Thus, whilst Merlin and his feats were retained as part of the historical record, it became more and more difficult to view any magician in a positive light. It is not surprising that Merlin the Prophet played such an important role in this period, whilst Merlin the Magician faded.

Merlin's magic, then, represents the essence of mediaeval magic: it was a mingling of ancient and 'modern' knowledge, and placed within a Christian world view. The complexity of this position, and of the issues raised by both Merlin's inspired prophecies and his part-demon nature, was such that it is scarcely surprising that writers about the historical Merlin were at pains to clarify that they were not attempting to analyse him. Those who were not trained theologians were only too happy to leave that to the professionals. But this caution is significant: in itself writing about Merlin could have had such serious ramifications only if he had indeed been a real figure.

Writers of fictional romances, on the other hand, felt free to elaborate Merlin's magical powers, and were far less interested in his self-imposed moral code. It is scarcely surprising that this fictional Merlin, a figure of such power that he himself both makes and dictates the whole course of history, had to be ruthlessly contained. The fact that his downfall took the form of a young girl, rather than a rival magician or an out-of-control demon, is less predictable for modern readers. But making Merlin into a self-sacrificing, courtly lover is entirely within the 'rules' of chivalric romance, as well as further demonstrating his strong sense of morality. The great magician and prophet is fully aware that his love will bring him only a temporary happiness and connection to another (almost equally magical) individual. That he is prepared to pay such a savage price perhaps says something about the cost of his self-imposed isolation. The fictional Merlin, however, is the subject of other books.

The historical Merlin may have performed only five great works of magic, rather than the countless feats attributed to the fictional Merlin, but these five works changed the writing of European history. The upstart realm of the Anglo-Norman and Angevin kings took on far greater significance than it had previously enjoyed. Proof of the status that Merlin could confer is provided by the enthusiasm with which the equally upstart rival states of Italy took him up as 'their' prophet and magician. Even the speed with which both monastic moralists and French poets began to emphasize the dangers of his demonic origins, and the temptation which his magic presented, provides a backhanded compliment of considerable force. For those concerned with the historical record, however, to change the facts of Merlin's magic was to interfere both with history and with matters beyond ordinary comprehension. Merlin and magic rose together and, inevitably, fell together – a process which, ironically, failed to strip them of glamour and power. The enthusiasm with which eighteenth-century antiquarians continued to search for sites associated with Merlin demonstrates not so much a stubborn attempt to prove that he was real after all, as the continuing significance of establishing a connection to the great magician. The real Merlin had put whole kingdoms on a new historical and political standing; even a legendary Merlin, in an 'enlightened' world, could transform space and transcend time.

NOTES

ഇറൠ

Introduction

1. Tennyson, 'Merlin and Vivien' (originally published in 1859, republished as the sixth poem in *Idylls of the King*, and in its final version in 1899), lines 411–14.
2. Quotations here are from T. H. White, *The Once and Future King*, HarperCollins (Voyager), London, 1996. The description of Merlyn's [*sic*] home is at pp. 26–27.
3. This was in the work of pseudo-history produced by Geoffrey of Monmouth, and now known as *Historia Regum Britanniae or* the *History of the Kings of Britain*. A good, recent edition and translation is Geoffrey of Monmouth, *History of the Kings of Britain*, ed. M. D. Reeve, trans. N. Wright, Boydell, Woodbridge, 2007. Henceforth: Geoffrey of Monmouth, *History*.
4. Ample evidence of this success is provided by the manuscripts discussed in J. C. Crick, *The Historia Regum Britannie of Geoffrey of Monmouth III: A summary catalogue of the manuscripts*, Brewer, Cambridge, 1989.
5. A helpful introduction is provided by A. O. H. Jarman, *The Legend of Merlin*, University of Wales Press, Cardiff, revised edn 1976.
6. See Bede, *Ecclesiastical History of the English People*, ed. B. Colgrave and R. A. B. Mynors, Clarendon, Oxford, 1969.
7. There is no English translation of this work. A complete digitized edition, based on the text of a fourteenth-century copy, now MS Douai 797, is available online at http://atilf.atilf.fr/bichard/ (accessed 17 October 2011). All citations refer to this version.
8. See William of Newburgh, *The History of English Affairs*, Book One, ed. and trans. P. G. Walsh and M. J. Kennedy, Aris & Phillips, Warminster, 1988, p. 28.
9. See *Faerie Queene*, Book Three, canto III, stanza 8.
10. Dryden's libretto is available online at http://opera.stanford.edu/Purcell/KingArthur/libretto.html (accessed 17 October 2011). An edition is given in V. A. Dearing, ed., *The Works of John Dryden*, vol. 16, University of California Press, Berkeley, 1997.

Chapter 1: The Discovery of Merlin

1. For Latin text and English translation of this work, see Geoffrey of Monmouth, *History*.
2. See Crick, *Historia Regum Britannie: A summary catalogue*, for evidence of the scale of the work's popularity. The separate transmission of the prophecies has been discussed by C. D. Eckhardt in 'The *Prophetia Merlini* of Geoffrey of Monmouth: Latin manuscript copies', *Manuscripta*, 26, 1982, pp. 167–76.
3. There is much debate about this complex work. See Nennius, *British History and the Welsh Annals*, ed. and trans. J. Morris, Phillimore, London and Chichester, 1980. The majority of twelfth-century sources attributed it to Gildas, although the earliest surviving (and best) copies are anonymous. Its attribution to Nennius seems to originate in Wales, but perhaps as late as the eleventh century. See also D. Dumville, *The Vatican Recension of the Historia Brittonum: Historia et genealogia Brittonum et de origine eorum necnon et expulsione*, Brewer, Cambridge, 1985.
4. This information is given in Geoffrey's Prologue. See Geoffrey of Monmouth, *History*, pp. 4–5. Geoffrey does seem to have known at least some of the poems about Myrddin which now survive in the (later) following works: *Black Book of Carmarthen* (now in the National Library of Wales, Peniarth MS 1), which can be viewed online at http://www.llgc.org.uk/index.php?id=blackbookofcarmarthen (accessed 19 October 2011); *White Book of Rhydderch* (National Library of Wales, Peniarth MS 4), see http://www.llgc.org.uk/index.php?id=whitebookofrhydderchpeniart (accessed 19 October 2011); and *Red Book of Hergest* (now in Oxford, Jesus College, MS 111), see http://image.ox.ac.uk/show?collection=jesus&manuscriptm=s111 (accessed 19 October 2011). These poems are the subject of a large secondary literature. Helpful translations are provided in A. O. H. Jarman, *The Cynfeirdd: Early Welsh poets and poetry*, Cardiff, University of Wales Press, 1981.
5. Geoffrey of Monmouth, *History*, pp. 138–9.
6. At least three detailed commentaries survive from the period 1139–79 alone. One is unpublished; another, believed to be by Alanus de Insulis, is available in an edition published in Frankfurt in 1603 (*Prophetia Anglicana Merlini Ambrosii Britanni una cum septem libris explanationum in eandem prophetiam*). More accessible are those published by J. Hammer in: 'A Commentary on the *Prophetia Merlini*', *Speculum*, 10, 1935, pp. 3–30, and *Speculum*, 15, 1940, pp. 409–31; 'Another Commentary on the *Prophetia Merlini*', *Bulletin of the Polish Institute of Arts and Sciences in America*, 1, 1942–3, pp. 589–601; and 'Bref commentaire de la *Prophetia Merlini* du ms 3514 de la bibliothèque de la cathédrale d'Exeter', in J. Hammer, ed., *Hommages à Joseph Bidez et à Franz Cumont*, Latomus, Brussels, 1949, pp. 111–19.
7. Geoffrey of Monmouth, *History*, p. 143. References to the Latin text are from this edition; translations are my own.
8. The main source for this account is William of Malmesbuy's *Historia Novella*, ed. E. King and trans. K. R. Potter, Clarendon, Oxford, 1999.
9. This information is placed in Book One, chapter 1, together with the description of Britain and its natural wonders. Bede, *Ecclesiastical History*.
10. Ibid., Book One, chapters 13 to 22.
11. This complex work exists in various versions, attested by seven manuscripts and two fragments. For discussion of the main versions, and a translation of the entries to 1042, see D. Whitelock, ed., *English Historical Documents c.500–1042*, Eyre Methuen and Oxford University Press, London and New York, 1979, pp. 109–25 and 145–261.
12. For William of Malmesbury's career, see R. M. Thomson, 'Malmesbury, William of (*b. c.*1090, *d.* in or after 1142)', *Oxford Dictionary of National Biography*, Oxford University Press, Oxford, 2004 (http://www.oxforddnb.com/view/article/29461, accessed 19 October 2011).

13. William of Malmesbury, *The Early History of Glastonbury: An edition, translation, and study of William of Malmesbury's De antiquitate Glastonie ecclesie*, ed. J. Scott, Brewer, Woodbridge, 1981.
14. William of Malmesbury, *Historia Novella*, ed. E. King, trans. K. R. Potter, Clarendon, Oxford, 1998.
15. Ibid., Book One, chapters 10 to 14.
16. See D. E. Greenway, 'Henry of Huntingdon (*c.*1088–*c.*1157)', *Oxford Dictionary of National Biography*, Oxford University Press, Oxford, 2004 (http://www.oxforddnb.com/view/article/12970, accessed 19 October 2011).
17. Henry of Huntingdon, *Historia Anglorum*, ed. D. E. Greenway, Clarendon, Oxford, 1996.
18. Orderic's work has been edited and translated in six volumes, as Orderic Vitalis, *The Ecclesiastical History of Orderic Vitalis*, ed. and trans. M. Chibnall, Clarendon, Oxford, 1969–1980. For Orderic's discussion of Merlin's prophecies see Chibnall vol. VI, 1978, pp. 380–88.
19. Robert produced both an updated history of the dukes of Normandy and a world chronicle, and these show his familiarity with older historical works. He included Henry of Huntingdon's letter about the *History of the Kings of Britain* in a collection of supplementary materials, whilst noting in the Prologue to his own work that the 'new' history was clearly unknown to Eusebius and Jerome. See L. Delisle, ed., *Chronique de Robert de Torigni, Abbé du Mont-Saint-Michel*, 2 vols, A. Le Brument, Rouen, 1872–3, at vol. 1, pp. 97–111. The letter was also later used by Henry himself in his *History of the English*.
20. For discussion, see N. Wright, ed., *The Historia Regum Britannie of Geoffrey of Monmouth: II, the First Variant Version*, Brewer, Woodbridge, 1988, p. lxxi, and references there.
21. For Geoffrey's addresses to both Robert of Gloucester and Waleran of Meulan, see Geoffrey of Monmouth, *History*, pp. 4 and 5.
22. Gaimar discusses his patrons, and the sources they provided, in his *Estoire des Engleis*. See A. Bell, ed., *L'Estorie des Engleis by Geffrei Gaimar*, Anglo-Norman Text Society, Oxford, 1960, at lines 6442 and 6458–9. For further discussion, see I. Short, 'Gaimar's Epilogue and Geoffrey of Monmouth's Liber vetustissimus', *Speculum*, 69, 2, 1994, pp. 323–43.
23. Ailred of Rievaulx, *Speculum Caritatis*, Book Two, chapter 17 (see *Patrologia Latina* CXCV, col. 565).
24. See T. Hearne, ed., *Aluredi Beverlacensis Annales sive Historia de Gestis Regum Britanniae*, E Theatro Sheldoniano, Oxford, 1716, at p. 2. In fact Alfred's account follows Geoffrey of Monmouth extensively, despite cross references to Gildas, Bede and a 'Roman history', e.g. on p. 51. The account of Merlin's discovery and birth is full, and based on the *History of the Kings of Britain*, including the comments of Mauguntius (p. 53). Merlin's great sequence of prophecies is, however, omitted, with a simple comment that it is long (p. 52). Merlin's prophetic powers are represented, as in vernacular translations, by his prophecies of Vortigern's coming death, and of the coming of the 'Boar of Cornwall' (Arthur).
25. For an edition and translation, see note 3, above.
26. Nennius, *British History*, chapters 31–56.
27. For further discussion of William of Newburgh, see A. Lawrence-Mathers, 'William of Newburgh and the Northumbrian Construction of English History', *Journal of Medieval History*, 33, 2007, pp. 339–57.
28. See William of Newburgh, *The History of English Affairs*, ed. and trans., G. Walsh and M. J. Kennedy, Warminster, 1988, Book One.
29. This is now in London at the British Library, MS Stowe 62.

Chapter 2: Writing the History of Merlin

1. For text and translation, see M. Winterbottom, ed., *The Ruin of Britain: History from the sources* vol. 7, Philimore, London and Chichester, 1978.
2. Bede, *Ecclesiastical History*, Book One, chapters 13–23.
3. Geoffrey of Monmouth, *History*, pp. 252–3.
4. Ibid., pp. 278–81.
5. For a discussion of this, see D. Dumville, 'Nennius and the *Historia Brittonum*', *Studia Celtica*, 10–11, 1975–77, pp. 78–95.
6. This is an extract from *Historia Brittonum*, chapter 42; Morris's translation of this passage is slightly different.
7. The resulting work does not survive in its earliest form. For the text and discussion, see William of Malmesbury, *The Early History of Glastonbury: An edition, translation, and study of William of Malmesbury's De antiquitate Glastonie ecclesie*, ed. J. Scott, Boydell, Woodbridge, 1981.
8. See William of Malmesbury, *Gesta Regum Anglorum: The History of the English kings*, 2 vols, ed. and trans. R. A. B. Mynors with R. M. Thomson and M. Winterbottom, Clarendon, Oxford, 1998.
9. Ibid., Book One, chapter 5.
10. Ibid., Book Two, under the year 1065.
11. Ibid., Book One, chapter 8.
12. As noted above, William's work does not survive in its original form, apart from some excerpts which he copied into his *Gesta Regum*; the rest survives only in the expanded version of the thirteenth-century chronicler Adam of Domerham. However, he does seem to have accepted the association of both Gildas and St Patrick with Glastonbury.
13. For discussion and further references, see A. Gransden, *Legends, Traditions and History in Medieval England*, Hambledon, London and Rio Grande, 1992, p. 158.
14. William of Malmesbury, *Gesta Regum*, Book Three, chapter 287.
15. The first witness to this is Gerald of Wales, who makes the identification in both his *De Principis Instructione* and the *Speculum Ecclesie*; he suggests that it was Henry II who was particularly interested in this identification. For texts and translation, see Gerald of Wales, *The Journey through Wales/The Description of Wales*, trans. L. Thorpe, Penguin, Harmondsworth, 1978, appendix 3, pp. 280–8.
16. Very little is known of Caradoc's career; one of the best discussions is still J. S. P. Tatlock, 'Caradoc of Llancarfan', *Speculum*, 13, 2, 1938, pp. 139–52.
17. On Caradoc's contribution to the legend of Gildas, see J. S. P. Tatlock, 'The Dates of the Arthurian Saints' Legends', *Speculum*, 14, 3, 1939, pp. 345–65. For an edition and translation, see *Two Lives of Gildas by a Monk of Ruys and Caradoc of Llancarfan*, ed. and trans., H. Williams. First published in the Cymmrodorion Record Series, 1899. Facsimile reprint: Llanerch Publishers, Felinfach, 1990.
18. Ibid., chapters 10–14.
19. This is also known as *liber Landavensis*, and is now MS 17110E in the National Library of Wales. Its historicity is discussed in W. Davies, *The Llandaff Charters*, National Library of Wales, Aberystwyth, 1979. The most comprehensive recent study is J. R. Davies, *The Book of Llandaf and the Norman Church in Wales*, Brewer, Woodbridge, 2003.
20. For William's Lives of Saints, see William of Malmesbury, *Saints' Lives*, ed. and trans. M. Winterbottom and R. M. Thomson, Clarendon, Oxford, 2002.
21. Geoffrey of Monmouth, *Vita Merlini (Life of Merlin)*, ed. and trans. B. Clarke, University of Wales Press, Cardiff, 1973.
22. For a version of the story from Iceland, see Gunnlaugr Leifsson, 'Merlinússpá', in F. Jonsson, ed., *Hauksbók, udgiven efter de Arnamagnoeanske handskrifter* No. 371, 544 og 675, Det kongelike nordiske Oldskrift-Sleskab, Copenhagen, 1892–6, pp. 271–83.
23. Clarke's translation, p. 2. Subsequent translations are my own.

24. For the poems, see chapter 1, note 4, above; for a discussion, see A. O. H. Jarman, 'Early Stages in the Development of the Myrddin Legend', in R. Bromwich and R. B. Jones, eds, *Studies in Old Welsh Poetry*, University of Wales Press, Cardiff, 1978, pp. 326–49.

25. Alfred of Beverley (Aluredi Beverlacensis), *Annales sive Historia de Gestis Regum Britanniae*, Book IX, ed. T. Hearne, E. Theatro Sheldoniano, Oxford, 1716.

26. See Sidney Lee, and J. C. Crick, 'Beverley, Alfred of (*d.* 1154–7)', rev. J. C. Crick, *Oxford Dictionary of National Biography*, Oxford University Press, Oxford, 2004 (http://www.oxforddnb.com/view/article/344 (accessed 23 October 2011).

27. Alfred of Beverley, *Annales*, p. 52

28. Ibid., pp. 56–7.

29. For Gaimar, see Chapter 1, note 22.

30. See (Master) Wace, *Roman de Brut*, (*A History of the British*), ed. and trans. J. Weiss, University of Exeter Press, Exeter, 2006.

31. Ibid., pp. 122–3.

32. Ibid., pp. 190–1 and note 1. Manuscript copies which insert the prophecies include Durham, Dean and Chapter Library, MS C IV 27, and Lincoln Cathedral Library MS 104.

33. For an edition and translation of the complete work, see F. Madden, *Layamon's Brut, or Chronicle of Britain: A Poetical Semi-Saxon Paraphrase of the Brut of Wace*, 3 vols, Society of Antiquaries, London, 1847.

34. Madden, *Layamon's Brut*, vol. 2, p. 246.

35. This is my rendition of the text; see Madden, *Layamon's Brut*, vol. 2, p. 249.

36. See Geoffrey of Monmouth, *History*, p. 139 for the Latin text.

37. Wace, *Roman de Brut*, p. 186.

38. See Madden, *Layamon's Brut*, vol. 2, pp. 233–5.

39. Wace, *Roman de Brut*, p. 202.

40. Madden, *Layamon's Brut*, vol. 2, p. 289.

41. Ibid., p. 445.

42. Ibid., vol. 3, pp. 145–6.

43. Ibid., pp. 294–5.

44. See Robert Bartlett, 'Gerald of Wales (*c.*1146–1220x23)', *Oxford Dictionary of National Biography*, Oxford University Press, 2004; online edn, October 2006 (http://www.oxforddnb.com/view/article/10769, accessed 23 October 2011).

45. See, for instance, the *Vita S. David* composed by Rhygyfarch ap Sulien, discussed by J. R. Davies, in *The Book of Llandaf and the Norman Church in Wales*, Woodbridge, Boydell, 2003, p. 76.

46. On Ireland, see Gerald's *The History and Topography of Ireland*, trans. J. J. O'Meara, Penguin, Harmondsworth, rev. edn, 1982. For the works on Wales, see Gerald's *The Journey through Wales/The Description of Wales*, trans. L. Thorpe, Penguin, Harmondsworth, 1978. Gerald's comments on Geoffrey of Monmouth are in ibid., pp. 117–18.

47. For this declaration, see ibid., pp. 192–3.

48. Ibid.

49. Ibid., Book One, chapter 16, pp. 246–51.

50. Ibid., pp. 116–21.

51. Ibid., Book Two, chapter 6, p. 183.

52. Ibid., pp. 121–2 and 166–8.

53. Gerald tells of the discovery of the grave of Arthur and Guinevere at Glastonbury in his work on the education of princes, *De principis instructione*, Book One, chapter 20; and on the Church, *Speculum Ecclesiae*, Book Two, chapters 8–10. For translations, see Gerald's *Journey through Wales* (trans. Thorpe), pp. 280–88.

54. For discussion of the complex issues raised by this text, see K. Grabowski and D. Dumville, eds, *Chronicles and Annals of Medieval Ireland and Wales: The Clonmacnoise group of texts*, Boydell, Woodbridge, 1984; and K. Hughes, 'The Welsh Latin chronicles: *Annales Cambriae* and related texts', in K. Hughes, ed., *Celtic Britain in the early Middle Ages*, Boydell, Woodbridge, 1980, pp. 67–85.

55. The Neath version of the chronicle is now at Kew, in the National Archives, E164/1. For the text, see J. Williams ab Ithel, ed., *Annales Cambriae (AD 444–1288)* London, Rolls Series 20, 1860; translated in P. M. Remfry, ed., *Annales Cambriae; A translation of Harleian 3859, PRO E164/1*, Cottonian Domitian A I, Exeter Cathedral Library MS 3514, and MS Exchequer DB Neath PRO E, Castle Studies Research and Publishing, Malvern, 2007.

56. See Jocelyn of Furness, *Life of St Kentigern*, ed. and trans. John Pinkerton, in *Lives of the Scottish Saints*, Alexander Gardner, Paisley, 1889–95.

57. This manuscript also contains the surviving text of the 'Herbertian' Life of St Kentigern (fols 76–80), suggesting a careful collection of materials.

58. A complete, digitized edition, based on the text of a fourteenth-century copy, now MS Douai 797, is available online at http://atilf.atilf.fr/bichard/ (accessed 17 October 2011). All references will be to this version.

Chapter 3: The British Merlin

1. For text and translation, see Geoffrey of Monmouth, *History*, pp. 144–59.

2. See Orderic Vitalis, *Ecclesiastical History*, Book Twelve, Vol. 6, chapter 46, ed. Chibnall, pp. 330–9.

3. Ibid.

4. *Deeds of Louis the Fat*, chapter 16; see R. Cusimano and J. Moorhead, trans. *Suger, Abbot of Saint Denis 1081–1151; The Deeds of Louis the Fat*, Catholic University of America Press, Washington, D.C., 1992.

5. For the text, see G. Waitz, ed., *Richardi Pictaviensis Chronica*, in *Monumenta Germaniae Historica Scriptores*, vol. XXVI, Impensis Bibliopolii, Hahniani, Hanover, 1882; and for discussion, see M. Saurette, 'Tracing the Twelfth-Century *Chronica* of Richard of Poitiers, Monk of Cluny', *Memini; Bulletin de la Société d'Etudes médiévales du Québec*, Vols 9–10, 2005/6, pp. 303–50.

6. Ralph of Diceto, *Images of History*, ed. W. Stubbs, in *Radulfi de Diceto decani Lundoniensis opera historica* 2 vols, Rolls Series 68, London, 1876, Vol. 2, pp. 64 and 67–8.

7. Both chroniclers refer to Merlin's prophecy in their discussions of the rebellions of Henry II's sons. See, Roger of Howden ed. W. Stubbs, 4 vols Chronica Rogeride Houedene, Rolls Series 51, London, 1868–71, Vol. 2, p. 47; and Benedict of Peterborough *The Chronicle of the Reigns of Henry II and Richard I, known commonly under the name of Benedict of Peterborough*, ed. W. Stubbs, 2 vols, Rolls Series 49, London, 1867, Vol. 1.

8. Diceto, sub anno 1189, vol. 2, pp. 67–8.

9. Ralph of Coggeshall is one of the main chroniclers for the reign of King John; see his *Chronicon Anglicanum*, ed. J. Stevenson, Rolls Series 66, London 1875, p. 146.

10. Gervase of Canterbury, *Historical Works* ed. W. Stubbs, 2 vols, Rolls Series 73, London, 1879–80, Vol. 2, sub anno 1210.

11. Matthew Paris, *Chronica Majora*, ed. H. R. Luard, 7 vols, Rolls Series 57, London, 1872–83.

12. This is now in London: British Library, MS Cotton Claudius B VII; the illumination is on fol. 224.

13. Paris, *Chronica Majora*, Vol. 5, pp. 204–22.

14. Ibid., p. 206.

15. Ibid., p. 208.
16. Ibid.
17. Ibid., p. 209; and Geoffrey of Monmouth, *History*, p. 149.
18. These two translations have been edited and translated by Jean Blacker, from Durham Cathedral Library, MS C IV 27, and Lincoln Cathedral Library, MS 104; an English translation is given for the first. See Jean Blacker, ed., *Anglo-Norman Verse Prophecies of Merlin*, Scriptorium Press, Dallas, TX, 2005.
19. W. A. Wright, ed., *The Metrical Chronicle of Robert of Gloucester*, 2 vols, Rolls Series 86, London, 1887, 1. 3109. See p. 133.
20. Ibid., pp. 200–1. An anonymous English prose translation of the fifteenth century has been edited, with extensive discussion; see C. D. Eckhardt, ed., *The Prophetia Merlini of Geoffrey of Monmouth: A Fifteenth-Century English Commentary*, Speculum Anniversary Monographs 8, Medieval Academy of America, Cambridge, MA. 1982.
21. See L. M. Matheson, *The Prose Brut: The development of a Middle English chronicle*, Medieval and Renaissance Texts and Studies, Tempe, AZ, 1998. For a list and description of manuscripts, see: http://www.qub.ac.uk/imagining-history/resources/short/index.php (accessed 24 October 2011).
22. See Anon., *The Brut or the Chronicles of England*, Part 1, ed. F. W. D. Brie. Early English Text Society, London, Original Series 131, 1906, pp. 58–9.
23. Ibid., pp. 72–6.
24. Ibid., (my translation).
25. Ibid., pp. 177–8.
26. For discussion, see T. M. Smallwood, 'The Prophecy of the Six Kings', *Speculum*, 60, 3, 1985, pp. 571–92. See also R. H. Robbins, 'Poems Dealing with Contemporary Conditions', in A. Hartung, ed., *A Manual of the Writings in Middle English 1050–1500*, Vol. 5, Yale, New Haven and London, 1975.
27. Walter of Coventry, *The Historical Collections of Walter of Coventry, from Brutus to 1225*, ed. W. Stubbs, 2 vols, Rolls Series 58, London, 1872–3, Vol. 1, p. 26.
28. Sir Thomas Gray, *Scalacronica*, ed. J. Stevenson, Maitland Society, London, 1856, Appendix II, 'Extracts from the early portion of the Scalacronica', p. 317.
29. Thomas Castleford, *Castleford's Chronicle or the Boke of Brut*, ed. C. D. Eckhardt, 2 vols, Oxford University Press for Early English Text Society, Oxford, 1996. The Prophecies of Merlin are on pp. 414–50. They follow Geofrey of Monmouth closely until the end of the world is reached, when the darkening of the sun and the ominous influence of Mars are simply followed by the statement 'tharof na mere to lerne' (line 16,730).
30. On these, see C. D. Eckhardt, 'The First English Translation of the *Prophetia Merlini*', *The Library*, 6th series, vol. 4, No. 1, March 1982, pp. 25–34.
31. See A. O. H. Jarman, 'The Merlin Legend and the Welsh Tradition of Prophecy', in P. H. Goodrich and R. H. Thompson, eds, *Merlin: A casebook*, Routledge, London, 2003, pp. 105–30.
32. M. J. Curley, 'A New Edition of John of Cornwall's *Prophetia Merlini*', *Speculum*, 57, 2, 1982, pp. 217–49.
33. STC (2nd ed.), 17841: ESTC Citation No. S100757.
34. See Eckhardt, 'First English Translation of the *Prophetia Merlini*'.
35. William Lilly, *History of his Life and Times, from the Year 1602 to 1681*, London 1715, reprinted London 1822, pp. 48–9.

Chapter 4: The Curious Career of Merlin the Astrologer

1. For the Latin text, see Geoffrey of Monmouth, *History*, p. 159.
2. See II Esdras, 5: 1–12 (also known in the mediaeval period as IV Esdras).
3. Geoffrey of Monmouth, *History*, pp. 178–9.

4. Halley's Comet is famously depicted in the Bayeux Tapestry, together with a crowd of anxious observers.
5. Geoffrey of Monmouth, *Life of Merlin*, see especially lines 421–51.
6. For a slightly different view, see J. Ziolkowski, 'The Nature of Prophecy in Geoffrey of Monmouth's *Vita Merlini*', in J. L. Kugel, ed., *Poetry and Prophecy: The beginnings of a literary tradition*, Cornell University Press, New York, 1990, pp. 151–62.
7. Geoffrey of Monmouth, *Life of Merlin*, pp. 11–12.
8. See Acts of the Apostles, 8: 9–25. For the growth of the legend of Simon Magus, see A. Ferreiro, *Simon Magus in Patristic, Medieval and early-Modern Traditions*, Brill, Leiden, 2005.
9. Geoffrey of Monmouth, *Life of Merlin*, p. 13.
10. The standard textbook on these calculations was by Bede: see *Bedae Opera de Temporibus*, ed. C. W. Jones, The Medieval Academy of America, Cambridge, MA, 1941; and Bede, *The Reckoning of Time*, ed. and trans. F. Wallis, University Press, Liverpool, 2004.
11. For a brief history of mediaeval astrology, see S. J. Tester, *A History of Western Astrology*, Boydell, Woodbridge, 1987, Chapter 5.
12. For a succinct account of mediaeval astrolabes, see J. D. North, 'The Astrolabe', in North, *Stars, Minds and Fate: Essays in ancient and medieval cosmology*, Hambledon Press, London and Ronceverte, 1989, pp. 211–20.
13. For the *Matheseos*, see Firmicus Maternus, *Matheseos Libri Octo (Ancient Astrology: Theory and Practice)*, ed. and trans. J. R. Bram, Noyes Press, Park Ridge, 1975.
14. Cited by R. M. Thomson, *William of Malmesbury*, rev. edn, Boydell, Woodbridge, 2003, p. 60.
15. Orderic Vitalis, *Ecclesiastical History*, Vol. 1, p. 156.
16. William of Malmesbury, *History of the English Kings*, p. 280.
17. For detailed analysis of the calculations involved, see J. D. North, 'Some Norman Horoscopes', in C. F. S. Burnett, ed., *Adelard of Bath, an English Scientist and Arabist of the Early Twelfth Century*, Warburg Institute, London, 1987, pp. 147–61.
18. On Adelard of Bath, see ibid. For Robert of Chester, see C. H. Haskins, *Studies in the History of Medieval Science*, Harvard University Press, Cambridge, MA, 1924, pp. 120–3.
19. The groundbreaking study is Haskins, 'The Court of Frederick II', in idem, *Medieval Science*, pp. 242–98.
20. This is now in Oxford: Bodleian Library, MS Ashmole 304. Some of the texts have been published: L. Brandin, 'Les Prognostica du Ms. Ashmole 304', in M. Williams and J. A. de Rothschild, eds, *Miscellany of Studies in Romance Languages and Literatures presented to L. E. Kastner*, Cambridge University Press, Cambridge, 1932, pp. 57–67.
21. See R. Vaughan, *Matthew Paris*, Cambridge University Press, Cambridge, 1958, pp. 252–4.
22. Gervase of Tilbury, *Otia Imperialia (Recreation for an Emperor)*, ed. and trans. S. E. Banks and J. W. Binns, Clarendon, Oxford, 2002. For an outline of Gervase's career, see ibid., Introduction, pp. xxv–xxxviii.
23. On Michael Scot, see Haskins, *Medieval Science*, pp. 272–98, and L. Thorndike, *Michael Scot*, Nelson, London, 1965.
24. For the text, see Haskins, *Medieval Science*, pp. 292–7.
25. Salimbene de Adam, *The Chronicle*, trans. J. L. Baird, G. Baglivi and J. R. Kane, Medieval Texts and Studies 40, Binghamton, 1986, p. 17. For the Latin text, see Salimbene de Adam *Cronica*, ed. C. Scalia, Turnhout, Brepols (Corpus Christianorum Continuatio Mediaevalis, vol. CXXV), Turnhout, 1998.
26. Haskins, *Medieval Science*, pp. 257–9.
27. *Les Prophesies de Merlin (Cod. Bodmer 116)*, ed. A. Berthelot, Fondation Martin Bodmer, Cologny-Geneva, 1992.

28. Middle English lunar prognostics also circulated; see I. Taavitsainen, 'Middle English Lunaries: A Study of the Genre', *Mémoires de la Société Néophilologique de Helsinki*, 47, Helsinki, 1988. For text and discussion of eleventh-century examples, see L. S. Chardonnens, *Anglo-Saxon Prognostics: 900–1100*, Brill, Leiden, 2007, pp. 393–465.

29. See J. Marvin, ed. and trans., *The Oldest Anglo-Norman Prose Brut Chronicle*, Boydell, Woodbridge, 2006.

30. See Matheson, *Prose Brut*, pp. 5–8.

31. Brie, ed., *The Brut*, p. 64.

32. See L. A. Smoller, *History, Prophecy, and the Stars: The Christian astrology of Pierre d'Ailly, 1350–1420*, Princeton University Press, Princeton, NJ, 1994.

33. J.-P. Boudet, ed., *Le Recueil des plus célèbres astrologues de Simon de Phares*, Champion, Paris, 1997.

34. Ibid., pp. 315–17.

Chapter 5: Merlin's Magic

1. Augustine, *Concerning the City of God Against the Pagans*, trans. H. Bettenson, reissued by Penguin, London, 2003, Book Ten, chapter 9 p. 383.

2. See William of Conches, *Dragmaticon Philosophiae* (*A Dialogue on Natural Philosophy*), trans. I. Ronca and M. Curr, University of Notre Dame Press, Notre Dame, IN, 1997.

3. William of Conches, *Patrologia Latina*, vol. CLXXII, 56.

4. For an introductory discussion of natural magic, see R. Kieckhefer, *Magic in the Middle Ages*, 2nd edn, Canto Series, Cambridge University Press Cambridge, 2000, pp. 14–17.

5. For the Stonehenge story, see Geoffrey of Monmouth, *History*, pp. 170–5.

6. Ibid., pp. 36–7.

7. Gervase of Tilbury, *Otia Imperialia*, Book Two, chapter 8, p. 265.

8. This poem is found in the tenth-century poetic anthology known as the *Exeter Book*, now in Exeter, Cathedral Library, MS 3501. Numerous translations are available. The poem is so lacking in specific reference that it is not possible to identify the place described with certainty (or even to be sure that an actual location is being described).

9. See B. Cunliffe, 'Saxon Bath', in J. Haslam, ed., *Anglo-Saxon Towns in Southern England*, Phillimore, Chichester, 1984, pp. 345–58.

10. This was in a 'letter' on the subject of the transitory nature of worldly fame, which he incorporated into Book Eight of his *History*. See D. E. Greenway, 'Henry of Huntingdon as Poet', *Medium Aevum*, vol. 74, No. 2, 2005, p. 108 (and also pp. 470–1).

11. For this description of Bath, see (Anon.), *Gesta Stephani*, ed. and trans. K. R. Potter and R. H. C. Davis, Clarendon, Oxford, 1976, p. 59.

12. F. Jones, *The Holy Wells of Wales*, 2nd. edn University of Wales Press, Cardiff, 1992; and *Vitae Sanctorum Britanniae et Genealogiae*, ed. A. Wade-Evans, University of Wales Press, Cardiff, 1944, pp. 290–8.

13. For positive comment on the water supply and baths at Vivarium itself, see Cassiodorus, *Institutiones*, 1.29.1, in *Institutions of Divine and Secular Learning On the Soul*, Third edn, ed. and trans. J. W. Halporn and M. Vessey, University Press, Liverpool, 2004. See also P. Squatriti. *Water and Society in Early Medieval Italy, 400–1000*, Cambridge University Press, Cambridge, 1998, p. 55. The recommendation of the health-giving properties of Baia is in a letter: Cassiodorus, *Variae*, IX, Letter 6, cited in C. M. Kauffmann, *The Baths of Pozzuoli*, Cassirer, London and Oxford, 1959, p. 4.

14. Solinus, *Polyhistor* or *Collectanea Rerum Mirabilium*, ed. and trans. A. Agnant, C. L. F. Panckoucke, Paris, 1847, chapter 23, p. 184.

15. Gervase of Tilbury, *Otia Imperialia*, III, 13, p. 586.

16. C. Burnett: 'Malvern, Walcher of (d. 1135)', *Oxford Dictionary of National Biography*, Oxford University Press, online, 2004 (http://www.oxforddnb.com/view/

article/41145, accessed 31 October 2011); and C. S. F. Burnett, 'Mathematics and Astronomy in Hereford and its Region in the Twelfth Century', in D. Whitehead, ed., *Medieval Art, Architecture and Archaeology at Hereford*, British Archaeological Association Conference Transactions, 15, Leeds 1995, pp. 50–9. See also Haskins, *Medieval Science*, pp. 112–17.

17. On the wells of Malvern, see: http://www.malvern-hills.co.uk/malvernspa/well-info/priors.html (accessed 25 February 2010).
18. Geoffrey of Monmouth, *Life of Merlin*, p. 12.
19. See B. R. Kemp, 'The Miracles of the Hand of St James', *Berkshire Archaeological Journal*, vol. 65, 1970, pp. 1–20, at p. 16.
20. Geoffrey of Monmouth, *Life of Merlin*, pp. 13 and 17–18.
21. Layamon, *Brut*, Vol. 1, pp. 120–5.
22. William of Malmesbury, *History of the English Kings*, p. 282.
23. See Walter Map, *De Nugis Curialium (Courtiers' Trifles)*, ed. and trans. M. R. James, rev. edn. C. N. L. Brooke and R. A. B. Mynors, Clarendon, Oxford, 1983, p. 353.
24. *Brut*, Layamon, Vol. 2, p. 308.
25. William of Malmesbury, *History of the English Kings*, p. 280.
26. Adelard of Bath, *'De Avibus Tractatus' (Treatise on Birds)*, in *Adelard of Bath: Conversations with His Nephew: On the Same and the Different; Questions on Natural Science; and On Birds*, ed. and trans. C. Burnett, Cambridge, Cambridge University Press. Cambridge, 1998, pp. 237–68.
27. Geoffrey of Monmouth, *Life of Merlin*, p. 17
28. Anon. *Bestiary*, ed. and trans. R. Barber, Boydell, Woodbridge, pp. 125 and 130. The relevant section of the Aberdeen Bestiary (Aberdeen UL MS 2b.), where this bird is called 'Caladrius', can be seen at www.abdn.ac.uk/bestiary/
29. See L. White, Jr, 'Eilmer of Malmesbury, An Eleventh Century Aviator', *Technology and Culture*, 2, 2, 1961, pp. 97–111.
30. Geoffrey of Monmouth, *History*, pp. 186–7.
31. Wace, *Roman de Brut*, p. 218, line 8702.
32. Ibid., lines 8704–14.
33. Ibid., p. 220, line 8727.
34. Layamon, *Brut*, Vol. 2, pp. 365–9.
35. Ibid., p. 370.
36. Ibid.
37. Ibid., pp. 384–5.
38. Wace, *Roman de Brut*, p. 208.
39. Layamon, *Brut* vol. 2, pp. 315–20.
40. Ibid., pp. 372–3.
41. John of Worcester, *Chronicle*, ed. and trans. P. McGurk, Vol. 3, Clarendon, Oxford, 1995, pp. 201–3.
42. This has been the subject of considerable discussion. For a recent view, see J. Collard, 'Henry I's Dream in John of Worcester's *Chronicle* (Oxford, Corpus Christi College, MS 157) and the Illustration of Twelfth-Century English Chronicles', *Journal of Medieval History*, 36, 2, 2010, pp. 105–25.
43. P. Horden, 'Faricius (d. 1117)', *Oxford Dictionary of National Biography*, Oxford University Press, 2004, online (http://www.oxforddnb.com/view/article/9157, accessed 30 October 2011).
44. On MS Bodley 130, see N. R. Ker, *Catalogue of Manuscripts Containing Anglo-Saxon*, Clarendon, Oxford, 1957, repr. 1990, item 153.
45. The canon was Philip Apostolorum, who gave six volumes to Worksop Priory in 1187, one of which was a luxurious bestiary now in the Morgan Library, New York. See W. B. Clark, *A Medieval Book of Beasts: The Second-Family Bestiary*, Boydell, Woodbridge, 2006, p. 12.

46. See D. E. Greenway, 'Henry of Huntingdon as Poet', *Medium Aevum*, 74, 2, 2005, pp. 329–32; and J. H. Harvey, 'The Square Garden of Henry the Poet', *Garden History*, 15, 1, 1987, pp. 1–11.
47. See Haskins, *Medieval Science*, pp. 169–71.

Chapter 6: A Demonic Heritage

1. This was 'Alanus' (usually identified as Alanus de Insulis) whose full-length commentary on the prophecies appeared *c.*1170. Despite his scepticism about Merlin's parentage, Alanus compared Merlin's prophetic gifts to those of the Sibyl and Job. See J. Crick, 'Geoffrey of Monmouth, Prophecy and History', *Journal of Medieval History*, 18, 4, 1992, pp. 357–71, at p. 369.
2. Geoffrey of Monmouth, *History*, pp. 136–41.
3. See Thomas of Monmouth, *The Life and Miracles of Saint William of Norwich*, ed. and trans. A. Jessopp and M. R. James, Cambridge University Press, Cambridge, 1896, pp. 79–83.
4. See Walter Map, *De Nugis Curialium*, ed. M. R. James, Clarendon, Oxford, 1914, pp. 159–73.
5. William of Newburgh, '*Historia Rerum Anglicarum*', in R. Howlett, ed., *Chronicles of the Reigns of Stephen, Henry II and Richard I*, Rolls Series 82, 2 Vols, Longman, London, 1884–5, Vol. 2, pp. 476–81.
6. On the Nephilim, see M. Black and O. Neugebauer, *The Book of Enoch, or, I Enoch*, Brill, Leiden, 1985, pp. 13–15. Saint Augustine's comments are in his *City of God*, Book Fifteen, chapter 22.
7. Geoffrey of Monmouth, *History*, pp. 18–21.
8. Ibid., pp. 36–7.
9. Ibid., pp. 26–9.
10. Ibid., pp. 20–1 and pp. 60–3.
11. Ibid., pp. 44–5.
12. William of Newburgh, *Historia Rerum Anglicarum* II, pp. 474–5.
13. Geoffrey of Burton, *Life and Miracles of St Modwenna*, ed. and trans. R. Bartlett, Clarendon, Oxford, 2002, pp. 192–9.
14. Geoffrey of Monmouth, *History*, pp. 128–33.
15. Ibid., pp. 138–9.
16. St Augustine was sufficiently concerned about Apuleius to make frequent reference to him in Books Eight and Nine of *The City of God*. For discussion of Apuleius' actual writings, see J. Beaujeu, ed. and trans. (in French) *Apulée, opuscules philosophiques et fragments*. Collection des Universités de France, Paris, 1973.
17. Geoffrey of Monmouth, *Life of Merlin*, pp. 11–12.
18. For a survey of new scholarship on angels in high mediaeval Europe, see D. Keck, *Angels and Angelology in the Middle Ages*, Oxford University Press, Oxford and New York, 1998, chapter 4.
19. See D. Luscombe, 'The Reception of the Writings of Denis the Pseudo-Areopagite into England', in D. E. Greenway et al., eds, *Tradition and Change: Essays in honour of Marjorie Chibnall*, Cambridge University Press, Cambridge, 1985, pp. 115–43.
20. See P. Rorem, *Pseudo-Dionysius: A Commentary on the Texts and an Introduction to their Influence*, Oxford University Press, Oxford and New York, 1993.
21. See Luscombe,'The Reception', p. 120.
22. The *Imago Mundi* has not been translated into English. For discussion, see V. I. J. Flint, 'The Career of Honorius Augustodunensis. Some Fresh Evidence', *Revue Benedictine*, 82, 1972, pp. 62–86.
23. See Keck, *Angels and Angelology*, pp. 75–94.

24. See D. Luscombe, 'Pullen, Robert (d. in or after 1146)', *Oxford Dictionary of National Biography*, Oxford University Press, Oxford, (2010, online http://www.oxforddnb.com/view/article/22877) (accessed 7 September 2011).
25. For Archdeacon Walter and his learning, see Henry of Huntingdon, *Historia Anglorum*, ed. Thomas Arnold, London, Rolls Series 74, 1879, p. 302.
26. See Peter Lombard, *The Sentences, Book Two: On Creation*, trans. G. Silano, Pontifical Institute of Mediaeval Studies, Toronto, 2008. A Latin text, with parallel English translation, is also being published via the Franciscan Archive website. For Book Two see http://www.franciscan-archive.org/lombardus/II-Sent.html (accessed 20 October 2011).
27. Ibid., Distinction VII, chapter 6.
28. Ibid., Distinction XI, chapter 1.
29. See Isidore of Seville, *The Etymologies*, trans. S. A. Barney, W. J. Lewis, J. A. Beach and O. Beighof, Cambridge University Press, Cambridge and New York, 2006.
30. Ibid., p. 184.
31. Ibid., p. 190.
32. Ibid., p. 182.
33. Ibid., pp. 181–3.
34. See Hugh of St Victor, *The Didascalicon*, trans. J. Taylor, Columbia University Press, New York, 1991.
35. Ibid., Appendix B, 'Concerning Magic and its Parts', pp. 154–5.
36. See John of Salisbury, *Ioannis Saresberiensis Episcopi Carnotensis, Policratici*, ed. C. C. I. Webb, Clarendon, Oxford, 1919.
37. Book One, chapters 8–12. For translation, see John of Salisbury, *Frivolities of Courtiers and Footprints of Philosophers*, trans. J. B. Pike, University of Minnesota Press, Minneapolis, 1938.
38. Roger Bacon, *Opus Majus*, ed. J. H. Bridges, 2 vols, Clarendon, Oxford, 1898, vol. 1, especially pp. 200–60.
39. Ibid., pp. 261–3.
40. See E. Peters, *The Magician, the Witch and the Law*, Harvester, Hassocks, 1978, pp. 89–90.
41. Ibid., p. 91.
42. Robert of Gloucester, *The Metrical Chronicle*, ed. W. A. Wright, 2 Vols, Rolls Series 86, London, 1887–8.
43. See ibid., vol. 1, pp. 128–33.
44. Ibid., pp. 145–9.
45. Ibid., pp. 158–9.
46. Anon., *The Abridged English Metrical Brut*, ed. U. O'Farrell-Tate, Universitätsverlag C. Winter, Heidelberg, 2002.
47. Ibid., lines 156–60.
48. Ibid., line 334.
49. See Thomas Castleford, *Castleford's Chronicle or the Boke of Brut*, ed. C. D. Eckart, Vol. 1, Early English Text Society, Original Series, Oxford, 2005.
50. Ibid., pp. 415–50.
51. Ibid., pp. 409–10.
52. Ibid., pp. 477–86 and pp. 495–6.
53. Ibid., p. 516.
54. Robert Mannyng of Brunne, *Chronicle*, ed. F. J. Furnivall, 2 Vols, Rolls Series 87, London, Vol. I, 1887, p. 4.
55. Ibid., p. 6.
56. Ibid., pp. 282–4.
57. Ibid., p. 288.
58. Ibid., p. 308.

59. Ibid., pp. 329–30.
60. Ranulf Higden, *Polychronicon Ranulphi Higden Monachi Cestrensis: together with the English Translations of John Trevisa and of an Unknown Writer of the Fifteenth Century*, eds C. Bobington & J. R. Lumby, 9 vols, Rolls Series 41, London, 1865–8.
61. This discussion is placed at the end of Book Five, chapter 1.
62. Ibid., Book Five, chapters 4 and 5.
63. Ibid., chapter 6.
64. Ibid., Rolls Series volume facing the Latin version, see Vol. 5, p. 339.
65. J. Iohn Hardyng, *Chronicle*, ed. H. Ellis, F. C. and J. Rivington et al., London, 1812.
66. Ibid., p.132.

Chapter 7: Merlin in Europe

1. The story of the journey is told in Geoffrey of Monmouth, *History*, Book Eight, chapters 130–1.
2. For discussion of these, see Chapter 8, below.
3. This claim appears in the Preface to the prophecies of Merlin when they appear as chapter 7 of the *History of the Kings of Britain*.
4. Orderic's *Ecclesiastical History* was written *c.*1123–37, and Book Twelve, which contains Orderic's comments on Merlin's prophecies (in chapter 47), was written before the death of Henry I in 1135. For the text, see Orderic Vitalis, *The Ecclesiastical History of Orderic Vitalis*, ed. and trans. M. Chibnall, 6 vols vol. 6, Clarendon, Oxford, 1978, pp. 380–8.
5. This was the famous occasion when Henry of Huntingdon, travelling with the archbishop of Canterbury, was shown a copy of the *History of the Kings of Britain* by the Bec chronicler, Robert of Torigny. See Henry of Huntingdon, *Historia Anglorum* (*The History of the English People*), ed. and trans. D. E. Greenway, Clarendon Press, Oxford, 1996, p. 559.
6. Abbot Suger of St Denis, in his *Life of Louis the Fat*, refers to Merlin's prophecies, and pays special attention to those relating to Henry I. See Suger, *Vie de Louis le Gros*, ed. H. Waquet, 2nd edn, Les Belles Lettres, Paris, 1964, pp. 12–14 and pp. 98–100.
7. For the Latin text, see Geoffrey of Monmouth, *History*, p. 149.
8. See, for instance, Morgan Kay, 'Prophecy in Medieval Welsh Manuscripts', *Proceedings of the Harvard Celtic Colloquium*, vols 26/27, 2006/2007, p. 76, where the argument of J. Crick is also discussed.
9. Isidore of Seville, *Etymologies* p. 166.
10. For the Latin, see Geoffrey of Monmouth, *History*, p. 151.
11. For John of Cornwall's own *Prophecies of Merlin*, see M. J. Curley, 'A New Edition of John of Cornwall's *Prophetia Merlini*', *Speculum*, 57, 2, 1982, pp. 217–49.
12. On these, see E. Wind, *Michelangelo's Prophets and Sibyls*, Oxford University Press, London, 1966.
13. The rediscovery of the Tiburtine Sibyl was especially important and influential; see A. Holdenried, *The Sibyl and her Scribes: Manuscripts and interpretation of the Latin Sibylla Tiburtina, 1050–1500*, Ashgate, Aldershot and Burlington, VT, 2006.
14. Augustine's most influential citation of the sibyl's prophecy of the coming of Christ was in *The City of God*, Book Ten, chapter 27, and Book Eighteen, chapter 23. However, he stated the superiority of the Old Testament prophecies relating to Christ in Book Eighteen, chapters 46–7.
15. Isidore of Seville, *Etymologies*, p. 181.
16. Virgil, *Aeneid*, Book Six, 42–155. For the mediaeval reception of the Sibylline texts, see B. McGinn, '*Teste David cum Sibylla*: The Significance of the Sibylline Tradition in the Middle Ages', in J. Kirshner and S. Wemple, eds, *Women of the Medieval World*, Blackwell, Oxford and New York, 1985, pp. 7–35.
17. See Geoffrey of Monmouth, *History*, pp. 218 and 280.

18. McGinn, 'Teste David cum Sibylla', pp. 9–13.
19. Anonymous, Oracula Sibyllina, Book Three, lines 809–29. For translation, see The Sibylline Oracles Books III–V, trans. H. N. Bate, Society for Promoting Christian Knowledge, London, 1919, pp. 82–3.
20. This anonymous twelfth-century guide remained popular until the fifteenth century. See Mirabilia Urbis Romae (Marvels of Rome), trans. F. M. Nichols, Ellis and Elvey, London, 1889.
21. See Holdenried, The Sibyl, pp. 31–52.
22. For discussion see B. McGinn, Visions of the End: Apocalyptic Traditions in the Middle Ages, 2nd edn, Columbia University Press, New York, 1998.
23. Philippe de Thaon, Le Livre de Sibile, ed. H. Shields, Blackwell, Oxford, 1979.
24. For a list of manuscripts and their contents, see Holdenried, The Sibyl, pp. 73–91.
25. See N. Cohn, The Pursuit of the Millennium, 2nd edn, Oxford University Press, Oxford, 1970, pp. 108–13.
26. For a contemporary account of Hildegard's career, see Gottfried of Disibodenberg, Life of the Saintly Hildegard, trans. H. Fess, Peregrina, Toronto, 1996.
27. For the Scivias, see Hildegard of Bingen, Scivias, trans. C. Hart and J. Bishop, Paulist Press, New York, 1990; for the Book of Divine Works, see Hildegard of Bingen, Liber Divinorum Operum, eds A. Derolez and P. Dronke, Corpus Christianorum Continuatio Medialvalis 92, Brepols, Turnhout, 1996.
28. Cited by R. W. Southern, 'History as Prophecy (Aspects of the European Tradition of Historical Writing, 3)', Transactions of the Royal Historical Society, 5th Series, 22, 1972, pp. 159–80, at p. 170.
29. The Pentachronon is unpublished; extracts are given in translation in Hildegard of Bingen, Selected Writings, ed. and trans. M. Atherton, Penguin, London, 2001, pp. 193–6.
30. The literature on Joachim is extensive; a helpful introduction to his prophetic technique is E. R. Daniel, 'Joachim of Fiore: Patterns of History in the Apocalypse', in R. K. Emmerson and B. McGinn, eds, The Apocalypse in the Middle Ages, Cornell University Press, New York, 1992, pp. 72–88.
31. Itinerarium Peregrinorum et Gesta Regis Ricardi, (The Deeds of King Richard), ed. W. Stubbs, 2 vols, Rolls Series 38, London, 1867, Vol. 2, pp. 80–4.
32. Ibid.
33. William of Tudela, The Song of the Cathar Wars: A history of the Albigensian Crusade, trans. J. Shirley, Ashgate, Aldershot, 1996.
34. Salimbene de Adam, The Chronicle, trans. J. L. Baird, G. Baglivi and J. R. Kane, Medieval and Renaissance Text Studies, vol. 40, Binghamton, NY, 1986, p. 113.
35. Gervase of Tilbury, Otia Imperialia (Recreation for an Emperor), ed. and trans. S. E. Banks and J. W. Binns, Clarendon, Oxford, 2002.
36. Ibid., p. 151.
37. Ibid., pp. 419 and 421, pp 488–9.
38. Ibid., p. 611.
39. Ibid., p. 1,006.
40. Bacon, Opus Majus, 268–9.
41. Les prophecies de Merlin, 2 vols, ed. L. Paton, Heath, New York, 1926–7.
42. For discussion, see L. Lahdensuu, 'Predicting History: Merlin's Prophecies in Italian XIIth–XVth Century Chronicles', in E. Kooper, ed., The Medieval Chronicle III, Rodopi, Amsterdam and New York, 2004, pp. 93–100.
43. J. Tarré, 'Las profecías del sabio Merlin u sus imitaciones', Analecta Sacra Taraconensis, vol. 16, 1943, pp. 135–71.
44. Cited by P. Zumthor, Merlin le Prophète, 2nd edn, Slatkine, Geneva, 2002, p. 78.
45. Christine de Pisan, Ditié de Jeanne d'Arc, ed. A. J. Kennedy and K. Varty, Society for the Study of Medieval Languages and Literature, Oxford, 1977, stanza 21.
46. See John of Cornwall, Prophetia Merlini (Propheues of Merlin), 'A New Edition', ed. M. J. Curley.

Chapter 8: Love and Death

1. Chrétien de Troyes, *Cligès*, lines 27–42, in Chrétien de Troyes, *Arthurian Romances*, trans. D. D. R. Owen, Dent, London, 1987, p. 93.
2. Higden, *Polychronicon*, eds C. Babington and J. R. Lumby, Vol. V, p. 336.
3. M. T. Bruckner, *Chrétien Continued: A study of the Conte du Graal and its verse continuations*, Oxford University Press, Oxford, 2009, esp. chapter 1.
4. Chrétien de Troyes, *Erec and Enide*, in *Arthurian Romances*, trans. Owen, p. 26, verses 1934–62.
5. Ibid., verses 5445–669.
6. Ibid., verses 6710–12.
7. Robert de Boron, *Merlin de Robert de Boron, roman en prose du XIIIe siècle*, ed. A. Micha, Droz, Paris-Geneva, 1980.
8. See in particular, 'L'Histoire de Merlin' (anon.) H. O. Sommer, ed., *The Vulgate Version of the Arthurian Romances*, in 8 vols, vol. 2 Carnegie Institute, Washington, 1908.
9. For an introduction to the issues, see K. Pratt, 'The Cistercians and the *Queste del Saint Graal*', *Reading Medieval Studies*, vol. 21, 1995, pp. 69–96.
10. *The Story of Merlin*, trans. R. T. Pickens, in N. J. Lacy, ed., *Lancelot–Grail: The Old French Arthurian Vulgate and Post-Vulgate in translation*, Vol. I, Garland, New York, 1993, pp. 167–424.
11. Ibid., p. xix.
12. Ibid., p. 172.
13. Ibid., p. 190.
14. Ibid., p. 196.
15. Ibid., p. 220.
16. Ibid., p. 234.
17. For discussion, see E. Peters, *The Magician the Witch and the Law*, esp. pp. 85–109.
18. This is the type of magic that John of Salisbury and later theologians had condemned as *praestigium*. For rituals and texts, see J. Lidaka, '*The Book of Angels, Rings, Characters and Images of the Planets*, Attributed to Osbern Bokenham', in C. Fanger, ed., *Conjuring Spirits: Texts and traditions of medieval ritual magic*, Sutton, Stroud, 1998, pp. 32–75.
19. St Augustine had condemned textual amulets in particular as demonic magic. See his *De doctrina Christiana*, 2.20.30: *Aurelii Augustini opera*, 4.1, Corpus Christianorum Series Latina vol. 32, Brepols, Turnhout, 1962, p. 54.
20. *Story of Merlin*, p. 329.
21. Ibid., p. 390.
22. See, for instance, Zumthor, *Merlin le Prophète*.
23. S. Knight, *Merlin: Knowledge and power through the ages*, Cornell University Press, Ithaca and London, 2009, p. 45.
24. *Story of Merlin*, pp. 317 and 399.
25. Ibid., p. 327.
26. Ibid., p. 399.
27. Ibid., pp. 415–20.
28. *The Post-Vulgate Merlin Continuation*, trans. M. Asher, Vol. V of N. J. Lacy, *Lancelot-Grail*.
29. Ibid., p. 158.
30. Ibid., pp. 69 and 13.
31. Ibid., p. 161.
32. Ibid., p. 190.
33. See F. Bogdanow, 'The Post-Vulgate *Roman du Graal*', in G. Burgess and K. Pratt, eds, *The Arthur of the French: The Arthurian Legend in Medieval French and Occitan Literature*, University of Wales Press, Cardiff, 2006, pp. 342–92.
34. See *Of Arthour and of Merlin*, ed. O. D. Macrae-Gibson, 2 vols Vol. I, Early English Text Society, OS 268, Oxford University Press, London, 1973.

35. Thomas Malory, *Morte Darthur, Le*, Caxton edition, re-edited by H. O. Sommer, David Nutt, London, 1889. Book Four, chapter 1.
36. See R. W. Ackerman, 'Henry Lovelich's *Merlin*', *PMLA*, 67, 4, 1952, pp. 473–84.
37. See R. Dalrymple, '"Evele knowen ye Merlyne in certain": Henry Lovelich's prose *Merlin*', in J. Weiss, J. Fellows and M. Dickins, eds, *Medieval Insular Romance*, Brewer, Cambridge, 2000, pp. 155–67.
38. For a complete translation, see A. C. Kors and E. Peters, eds, *Witchcraft in Europe, 400–1700*, 2nd edn, University of Pennsylvania Press, Philadelphia, 2001, pp. 177–79.
39. Ibid., p. 229.
40. E. Peters, *The Magician the Witch and the Law*, pp. 120–5.
41. Ibid., pp. 129–35.
42. See J. Freeman, 'Sorcery at Court and Manor: Margery Jourdemayne, The Witch of Eye Next Westminster', *Journal of Medieval History*, 30, 2004, pp. 343–57.

BIBLIOGRAPHY

࿓

Manuscripts

Aberdeen, University Library MS 24; the Aberdeen Bestiary. See www.abdn.ac.uk.
  bestiary/
Aberystwyth, National Library of Wales, MS Peniarth 1; *Black Book of Carmarthen*.
  See http://www.llgc.org.uk/index.php?id=blackbookofcarmarthen
Aberystwyth, Nat. Lib. Wales, MS Peniarth 4; *White Book of Rhydderch*. See http://www.
  llgc.org.uk/index.php?id=whitebookofrhydderchpeniart
London, British Library, MS Stowe 62 (William of Newburgh, *Historia rerum Anglicarum*)
Oxford, Jesus College MS 111; *Red Book of Hergest*. See http://image.ox.ac.uk/show?colle
  ction=jesus&manuscript—s111

Printed Primary Sources

Adelard of Bath, '*De Avibus Tractatus*' (*Treatise on Birds*), in C. Burnett, ed. and trans.,
  *Adelard of Bath, Conversations with his Nephew: On the Same and the Different; Questions
  on Natural Science; and On Birds*, Cambridge University Press, Cambridge, 1998,
  pp. 237–68.
Ailred of Rievaulx, *Speculum Caritatis* see *Patrologia Latina* CXCV, col. 565.
Alanus de Insulis (attrib.), *Prophetia Anglicana Merlini Ambrosii Britanni una cum septem
  libris explanationum in eandem prophetiam*, Frankfurt, 1603.
Alfred of Beverley, (Aluredi Beverlacensis), *Annales sive Historia de Gestis Regum Britanniae*,
  Book IX, ed. T. Hearne, E Theatro Sheldoniano, Oxford, 1716.
Anglo-Norman Verse Prophecies of Merlin, ed. and trans. J. Blacker, Scriptorium Press,
  Dallas, TX, 2005.
Anglo-Saxon Chronicle, in D. Whitelock, ed., *English Historical Documents c.500–1042*,
  Eyre Methuen and Oxford University Press, London and New York, 1979,
  pp. 145–261.
Annales Cambriae, ed. J. Williams ab Ithel, Rolls Series 20, London, 1860.

Annales Cambriae. A translation of Harleian 3859, PRO E164/1, Cottonian Domitian A I, Exeter Cathedral Library MS 3514, and MS Exchequer DB Neath PRO E, ed. and trans. P. M. Remfry, Castle Studies Research and Publishing, Malvern, 2007.

Anonymous, *The Abridged English Metrical Brut*, ed. U. O'Farrell-Tate, Universitätsverlag C. Winter, Heidelberg, 2002.

Apuleius, *Apulée, opuscules philosophiques*, ed. and trans. J. Beaujeu, Collection des Universités de France, Paris, 1973.

Augustine, *Concerning the City of God Against the Pagans*, trans. H. Bettenson, Penguin, London, 2003.

Augustine, *De doctrina Christiana*, in *Aurelii Augustini opera*, 4.1, Corpus Christianorum Series Latina, 32, Brepols, Turnhout, 1962.

Bacon, Roger, *The Opus Majus of Roger Bacon*, ed. J. H. Bridges, 2 vols, Clarendon, Oxford, 1898.

Bede, *Bedae Opera de Temporibus*, ed. C. W. Jones, Medieval Academy of America, Cambridge, Mass. 1941.

Bede, *Ecclesiastical History of the English People*, ed. B. Colgrave and R. A. B. Mynors, Clarendon, Oxford, 1969.

Bede, *The Reckoning of Time*, ed. and trans. F. Wallis, Liverpool, University Press, 2004.

Benedict of Peterborough, *Chronicle of the Reigns of Henry II and Richard I*, known commonly under the name of Benedict of Peterborough, ed. W. Stubbs, 2 vols, Rolls Series 49, London, 1867.

Bestiary, ed. and trans. R. Barber, Boydell, Woodbridge, 1992.

Boudet, J.-P., ed., *Le Recueil des Plus Célèbres Astrologues de Simon de Phares*, Champion, Paris, 1997.

Brut, The, or the Chronicles of England, Part 1, ed. F. W. D. Brie, Early English Text Society, Original Series 131, London, 1906.

Caradoc of Llancarfan, *Life of Gildas*, in H. Williams ed. and trans., *Two Lives of Gildas by a Monk of Rus and Caradoc of Llancarfan*, facsimile reprint, Llanerch Publishers, Feninfach, 1990.

Cassiodorus, *Institutiones*, 1.29.1, in J. W. Halporn and M. Vessey, ed. and trans., *Cassiodorus: Institutions of Divine and Secular Learning On the Soul*, Third edn, Liverpool, University Press, 2004.

Castleford, Thomas, *Castleford's Chronicle or the Boke of Brut*, ed. C. D. Eckhardt, 2 vols, Oxford University Press for the Early English Text Society, Oxford, 1996.

Chrétien de Troyes, *Cligès*, and *Erec and Enide*, in *Chrétien de Troyes: Arthurian Romances*, trans. D. D. R. Owen, Dent, London, 1987.

Christine de Pisan, *Ditié de Jeanne d'Arc*, ed. A. J. Kennedy and K. Varty, Society for the Study of Medieval Languages and Literature, Oxford, 1977.

Chronicon Anglicanum, in J. Stevenson, ed., Rolls Series, 66, London 1875, p. 146.

Clonmacnoise Annals, in K. Grabowski and D. Dumville, eds, *Chronicles and Annals of Medieval Ireland and Wales: The Clonmacnoise Group of Texts*, Boydell, Woodbridge, 1984.

Dryden, John, libretto for *King Arthur*. See http://opera.stanford.edu/Purcell/KingArthur/libretto.html (accessed 17 Oct. 2011). Dryden, John, *The Works of John Dryden* Vol 16, University of California Press, Berkeley, 1997.

Firmicus Maternus, Julius, *Matheseos Libri Octo (Ancient Astrology: Theory and Practice)*, ed. and trans. J. R. Bram, Noyes Press, Park Ridge, 1975.

Gaimar, Geoffrey, *L'Estorie des Engleis*, ed. A. Bell, Anglo-Norman Text Society, Oxford, 1960.

Geoffrey of Burton, *Life and Miracles of St Modwenna*, ed and trans. R. Bartlett, Clarendon, Oxford, 2002.

Geoffrey of Monmouth, *Vita Merlini*, (*Life of Merlin*); ed. and trans. B. Clarke, University of Wales Press, Cardiff, 1973.

Geoffrey of Monmouth, *Historia Regum Britannie* (*History of the Kings of Britain*), ed. M. D. Reeve, trans. N. Wright, *Arthurian Studies LXIX*, Boydell, Woodbridge, 2007.
Geoffrey of Monmouth, *Historia Regum Britannie of Geoffrey of Monmouth II: The First Variant Version*, ed. N. Wright, Boydell, Woodbridge, 1988.
Gerald of Wales, *The History and Topography of Ireland*, trans. J. J. O'Meara, rev. edn, Penguin, Harmondsworth, 1982.
Gerald of Wales, *The Journey through Wales/The Description of Wales*, trans. L. Thorpe, Penguin, Harmondsworth, 1978.
Gerald of Wales, *The Conquest of Ireland*, trans. T. Forester, ed. T. Wright, In Parentheses Publications, Medieval Latin Series, Cambridge, Ontario, 2001.
Gervase of Canterbury, *Historical Works*, ed. W. Stubbs, 2 vols, Rolls Series 73, London, 1879–80.
Gervase of Tilbury, *Otia Imperialia* (*Recreation for an Emperor*), ed. and trans. S. E. Banks and J. W. Binns, Clarendon, Oxford, 2002.
Gesta Stephani, ed. and trans. K. R. Potter and R. H. C. Davis, Clarendon, Oxford, 1976.
Gildas, *De excidio et Conquestu Britanniae*, ed. M. Winterbottom in *The Ruin of Britain: History from the Sources*, vol. 7, Philimore, London and Chichester, 1978.
Gottfried of Disibodenberg, *Life of the Saintly Hildegard*, trans. H. Fess, Peregrina, Toronto, 1996.
Gray, Sir Thomas, *Scalacronica*, ed. J. Stevenson, Maitland Society, London, 1856.
Gunnlaugr Leifsson, *Merlinússpá*, ed. F. Jonsson in *Hauksbók, udgiven efter de Arnamagnoeanske handskrifter* No. 371, 544 og 675, Det kongelike nordiske Oldskrift-Sleskab, Copenhagen, 1892–96, pp. 271–83.
Henry of Huntingdon, *Historia Anglorum*, ed. Arnold, London, Rolls Series, 1879, p. 302.
Henry of Huntingdon, *Historia Anglorum* (*The History of the English People*), ed. and trans. D. E. Greenway, Clarendon Press, Oxford, 1996.
Hildegard of Bingen, *Scivias*, trans. C. Hart and J. Bishop, Paulist Press, New York, 1990.
Hildegard of Bingen, *Liber Divinorum Operum* (*Book of Dinne Work*), ed. A. Derolez and P. Dronke, Corpus Christianorum Continuatio Medialvalis 92, Brepols, Turnhout, 1996.
Hildegard of Bingen, *Selected writings*, ed. and trans. M. Atherton, Penguin, London, 2001, pp. 193–6
Histoire de Merlin, ed. H.O. Sommer, *The Vulgate Version of the Arthurian Romances*, 8 vols Carnegie Institute, Washington, 1908.
Hugh of Saint Victor, *The Didascalicon of Hugh of St Victor*, trans. J. Taylor, Columbia University Press, New York, 1991.
Isidore of Seville, *The Etymologies of Isidore of Seville*, trans. S. A. Barney, W. J. Lewis, J. A. Beach and O. Beighof, Cambridge University Press, Cambridge and New York 2006.
Itinerarium Peregrinorum et Gesta Regis Ricardi, ed. W. Stubbs, 2 vols, Rolls Series 38, London, 1864.
Jocelyn of Furness, *Life of St Kentigern*, ed. and trans. John Pinkerton, in *Lives of the Scottish Saints*, Alexander Gardner, Paisley, 1889–95.
John of Cornwall, *Prophetiae Merlini* (*Prophecies of Merlin*), ed. M. J. Curley, 'A New Edition of John of Cornwall's *Prophetia Merlini*', *Speculum* 57, 2, 1982, pp. 217–49.
John of Salisbury, *Frivolities of Courtiers and Footprints of Philosophers*, trans. J. B. Pike, University of Minnesota Press, Minneapolis, 1938.
John of Salisbury, *Ioannis Saresberiensis Episcopi Carnotensis, Policratici*, ed. C. C. I. Webb, Clarendon, Oxford, 1919.
John of Worcester, *The Chronicle of John of Worcester*, ed. and trans. P. McGurk, Vol. 3, Clarendon, Oxford, 1995.
John Hardyng, *Chronicle*, ed. H. Ellis, F.C. and J. Rivington et al., London, 1812.
Layamon, *Brut, or Chronicle of Britain: A Poetical Semi-Saxon Paraphrase of the Brut of Wace*, ed. and trans. F. Madden, 3 vols, Society of Antiquaries, London, 1847.
Lilly, William, *History of his Life and Times from the Year 1602 to 1681*, London, 1715, repr. London, 1822.

Llandaff Charters, ed. W. Davies, Aberystwyth, National Library of Wales, 1979.

Malory, Thomas, *Morte Darthur, Le*, Caxton edition, re-edited H. O. Sommer, David Nutt, London, 1881.

Matthew Paris, *Chronica Majora*, ed. H. R. Luard, 7 vols, Rolls Series 57, London, 1872–83.

Matthew Paris, *Prognostica*, ed. L. Brandin, 'Les Prognostica du Ms. Ashmole 304', in M. Williams and J. A. de Rothschild, eds, *Miscellany of Studies in Romance Languages and Literatures presented to L.E. Kastner*, Cambridge University Press, Camrbridge, 1932, pp. 57–67.

Mirabilia Urbis Romae (Marvels of Rome), trans. F. M. Nichols, London, 1889.

Nennius, *British History and The Welsh Annals*, ed. and trans. J. Morris, Phillimore, London and Chichester, 1980.

Of Arthour and of Merlin, ed. O. D. Macrae-Gibson, 2 vols, Vol. 1, Early English Text Society, O.S. 268, Oxford University Press, London, 1973.

Oldest Anglo-Norman Prose Brut Chronicle, The: An Edition and Translation, ed. and trans. J. Marvin, Boydell, Woodbridge, 2006.

Oracula Sibyllina, The Sibylline Oracles Books III–V, trans. H. N. Bate, Society for Promoting Christian Knowledge, London, 1919.

Orderic Vitalis, *The Ecclesiastical History of Orderic Vitalis*, ed. and trans. M. Chibnall, 6 vols, Clarendon, Oxford, 1969–80.

Peter Lombard, *The Sentences, Book 2: On Creation*, trans. G. Silano, Pontifical Institute of Mediaevel Studies, Toronto, 2008.

Philippe de Thaon, *Le Livre de Sibile*, ed. H. Shields, Blackwell, Oxford, 1979.

Post-Vulgate Merlin Continuation, trans. M. Asher, in N. J. Lacy, ed., *Lancelot-Grail*, Volume 5, D. S. Brewer, Cambridge, 2010.

Prophecies de Merlin, Les ed. L. Paton, 2 vols, Heath, New York, 1926–7.

Prophesies de Merlin, Les, ed. A. Berthelot, Martin Bodmer Foundation, Cologny, Geneva, 1992.

Ralph of Coggeshall, *Chronicon Anglicanum*, ed. J. Stevenson, Rolls Series 66, London, 1875.

Ralph of Diceto, *Images of History*, ed. W. Stubbs, in *Radulfi de Diceto decani Lundoniensis opera historica*, 2 vols, Rolls Series 68, London, 1876.

Ranulph Higden, *Polychronicon Ranulphi Higden Monachi Cestrensis; together with the English Translations of John Trevisa and of an Unknown Writer of the Fifteenth Century*, ed. C. Babington and J. R. Lumby, 9 vols, Rolls Series 41, London, 1865–68.

Richard of Poitiers, *Richardi Pictaviensis Chronica*, ed. G. Waitz, in *Monumenta Germaniae Historica Scriptores*, vol. XXVI, Impensis Bibliopolii, Hahniani, Hanover, 1882.

Robert de Boron, *Merlin de Robert de Boron, roman en prose du XIIIe siècle*, ed. A. Micha, Droz, Paris and Geneva, 1980.

Robert of Gloucester, *The Metrical Chronicle*, ed. W. A. Wright, 2 Vols, Rolls Series 86, London, 1887–88.

Robert Mannyng of Brunne, *Chronicle*, ed. F. J. Furnivall, 2 vols Rolls Series 87, Vol. 1 London, 1887.

Robert of Torigny, *Chronique de Robert de Torigni, Abbé du Mont-Saint-Michel*, 2 vols, ed. L. Delisle, Rouen, 1872–73.

Roger of Howden, *Chronica Rogeri de Houedene*, ed. W. Stubbs, 4 vols, Rolls Series 51, London, 1868–71.

Salimbene de Adam, *Cronica*, ed. G. Scalia, Corpus Christianorum Continuatio Mediaevalis CXXV, Brepols, Turnhout, 1998.

Salimbene de Adam, *The Chronicle*, trans. J. L. Baird, G. Baglivi and J. R. Kane, Medieval and Renaissance Text Studies Vol. 40, Binghamton, NY, 1986.

Simon de Phares, *Le Recueil des Plus Célèbres Astrologues*, ed. J.-P. Boudet, Champion, Paris, 1997.

Solinus, *Polyhistor* or *Collectanea rerum mirabilium*, ed. and trans. A. Agnant, Paris, 1847.

Spenser, Edmund, *Faerie Queene*, ed. T. P. Roche, Jr., Penguin, London, 1978.

Story of Merlin, trans. R. T. Pickens, in N. J. Lacy, ed., *Lancelot-Grail: The Old French Arthurian Vulgate and Post-Vulgate in Translation*, Vol. 1, Garland, New York, 1993.

Suger of St Denis, *Vie de Louis le Gros (Life of Louis the Fat)*, ed. H. Waquet, 2nd edn, Les Belles Lettres, Paris 1964.

Suger of St Denis, *Suger, Abbot of Saint Denis 1081–1151: The Deeds of Lovis the Fat*, trans. 'Cusimano and J. Moorhead, Catholic University of America Press, Washington D. C., 1992.

Tennyson, Alfred; ed. J. M. Gray, *Idylls of the King*, Penguin, Harmondsworth, 1983.

Thomas of Monmouth, *The Life and Miracles of Saint William of Norwich*, ed. and trans. A Jessopp and M. R. James, Cambridge University Press, Cambridge, 1896.

Vincent of Beauvais, *Speculum Historiale*; for text of Douai, MS 797, see http://atilf.atilf.fr/bichard/.

Virgil, *Aeneid*, trans. J. Dryden, Penguin.

Vitae Sanctorum Britanniae et Genealogiae, ed. A. Wade-Evans, University of Wales Press, Cardiff, 1944.

Wace (Master), *Roman de Brut (A History of the British)*, ed. and trans. J. Weiss, University of Exeter Press, Exeter, 2006.

Walter of Coventry, *The Historical Collections of Walter of Coventry, from Brutus to 1225*, ed. W. Stubbs, 2 vols, Rolls Series 58, London.

Walter of Coventry, *Les Prophesies de Merlin (Cod. Bodmer 116)*, ed. A. Berthelot, Fondation Martin Bodmer, Cologny-Geneva,1992.

Walter Map, *De Nugis Curialium (Courtiers' Trifles)*, ed. and trans. M. R. James, 1914, rev. edn C. N. L. Brooke and R. A. B. Mynors, Clarendon, Oxford, 1983.

White, T. H., *The Once and Future King: the Complete Edition*, HarperCollins (Voyager), London, 1996.

William of Conches, *Dragmaticon Philosophine, (A Dialogue on Natural Philosophy)*, trans. I. Ronca and M. Curr, University of Notre Dame Press, Ind., 1997.

William of Malmesbury, *Gesta Regum Anglorum (The History of the English Kings)*, ed. and trans. R. A. B. Mynors with R. M. Thomson and M. Winterbottom, 2 vols, Clarendon, Oxford, 1998.

William of Malmesbury, *Historia Novella*, ed. E. King, trans. K. R. Potter, Clarendon Oxford, Press, 1999.

William of Malmesbury, *The Early History of Glastonbury: An edition, Translation, and Study of William of Malmesbury's De antiquitate Glastonie ecclesie*, ed. J. Scott, Boydell, Woodbridge, 1981.

William of Malmesbury, *Saints' Lives*, ed. and trans. M. Winterbottom and R. M. Thomson, Clarendon, Oxford, 2002.

William of Newburgh, '*Historia Rerum Anglicarum*', in R. Howlett, ed., *Chronicles of the Reigns of Stephen, Henry II and Richard I*, 2 vols, Rolls Series 82, Longman, London, 1884–85.

William of Newburgh, *The History of English Affairs, Book One*, ed. and trans. P. G. Walsh and M. J. Kennedy, Aris and Phillips Warminster, 1988.

William of Tudela, *The Song of the Cathar Wars; A History of the Albigensian Crusade*, trans. J. Shirley, Ashgate, Aldershot, 1996.

Wynkyn de Worde, *A Lytel Treatys of the Byrth and Prophecye of Merlin*, London, 1510. ESTC No. S100757.

Secondary Sources

Ackerman, R. W., 'Herry Lovelich's *Merlin*', *Proceedings of the Modern Language Association*, 67, 4, 1952.

Bartlett, R., 'Gerald of Wales (*c*.1146–1220×23)', *Oxford Dictionary of National Biography*, Oxford University Press, 2004; online edn, Oct. 2006 http://www.oxforddnb.com/view/article/10769 (accessed 23 Oct. 2011).

Black, M., and O. Neugebauer, *The Book of Enoch, or, I Enoch*, Brill, Leiden, 1985.

Bogdanow, F., 'The Post-Vulgate *Roman du Graal*', in G. Burgess and K. Pratt, eds, *The Arthur of the French: The Arthurian Legend in Medieval French and Occitan Literature*, University of Wales Press, Cardiff, 2006.

Brandin, L., 'Les Prognostica du Ms. Ashmole 304', in M. Williams and J. A. de Rothschild, eds, *Miscellany of Studies in Romance Languages and Literatures presented to L. E. Kastner*, University Press, Cambridge, 1932, pp. 57–67.

Bruckner, M. T., *Chrétien Continued: A Study of the Conte du Graal and its Verse Continuations*, Oxford University Press, Oxford 2009.

Burnett, C., 'Malvern, Walcher of (d. 1135)', *Oxford Dictionary of National Biography*, Oxford University Press, 2004 http://www.oxforddnb.com/view/article/41145 (accessed 31 Oct. 2011).

Burnett, C., 'Mathematics and Astronomy in Hereford and its region in the twelfth century', in D. Whitehead, ed., *Medieval Art, Architecture and Archaeology at Hereford*, British Archaeological Association Transactions Conference, 15, 1995, pp. 50–59.

Chardonnens, L. S., *Anglo-Saxon Prognostics: 900–1100*, Brill, Leiden, 2007.

Clark, W. B., *A Medieval Book of Beasts: The Second-Family Bestiary*, Boydell, Woodbridge, 2006.

Cohn, N., *The Pursuit of the Millennium*, 2nd edn, Oxford University Press, Oxford 1970.

Collard, J., 'Henry I's Dream in John of Worcester's *Chronicle* (Corpus Christi College, Oxford, MS 157) and the Illustration of Twelfth-Century English Chronicles', *Journal of Medieval History* 36, 2, 2010, pp. 105–25.

Crick, J. C., 'Geoffrey of Monmouth, Prophecy and History', *Journal of Medieval History* 18, 4, 1992, pp. 357–71.

Crick, J. C., *The Historia regum Britannie of Geoffrey of Monmouth III: A Summary Catalogue of the Manuscripts*, Brewer, Cambridge, 1989.

Cunliffe, B., 'Saxon Bath', in J. Haslam, ed., *Anglo-Saxon Towns in Southern England*, Chichester, Phillimore, 1984.

Dalrymple, R., '"Evele knowen ye Merlyne in certain"; Henry Lovelich's Prose *Merlin*', in J. Weiss, J. Fellows and M. Dickins, eds., *Medieval Insular Romance*, Brewer, Cambridge, 2000.

Daniel, E. R., 'Joachim of Fiore; Patterns of History in the Apocalypse', in R. K. Emmerson and B. McGinn, eds, *The Apocalypse in the Middle Ages*, Cornell University Press, New York, 1992.

Davies, J. R., *The Book of Llandaf and the Norman Church in Wales*, Boydell, Woodbridge, 2003.

Davies, W., *The Llandaff Charters*, National Library of Wales, Aberystwyth, 1979.

Dumville, D., 'Nennius and the *Historia Brittonum*', *Studia Celtica* 10–11, 1975–77, pp. 78–95.

Dumville, D., *The Vatican Recension of the Historia Brittonum: Historia et genealogia Brittonum et de origine eorum necnon et expulsione*, Brewer, Cambridge, 1985.

Eckhardt, C. D., 'The First English Translation of the *Prophetia Merlini*', *The Library*, 6th series, 4, vol. no. 1, March 1982.

Eckhardt, C. D., 'The *Prophetia Merlini* of Geoffrey of Monmouth: Latin manuscript copies', in *Manuscripta* 26, 1982.

Eckhardt, C. D., ed., *The Prophetia Merlini of Geoffrey of Monmouth: A Fifteenth-Century English Commentary*, Speculum Anniversary Monographs 8, Medieval Academy of America, Cambridge, Mass, 1982.

Ferreiro, A., *Simon Magus in Patristic, Medieval and early-Modern Traditions*, Brill, Leiden, 2005.

Flint, V. I. J., 'The Career of Honorius Augustodunensis. Some Fresh Evidence', *Revue Bénédictine*, 82, 1972, pp. 62–86.

Freeman, J., 'Sorcery at Court and Manor: Margery Jourdemayne, The Witch of Eye Next Westminster', *Journal of Medieval History*, 30, 2004, pp. 343–57.

Gransden, A., *Legends, Traditions and History in Medieval England*, Hambledon, London and Rio Grande, 1992.

Greenway, D. E., 'Henry of Huntingdon as Poet', *Medium Aevum*, 74, 2, 2005, pp. 329–32.

Greenway, D. E., 'Henry of Huntingdon (*c.*1088–*c.*1157)', *Oxford Dictionary of National Biography*, Oxford University Press, 2004, http://www.oxforddnb.com/view/article/12970, accessed 19 Oct. 2011.

Hammer, J., 'A Commentary on the *Prophetia Merlini*', *Speculum*, 10, 1935, pp. 3–30, and *Speculum*, 15, 1940, pp. 409–31.

Hammer, J., 'Another Commentary on the *Prophetia Merlini*', *Bulletin of the Polish Institute of Arts and Sciences in America*, 1, 1942–43, pp. 589–601.

Hammer, J., 'Bref commentaire de la *Prophetia Merlini* du ms 3514 de la bibliothèque de la cathédrale d'Exeter', in J. Hammer, ed., *Hommages à Joseph Bidez et à Franz Cumont*, Latomus, Brussels, 1949, pp. 111–19.

Harvey, J. H., 'The Square Garden of Henry the Poet', *Garden History*, 15, 1, 1987, pp. 1–11.

Haskins, C. H., 'The Court of Frederick II', in idem, *Medieval Science*, pp. 242–98.

Haskins, C. H., *Studies in the History of Medieval Science*, Harvard University Press, Cambridge, Mass., 1924, pp. 120–23.

Holdenried, A., *The Sibyl and her Scribes; Manuscripts and Interpretation of the Latin Sibylla Tiburtina, 1050–1500*, Ashgate, Aldershot and Burlington, VT, 2006.

Horden, P., 'Faricius (d. 1117)', *Oxford Dictionary of National Biography*, Oxford University Press, 2004 http://www.oxforddnb.com/view/article/9157 (accessed 30 Oct. 2011).

Hughes, K., 'The Welsh Latin chronicles; *Annales Cambriae* and related texts', in K. Hughes, ed., *Celtic Britain in the Early Middle Ages*, Boydell, Woodbridge, 1980, pp. 67–85.

Jarman, A. O. H., 'Early Stages in the Development of the Myrddin Legend', in R. Bromwich and R. B. Jones, eds, *Studies in Old Welsh Poetry*, Cardiff, 1978, pp. 326–49.

Jarman, A. O. H., 'The Merlin Legend and the Welsh Tradition of Prophecy', in P. H. Goodrich and R. H. Thompson, eds, *Merlin: A Casebook*, Routledge, London, 2003, pp. 105–30.

Jarman, A. O. H., *The Cynfeirdd: Early Welsh Poets and Poetry*, University of Wales Press, Cardiff, 1981.

Jarman, A. O. H., *The Legend of Merlin*, revised edn, University of Wales Press, Cardiff, 1976.

Jones, F., *The Holy Wells of Wales*, 2nd edn, University of Wales Press, Cardiff, 1992.

Kauffmann, C. M., *The Baths of Pozzuoli*, Cassirer, London and Oxford, 1959.

Kay, M., 'Prophecy in Medieval Welsh Manuscripts', *Proceedings of the Harvard Celtic Colloquium*, Vols 26/27, 2006/2007.

Keck, D., *Angels and Angelology in the Middle Ages*, Oxford University Press, Oxford and New York, 1998.

Kemp, B. R., 'The Miracles of the Hand of St James', *Berkshire Archaeological Journal*, 65, 1970, pp. 1–20.

Ker, N. R., *Catalogue of Manuscripts Containing Anglo-Saxon*, Oxford, Clarendon, 1957 (repr. 1990).

Kieckhefer, R., *Magic in the Middle Ages*, 2nd edn, Canto series, Cambridge University Press, Cambridge, 2000.

Knight, S., *Merlin; Knowledge and Power Through the Ages*, Cornell University Press, Ithaca and London, 2009.

Kors, A. C., and E. Peters, eds., *Witchcraft in Europe, 400–1700*, 2nd edn, University of Pennsylvania Press, Philadelphia, 2001.

Lahdensuu, L., 'Predicting History: Merlin's Prophecies in Italian XIIth–XVth Century Chronicles', in E. Kooper, ed., *The Medieval Chronicle III*, Rodopi, Amsterdam and New York, 2004, pp. 93–100.

Lawrence-Mathers, A., 'William of Newburgh and the Northumbrian Construction of English History', *Journal of Medieval History*, 33, 2007, pp. 339–57.

Lee, S., and J. C. Crick, 'Beverley, Alfred of (*d.* 1154×7?)', rev. J. C. Crick, *Oxford Dictionary of National Biography*, Oxford University Press, 2004 http://www.oxforddnb.com/view/article/344 (accessed 23 Oct. 2011).

Lidaka, J., '*The Book of Angels, Rings, Characters and Images of the Planets*, Attributed to Osbern Bokenham', in C. Fanger, ed., *Conjuring Spirits: Texts and Traditions of Medieval Ritual Magic*, Sutton, Stroud, 1998.

Luscombe, D., 'Pullen, Robert (d. in or after 1146)', *Oxford Dictionary of National Biography*, Oxford University Press, Oxford, 2010 http://www.oxforddnb.com/view/article/22877 (accessed 7 September 2011).

Luscombe, D., 'The Reception of the Writings of Denis the Pseudo-Areopagite into England', in D. E. Greenway et al., eds, *Tradition and Change: Essays in Honour of Marjorie Chibnall*, Cambridge University Press, Cambridge 1985.

Macrae-Gibson, O. D., ed., *Of Arthour and of Merlin*, Vol. 1, Early English Text Society, OS 268, Oxford University Press, London, 1973.

Matheson, L. M., *The Prose Brut: The Development of a Middle English Chronicle*, Medieval and Renaissance Texts and Studies, Tempe, Arizona, 1998.

McGinn, B., '*Teste David cum Sibylla:* The Significance of the Sibylline Tradition in the Middle Ages', in J. Kirshner and S. Wemple, eds, *Women of the Medieval World*, Blackwell, Oxford and New York, 1985 pp. 7–35.

McGinn, B., *Visions of the End: Apocalyptic Traditions in the Middle Ages*, 2nd edn, Columbia University Press, New York, 1998.

North, J. D., 'Some Norman horoscopes', in C. F. S. Burnett, ed., *Adelard of Bath, an English Scientist and Arabist of the Early Twelfth Century*, Warburg Institute, London, 1987, pp. 147–61.

North, J. D., 'The Astrolabe', in idem, *Stars, Minds and Fate: Essays in Ancient and Medieval Cosmology*, Hambledon Press, London and Ronceverte, 1989, pp. 211–20.

Peters, E., *The Magician the Witch and the Law*, Harvester, Hassocks, 1978.

Pratt, K., 'The Cistercians and the *Queste del Saint Graal*', *Reading Medieval Studies* 21, 1995.

Robbins, R. H., 'Poems Dealing with Contemporary Conditions', in A. Hartung ed., *A Manual of the Writings in Middle English 1050–1500*, Vol. 5, Yale, New Haven and London, 1975.

Rorem, P., *Pseudo-Dionysius; A Commentary on the Texts and an Introduction to their Influence*, Oxford University Press, Oxford and New York, 1993.

Saurette, M., 'Tracing the Twelfth-Century *Chronica* of Richard of Poitiers, Monk of Cluny', *Memini; Bulletin de la Société d'Etudes médiévales du Québec*, 9–10, 2005/06, pp. 303–50.

Short, I., 'Gaimar's Epilogue and Geoffrey of Monmouth's Liber vetustissimus', *Speculum*, 69, 2, 1994, pp. 323–43.

Smallwood, T. M., 'The Prophecy of the Six Kings', *Speculum* 60, 3, 1985, pp. 571–92.

Smoller, L. A., *History, Prophecy, and the Stars: The Christian Astrology of Pierre d'Ailly, 1350–1420*, Princeton University Press, NJ, 1994.

Southern, R. W., 'History as Prophecy (Aspects of the European Tradition of Historical Writing, 3)', *Transactions of the Royal Historical Society*, 5th series, 22, 1972.

Squatriti, P., *Water and Society in Early Medieval Italy, 400–1000*, Cambridge University Press, Cambridge, 1998.

Taavitsainen, I., *Middle English Lunaries: A Study of the Genre*, Mémoires de la société néophilologique de Helsinki, 47, Helsinki, 1988.

Tarré, J., 'Las profecías del sabio Merlin u sus imitaciones', *Analecta Sacra Taraconensia* 16, 1943, pp. 135–71.

Tatlock, J. S. P., 'Caradoc of Llancarfan', *Speculum* 13, 2, 1938, pp. 139–52.

Tatlock, J. S. P., 'The Dates of the Arthurian Saints' Legends', *Speculum* 14, 3, 1939, pp. 345–65.

Tester, S. J., *A History of Western Astrology*, Boydell, Woodbridge, 1987.

Thomson, R. M., 'Malmesbury, William of (*b. c.* 1090, *d.* in or after 1142)', *Oxford Dictionary of National Biography*, Oxford University Press, 2004, http://www.oxforddnb.com/view/article/29461 (accessed 19 Oct. 2011).

Thomson, R. M., *William of Malmesbury*, rev. edn, Boydell, Woodbridge, 2003.

Thorndike, L., *Michael Scot*, Nelson, London, 1965.

Vaughan, R., *Matthew Paris*, Cambridge University Press, Cambridge 1958.

White, L., Jr., 'Eilmer of Malmesbury, An Eleventh Century Aviator', *Technology and Culture*, 2, 2, 1961, pp. 97–111.

Wind, E., *Michelangelo's Prophets and Sibyls*, Oxford University Press, London, 1966.

Winterbottom, M., ed., *The Ruin of Britain: History from the sources* vol. 7, Philimore, London and Chichester, 1978.

Ziolkowski, J., 'The Nature of Prophecy in Geoffrey of Monmouth's *Vita Merlini*', in J. L. Kugel, ed., *Poetry and Prophecy: The Beginnings of a Literary Tradition*, Cornell University Press, New York, 1990, pp. 151–62.

Zumthor, P., *Merlin le Prophète*, 2nd edn, Slatkine, Geneva, 2002.

INDEX

ℰℷℭℛ